THE BOOK BEAUTIFUL

THE BOOK BEAUTIFUL

WALTER PATER AND THE HOUSE OF MACMILLAN

EDITED BY

ROBERT M. SEILER

THE ATHLONE PRESS
LONDON AND NEW BRUNSWICK, NJ

First published in 1999 by
THE ATHLONE PRESS
1 Park Drive, London NW11 7SG
and New Brunswick, New Jersey

British Library Cataloguing in Publication Data
A catalogue record for this book is available from the British Library

ISBN 0 485 11535 2

Library of Congress Cataloging in Publication Data

The book beautiful : Walter Pater and the House of Macmillan / edited by Robert M. Seiler.
p. cm.
Includes bibliographical references and index.
ISBN 0-485-11535 2 (cloth)
1. Pater, Walter, 1839-1894--Correspondence. 2. Authors and publishers--Great Britain--History--19th century. 3. Literature publishing--Great Britain--History--19th century. 4. Fine books--Publishing--Great Britain--History--19th century. 5. Publishers and publishing--Great Britain--Correspondence. 6. Macmillan & Co.
I. Seiler, R. M. (Robert Morris)
PR5136.A4 1999
824'.8--dc21
[B] 98-54257
CIP

Distributed in the United States, Canada and South America by
Transaction Publishers
390 Campus Drive
Somerset, New Jersey 08873

Typeset by Bibloset
Printed and bound in Great Britain by
Cambridge University Press

In Grateful Memory of
Ian Fletcher
1920–1988

CONTENTS

PREFACE

The letters reproduced in this volume make up a small but important chapter in the story of Walter Pater's literary career. They do so by virtue of recording in some detail the relations between this Victorian man of letters and his publisher, Macmillan and Co., as they affected the form as well as the content of the books they produced. Of course, such relations are difficult at the best of times. This was doubly so with Pater who, like Dante Gabriel Rossetti before him and William Morris, James MacNeill Whistler, and Oscar Wilde after him, believed that the book should be thought of as an aesthetic object. All too often these relations between author and publisher go unnoticed, because the letters and the documents exchanged regarding their joint enterprise are not preserved. Fortunately, this is not the case with Pater. The letters reproduced here make accessible valuable literary as well as historical information. Moreover, they offer insight into the principles as well as the practices of modern bookmaking.

In this complex undertaking, we can take our bearings from two students of bookmaking. First, James G. Nelson (1971) helps readers see bookmaking through the eyes of the Bodley Head, the small bookshop and publishing firm that produced the books which summed up the aesthetic milieu of the early 1890s. Secondly, Jerome J. McGann (1991) helps us appreciate the signifying mechanisms which are comprised in the physical aspects of the book, the linguistic and the bibliographical features. The lesson we learn here is that any literary text comes down to us via complex 'social' processes, which together constrain the way the reader 'decodes' the meaning. An author may exercise some control over the linguistic aspects of textual production, namely, the words, but in the vast majority of instances the publisher exercises total control over the bibliographical aspects, such as page layout, typography, paper, and binding. Consider the way Pater's 'texts' have come down to the twentieth century. Initially, he wrote for a variety of periodicals; subsequently, he revised many of these works for publication in book-form; moreover, much of the remaining material (unfinished or uncollected) has come down to us via the mediation of his literary executor, Charles L. Shadwell, who had his own ideas as to what Pater wanted to convey to his readers (Brake and Small, 1991b). In other words, the 'Pater' we read is the product of a number of decisions, some authorial but many editorial. Gerald Monsman (1991) and Ian Small (1991a) have shown that choosing a copy-text is no easy matter. Pater supervised the production of his texts, from first draft to printed book, with close attention, but much of the material needed to construct the pedigree of any one work has not survived (Small, 1991a, 34).

My goal in the Introduction is to establish an appropriate context for appreciating the collaboration represented in the letters presented here; I try to indicate a line of thought from Rossetti, through Whistler, to commercial bookmakers at work around the turn of the last century, with the solitary figure of Pater in the background. For reasons of coherence, I present the narrative in a number of parts: I start with Pater's apprenticeship as a writer, and then shift to the apprenticeship of Daniel and Alexander, who founded the House of Macmillan in 1843. Next, I glance at commercial bookmaking during the last part of the nineteenth century, with an emphasis on the small private presses, and then notice the pre-eminence of Macmillan and Co. in the field of quality bookmaking. Finally, I survey Pater's literary career as a Macmillan author, glancing at the efforts his sisters, Hester and Clara, made to preserve if not enhance their brother's literary reputation after his death.

Many people, friends and colleagues, have helped me prepare this book, which took shape in my mind during conversations I had with the late Kenneth Allott. I am deeply indebted to Miriam Allott, James Black, Laurel Brake, William E. Buckler, Barrie Bullen, Denis Donoghue, Lawrence Evans, the late Ian Fletcher, W.E. Fredeman, Warwick Gould, Michael Holroyd, Billie Andrew Inman, the late Robin Peedell, Bernard Richards, William F. Shuter, Ian Small, Patricia Srebrnik, and Samuel Wright for their comments and suggestions.

I wish to thank Auriol Milford, Copyright Manager, Oxford University Press, for granting me permission to reprint letters that appeared in *Letters of Walter Pater*, ed. Lawrence Evans (1970); Ms Catherine L. Jones, Reigate, Surrey, for granting me permission to print the Pater letters that have not appeared in *Letters of Walter Pater*; and Mr T.M. Farmiloe, Publishing Director, Macmillan Press Ltd, Basingstoke, for granting me permission to print the Macmillan letters.

I am indebted to Michael Bott, Keeper of Archives and Manuscripts, University of Reading, and Chris Sheppard, Brotherton Collection, Leeds University Library, for providing me with photocopies of original letters, and to Leslie Morris, Curator of Manuscripts, Houghton Library, Harvard University, for providing me with copies of Pater MSS there.

I would like to thank John Handford, Archivist, Macmillan Publishers Ltd, Basingstoke, and Philip V. Blake-Hill, Department of Manuscripts, and Elizabeth James, Early Collections Service, the British Library, for sharing their knowledge about Macmillan and Co., and Peter Salt, Archivist, Jarrold and Sons Ltd, Norwich, and J.W.L. Nichols, Director, Richard Clay Ltd, Bungay, for providing me with important background materials on the publishing firms of Jarrold and Sons Ltd. and Richard Barclay Ltd.

For helping me answer questions about writers and publishers, I thank Penelope Bullock, Librarian, Balliol College, David Cooper, Librarian, Corpus Christi College, and Mrs J.E. Robinson, Librarian, Keble College, Oxford; as well as Mark Lawrence, Senior Librarian, Central Library, Westgate, Oxford; D.G. Neill, Dept. of Western Manuscripts, Bodleian Library; and L. White, County Librarian, Oxfordshire County Council; John R. Adams, Assistant Librarian, and Pamela G. Roberts, Collection Librarian, the University of London; Louise Craven and J. Mosley, Librarians, St Bride Printing Library, Fleet Street; and Jane With, Information Officer, National Book League, London; D.S. Goodes, Walpole Librarian, King's School, Canterbury; J. Hilton, Librarian, Atkinson Library, Southport; Iaian Brown, Assistant Keeper, National Library of Scotland, and Lorna Cheyne, Librarian, Edinburgh University Library, Edinburgh; H. Lansing Mace, Assistant Reference Librarian, the University of the State of New York, Albany; Earle E. Coleman, University Archivist, Princeton University; Virginia Francis, Associate Librarian, University Library, the University of Florida, Gainesville; and Judith Ann Schiff, Chief Research Archivist, Yale University Library, New Haven.

I am grateful to Richard H. Laver, Assistant Librarian, and to Mrs Elizabeth Boardman, College Archivist, Brasenose College, Oxford, for providing me with the materials upon which I base my outline of Pater's financial situation; and to Laura De'Giovanni, Public Enquiries Group, the Bank of England; Angela Raspin, Archivist, the London School of Economics; and members of the Historical Association, 59A Kennington Park Road, London, for their expert advice on converting Victorian money to 1997 values.

For providing me with photocopies of documents central to my project, I would like to thank the personnel at the British Library; the Bodleian Library; the Harold Cohen Library; the National Library of Scotland; and the New York Public Library; and at the libraries at the following universities: the University of Alberta, the University of British Columbia, the University of Calgary, the University of Manitoba, McGill University, the University of Minnesota, and the University of Washington.

Finally, I wish to thank the members of the Research Committee, the University of Calgary, for three research grants, which enabled me to spend time in Oxford, and to the Faculty of General Studies, particularly the Dean, Dr. Michael McMordie, for recommending me for a sabbatical leave for the academic year 1996-97, which enabled me to complete this book.

I am pleased to acknowledge the invaluable assistance of my wife Tamara P. Seiler, who read and commented on the manuscript at various stages of completion.

Robert M. Seiler
Calgary
April 1997

INTRODUCTION

> I had been writing verse all my life, and what Browning was to me in verse, Pater from about the age of seventeen had been to me in prose. Meredith made the third; but his form of art was not, I knew never could be, mine. Verse, I suppose, requires no teaching, but it was from reading Pater's *Studies in the History of the Renaissance*, in its first edition on ribbed paper (I have the feel of it still in my fingers) I realised that prose also could be a fine art. That book opened a new world to me or, rather, gave me the key or secret of the world in which I was living.
>
> Arthur Symons remembering Pater (1906)

I BEGINNINGS

Walter Horatio Pater, critic and aesthete, was born in Shadwell, between Wapping and Stepney, East London, on 4 August 1839, the second son of Richard Glode Pater, surgeon, and Maria Hill Pater, thought to be descendants of the Dutch who had moved to England with William of Orange. Pater liked to believe that he was related to Jean Baptiste Pater, a minor Dutch painter and friend of Watteau.

Pater attended the King's School, Canterbury, where during the sixth form he resolved to live the life of the mind (Benson, p. 3). Not surprisingly, he was fascinated by the major figures of the age, John Ruskin and Matthew Arnold, reading *Modern Painters* (1843-60) and *Poems* (1853), especially 'The Scholar Gypsy,' with enthusiasm (Wright, T., i, 173). During the years 1857-67, Arnold was Professor of Poetry at Oxford, and during the years 1870-84 Ruskin was Slade Professor of Fine Art at Oxford. These writers piqued his interest in the cultural debates of the day, such as the possibility of balancing Hebraism and Hellenism (DeLaura, 1969: 169; Adams, p. 153). Pater left school in June 1858, hoping to become a clergyman, and entered Queen's College, Oxford, as a commoner, with a scholarship from Canterbury (Gosse, p. 798). In October, he went into residence, where he met Ingram Bywater (1840-1914), the future classical scholar. The two became close friends. Many years later, Bywater (quoted in Jackson, p. 79) wrote that they attended the same classes: Pater's 'mind was much more mature than mine and he completely subjugated me by his verve, and originality of view.' As it happened, they studied with some of the most gifted teachers of the time, including the charismatic William Wolfe Capes (1834-1914), Tutor and Lecturer (1856-65) at Queen's College, rector (from 1869) of Bramshott, Hants., Reader (1870-77) in Ancient History at Oxford, and Fellow (1878-86) at Hertford College, Oxford. Pater attended Arnold's lectures, enjoying the latter's 'impudence' and 'onslaught on the Philistines' (Wright, T., i, 173). During Lent Term 1861, they studied with the remarkable classics scholar Benjamin Jowett (1817-93), for whom they prepared an essay every week. At this time, Jowett was Fellow (from 1840) and Tutor (1840-70) of Balliol College, Oxford, and Regius Professor of Greek (1855-93). According to Geoffrey Faber (1957), Jowett had a genius for helping students think for themselves: he criticised students' work without discouraging them, and in setting lofty goals he inspired a strong belief in powers yet to be developed (pp. 166-7). Jowett told Pater: 'I think you have a mind that will come to great eminence' (Benson, p. 9). During this period, he acquired a good knowledge of German, and read the 'new' German philosophy with enthusiasm. In December 1862, he graduated BA with second-class honours in *Literae Humaniores*.

Two years later, Pater was elected to a Fellowship at Brasenose College, Oxford. He went into residence as BNC's first non-clerical fellow, and immediately he abandoned his plan to become a (Unitarian) minister (Buchan, p. 23). At 25, then, Pater made Oxford the center of his life. As one biographer put it, he was 'a happy man in the sense that he had fallen into precisely the niche that was most suited for his peculiar genius' (Wright, T., i, 212). By way of celebrating his good fortune, Pater and another close friend, Charles Lancelot Shadwell (1840-1919), Fellow (1864-98) and later (1905-14) Provost of Oriel College, Oxford, travelled (1865) to Italy. The two junior 'academics' visited Ravenna, Pisa, and Florence, and the trip was nothing if not a great revelation (Donoghue, p. 31): Pater divined from the Renaissance paintings he saw the imagery of a richer, more daring sense of life than any he had so far seen in Oxford.

In organising this survey, I take my cue from Billie Andrew Inman (1991) and delineate three stages in Pater's career (pp. xxiv-xxv): (a) the early period 1858-73, during which he established himself as a writer with a daring (pagan) philosophy of life, which became irresistible to a certain type of young man (Clark, p.11); (b) the middle period 1874-77, during which he changed direction a number of times, exploring new themes and developing new techniques, answering his critics, and reconciling his attitudes and beliefs with those of the time; and finally, (c) the later period from 1878, during which he concentrated on maintaining his hard-won place at BNC and mastering his craft (p. l).

The early period: 1858-73

Almost immediately, Pater launched his career as a writer, with a view to making his mark as a 'cultural' critic. Like most journalists of the time, he produced relatively short pieces (Brake, 1994: 16), including review-essays, articles, and lectures, as opposed to the heavily documented monographs serious academics[1] were starting to produce, and in turn he 'recycled' these pieces in book-form. Collecting and then reprinting essays had become an attractive proposition, thanks in part to the rapid growth of the periodical press. In this regard, he followed the example offered by such writers as Arnold, who routinely collected and reprinted essays which had appeared in periodicals (Super, 1966), the immediate instance being the first series (1865) of *Essays in Criticism*. In this way, writers modified their arguments on the basis of the criticisms which were made when the pieces first appeared.

From 1866-68, Pater published his work[2] in the *Westminster Review*, the mouthpiece for advanced theological and philosophical thought, and from 1869 he published his work in (for example) the *Fortnightly Review*, the mouthpiece for advanced liberal thought. John Chapman (1821-94), editor of the *Westminster Review*, encouraged Pater, giving the would-be journalist plenty of space and sufficient time to get his bearings intellectually, hoping that he would become a regular contributor (Levey, p. 132). He took advantage of the opportunity, especially the anonymity, making what he could of the assortment of recent publications Chapman sent to him (Brake, 1994: 17). In these, his very first compositions, Pater introduced a group of related topics he would explore throughout his career (Fletcher, 1971: 10), including human isolation within the flux, the relative spirit of the modern world, the Greek ideal, and the importance of temperament. In addition, he developed (Bullen, p. 280) the 'self-conscious and carefully measured prose style' a number of readers would find beguiling.

Pater's first review-essay, based on a selection of conversations, letters, and recollections of S.T. Coleridge, edited (1864) by Thomas Allsop, appeared (unsigned) in the January (1866) issue of the *Westminster Review*. Pater contextualises his analysis of Coleridge's 'intellectual position' in terms of the conflict between the pursuit of the 'absolute,' characteristic of ancient thought, and the cultivation of the 'relative' spirit, characteristic of modern thought. Surprisingly, he focuses not on Coleridge's poetry or criticism – as his readers would expect – but on Coleridge's metaphysics, attacking him for pursuing the absolute, that expression of mental sickliness which (he claims) is in revolt against the patient tentativeness of the scientific method (Fletcher, 1971, p. 11). According to the modern spirit, he writes, one can know nothing rightly except relatively, that is, under very specific conditions. He rejects Coleridge's critical method (the attempt to define the universal element in any artistic effort) and instead posits the practical (empirical) test of an individual's response to a work. In addition, he rejects orthodox Christianity, because (in his words) the worship of sorrow and the 'crucifixion' of the senses frustrate creativity.

Pater's second review-essay, based on Otto Jahn's biography (1866) of Johann Winckelmann (in German) and G. Henry Lodge's (1850) translation of Winckelmann's seminal book, *The History of Ancient Art* (1764), appeared (unsigned) in the January (1867) issue of the *Westminster Review*. Pater's goal in this, the most 'weighty' (DeLaura, 1969: 203; Bullen, p. 278; Adams, pp. 154-81), of his early pieces, is to put Winckelmman in intellectual perspective, with Goethe in the foreground. As Ian Fletcher (1971: 13-14) writes, the German Hellenist stands apart from Pater's other Renaissance types: these figures, painters and poets alike, exude the sense of discovering in the classical world something new, together with the possibility of renewed creation; however, Winckelmann (their descendent) exudes the sense of recovering something lost, that is, the Greek ideal. That Pater identifies with the persona of Winckelmann as scholar and writer is obvious (Benson, p. 29; Clark, p. 13; Potts, pp. 238-53). He offers readers the following portrait: After a rather depressing apprenticeship in 'the tarnished intellectual world' of Germany, Winckelmann discovered the beauty of Greek art (he had to be his own teacher); in fact, he possessed the key to appreciating Hellenism in his own temperament; in other words, his affinity with paganism enabled him to apprehend Hellenic art not in the abstract but in the concrete, so that when he moved to Rome he could 'finger' those marble classical male nudes without shame; moreover, this affinity is demonstrated by his 'romantic friendships' with young men, which brought him into contact with 'the pride of the human form.' In a word, appreciating the beauty of the male form is the key to appreciating Greek art. In this way, Winckelmann acts as a bridge, bringing classical culture from the distant past to the present (Bullen, pp. 277-9), and this discussion of Winckelmann's pagan temperament takes us right to the very heart of Pater's early Renaissance studies: (a) his personal concept of the Renaissance as a process of renewal, the rebirth of individuality, (b) his notion of self-culture as a vehicle for achieving unity with oneself, and (c) his urgent plea for a fresh approach to appreciating art.

Pater's third review-essay, based on William Morris' *The Defence of Guenevere and other Poems* (1858), *The Life of Jason: A Poem* (1867), and

The Earthly Paradise: A Poem (1868), appeared (unsigned) in the October (1868) issue of the *Westminster Review*. What fascinates Pater about Morris' narrative poems is how ably they exude the pagan spirit: 'the sense of death and the desire of beauty; the desire of beauty quickened by the sense of death.' The (secret) enjoyment he gets from this poetry – it is an imitation of neither Greek nor medieval poetry – derives from that 'inversion of homesickness known to some, that incurable thirst for the sense of escape, which no actual form of life satisfies, no poetry even, if it be merely simple and spontaneous.' The last paragraphs of this composition are central, because here Pater outlines his solution to this dilemma, which runs through most of his work (cf. Crinkley, p. 57).

Pater takes as his point of departure an observation he made in the essay on Winckelmann, namely, what modern art should be doing in the service of culture is to rearrange the details of modern life so as to reflect it, thereby satisfying the human spirit.

The last section of the essay (it makes up the 'Conclusion' to *The Renaissance*) reads like a manifesto for the liberation of the human spirit from the trammels of the modern world, with its complex technology and morbid introspection. Pater begins with the observation that modern empirical science has atomised life so completely that we feel caught up in 'a magic web,' necessity or natural law, which has produced a kind of psychological paralysis. That is, empirical science has completely reduced life to its 'natural elements' and basic processes. These reflections (he adds) produce the 'the impression of the individual in his isolation,' surrounded by 'that thick wall of personality,' whereby each mind keeps as a solitary prisoner its own dream of a world. In fact, further analysis reveals that all that is actual or real for us is the 'single moment,' which vanishes when we try to apprehend it. Pater thus asks us to cast off our psychic inertia by courting new and intense experiences. Our one chance (he says) is to expand those brief intervals, to get 'as many pulsations as possible' into those moments. What makes life as intense and as complete as possible (this is the real aim of culture) is 'the love of art for its own sake.' Thus, since works of art present the most complete forms of idealised life, spirit and matter alike under their purest and most perfect conditions, they are the most appropriate objects for 'impassioned contemplation.' In this way, Pater invites us to live life in the spirit of art, to mould life to artistic perfection.

Pater lived the life of an 'academic,' a fact not unconnected with his claim on our attention, and contrary to reports (Benson, p. 23) alleging that he never considered himself a 'professional' educator,[3] the evidence suggests that he attached a great deal of importance to his work as a teacher and that he was more involved in 'the life of the College' (Buchan, p. 24) than these judgments otherwise suggest (Shuter, 1988: 41). Pater was elected Fellow of BNC in large part because he had just passed through the revised program called *Literae Humaniores,* that in-depth inquiry into the nature of Greek and Roman civilization via the minds of its greatest exponents. That is, Pater was qualified to prepare others for the two quite different sets of examinations involved (Shuter, 1988: 42). Under the revised regulations, which were formulated in 1850 (Mallet, iii, 297), students wrote (a) Classical Moderations, a test of their grasp of Latin and Greek language and literature, in their second year, and (b) the Final Honour School, a test of their grasp of Latin and Greek history and philosophy, in their fourth year. As Tutor during the period 1867-83 (Inman, 1990: 28), Pater prepared students for Classical Moderations. This examination included (a) translating passages (unseen) from Latin and Greek into English, (b) rendering passages of English prose into Latin and Greek in the style of the great classical writers and orators, and (c) critiquing (textually) selected texts. In order to engage in more 'specialised' teaching, he joined (in the late 1860s) the 'combination system,' an informal association which had been organised by four tutors, including his friend Shadwell, for the purpose of offering (combined) lectures to students of the colleges participating in the system (Engel, pp. 81-93). As philosophy lecturer during the period 1872-92, Pater prepared students for the Final Honour School. Over the years, he offered no less than 38 courses of lectures (Shuter, 1988: 43), concentrating on Plato's *Republic* and Aristotle's *Ethics,* texts at the centre of the newly revised curriculum.

According to the testimony of many former students, including T.H.S. Escott, Edward Manson, Samuel Waddington, and Thomas Humphry Ward, Pater soon became a cult figure. One acquaintance (Anon., 1894) put the matter in these terms: 'No man ever came into the presence of Mr Pater without feeling a certain spell come over him.' Humphry Ward (1845-1926), Fellow (1869) and Tutor (from 1870) of BNC before moving (1881) to London, to become 'leader writer' and later art critic for *The Times,* recalls (p. 74) that, when the review-essays on Coleridge and Winckelmann appeared in 1866 and 1867 respectively, a small group of admirers formed, in Oxford and in London, and this mixture of curiosity and admiration became general when the essay on Leonardo da Vinci appeared (1869) in the *Fortnightly Review.* But, as Humphry Ward puts it (quoted in Benson, p. 22), Pater was no scholar[4] as Oxford and Cambridge understood the word. Unlike Mark Pattison (1813-84), Fellow (from 1839) and Rector (from 1861) of Lincoln College, Oxford, and Bywater, he had little patience for getting to the bottom of a subject (Pattison, quoted in Mrs. Humphry Ward, p. 105; see Pattison, 1885) or for the conventions of scholarship. Moreover, his range of interests was unusually wide (Shuter, 1988: 56; Small, 1991a: 93-5).

Perhaps to conceal his mixed feelings about all the forms of intellectual authority he encountered as a teacher and as a writer (Small, 1991a: 106-10), Pater developed a cavalier attitude. At Oxford dinner-parties, he liked to engage in 'brilliant and paradoxical' talk (Benson, p. 32), taking great delight in shocking acquaintances with quips about religion and art. At one dinner-party, he said that no reasonable person could govern his life 'by the opinions or actions of a man who died eighteen centuries ago' (quoted in Seiler, 1987: 29).

In this way, Pater declared that he no longer considered himself a 'provincial' philosopher, but rather a cosmopolitan critic who moved in the wider world of the fine arts. First, he transferred his work to a new periodical, the *Fortnightly Review*, thereby abandoning book-reviewing, with its cover of anonymity, and giving himself the freedom to choose his own subjects (Brake, 1994: 16, 25). Founded (in 1865) to promote independent thought, this periodical eventually appeared monthly, featuring articles surveying current social and cultural matters, as well as critiques of new books, and (as a matter of policy) identifying each contributor. John, later Viscount Morley of Blackburn (1838-1923), journalist, biographer, radical politician, and statesman, edited the *Fortnightly Review* from 1867-82 and the *Pall Mall Gazette* from 1880-93.

Pater's association with the *Fortnightly Review* proved fruitful. First, he refined his critical method (aesthetic criticism), the foundation for which he laid in the essay on Winckelmann. Secondly, he published (1869-71) a sequence of articles on the culture of the Italian Renaissance: Leonardo da Vinci, Sandro Botticelli, Pico della Mirandola, and Michelangelo, thereby establishing a theme for his first book. In 1872, he produced three articles especially for *The Renaissance*, the book which would secure his place in intellectual history.

Meanwhile, Pater declared his heterodoxy when he discarded 'the ordinary academic dress of the period' for that of the dandy, appearing in May 1869 at the Private Showing of the Royal Academy in top hat, high stiff collar, silk tie of brilliant apple-green, black tailcoat, dog-skin gloves, dark-striped trousers, and patent leather boots (Gosse, p. 801). In making his aestheticism public this way, he courted censure, for in the popular mind the dandy (and the aesthete) was associated with homosexuality.

In December 1869, Pater rented the house at 2 Bradmore Road, north of the Parks, in what was the newest part of Oxford; here, he and his sisters, Hester Maria Pater (1837-1922) and Clara Ann Pater (1841-1910), lived as a family until summer 1885, when they moved to London. Humphry Ward, now his colleague, bought (in 1870) the house at 5 Bradmore Road, paying about £2,000 (equivalent to £77,200 in 1997) for it (Sutherland, p. 56), where he and his wife, Mary (Arnold) Ward (1851-1920) lived for nine years (1872-81). Grand-daughter of Dr Thomas Arnold, Headmaster of Rugby, and niece of the Professor of Poetry at Oxford, Mrs. Humphry (hereafter Mary) Ward made a name for herself as novelist and social worker.

It can be argued that the Paters – who lived on one salary – struggled to make ends meet (Richards, p. 6). Mary Ward (1918) writes that nobody under the rank of Head of College – she might have had the Rev. Edward Hartopp Cradock (1810-86), Principal of BNC from 1853-86, in mind – earned as much as £1,000 a year and that non-clerical tutors (such as Humphry and Pater) earned not much more than half that sum (p. 119). One historian of the period (Engel, 1983) claims that, during the 1870s, college tutorships and lectureships were worth £500 to £800 p.a. (p. 113). Mary Ward adds that the families of these young university teachers lived rather well on their stipends, giving dinner-parties and furnishing their houses in the latest Pre-Raphaelite fashion. Judging by these standards, I would say that Pater earned a 'modest' salary.[5] Based on the figures we find in the Junior Bursar's Dividend Books 1855-83 and in the Senior Bursar's Dividend Books 1867-93, now in the BNC Archives, I can present a very rough sketch of his earnings. For example, in 1870, Pater earned £266.16.08, whereas the Principal earned £476.10.06 (equivalent to £10,298.48 and £18,392.90 in 1997); in 1880, he earned £392.05.04, whereas the Principal earned £454.14.0 (equivalent to £15,935,09 and £18,480.56 in 1997); and in 1890 he earned £575.00.08, whereas the Principal earned £1,500 (equivalent to £27,743.75 and £72,375.00 in 1997). We get a sharper picture of Pater's financial situation if we compare the figures just cited with the figures that follow. According to B.R. Mitchell, the average money wages in the United Kingdom (allowing for unemployment) for 1870, 1880, and 1890 were £133, £144, and £166 respectively (equivalent to £5,133.80, £5,850.72, and £8,009.50 respectively in 1997).

This modest salary enabled Hester and Clara to create precisely the domestic environment Pater needed to organize his thoughts and feelings (cf. Mary Ward, pp. 119-25). Hester (known as 'Tottie') acted as the hostess for the family; she seems to have been more domestic than her younger sister. Clara distinguished herself as a woman of considerable intellect: she taught herself Latin and Greek, and during the 1870s many people regarded her as 'one of the best female conversationists in Oxford' (Evans, p. xxiii). She helped her brother with his projects: portions of Pater's MSS, including an early piece entitled 'Arezzo' and parts of the unfinished *Gaston de Latour* are in her hand. Possibly (Levey, p. 151), they engaged in collaboration of a sort. Clara promoted higher education for women at Oxford during the period 1879-94, serving as Vice-Principal (from 1886) and Classics Tutor (1887-94) of Somerville College (cf. Brittain, p. 82). Like her brother, she lived in Oxford during term time, and spent the vacation and the occasional week-end in London. Clara was an attractive, high strung, dominant woman, severe and reserved in manner, but capable of warm and abiding friendship (Mary Ward, p. 124).

With his domestic life comfortably settled, Pater blossomed 'into considerable sociability, entertaining and being entertained in the cordial Oxford way' (quoted in Seiler, 1987: 89). He acquired a wide circle of acquaintances, but he made few 'intimate' friends. Thanks in part to the on-going presence of Hester and Clara, Pater felt that now he could pursue another ambition, namely, to persuade Macmillan and Co. to publish the books he had in mind.

II DANIEL AND ALEXANDER

The fortunes of Alexander Macmillan (1818-96), especially early on, were so closely linked to the fortunes of his brother Daniel Macmillan (1813-57) that to talk of one is to talk of both (Cohen and Gandolfo, p. 2). Thanks in large part to their policy of taking a personal interest in their authors (Morgan, C., pp. 31-2), these Scots of humble origin and little formal education established one of the foremost publishing houses in the world.

Daniel and Alexander grew up at Irvine, Ayrshire, where the Macmillan family had settled in 1816. Their life was austere, but in spite of their poverty, accentuated by the early death in 1823 of Mr Macmillan (Duncan), Mrs Macmillan (Katharine) created a milieu which had much to do with the prosperity this family of book sellers and book publishers enjoyed much later. Duncan had toiled hard as a crofter and as a carter, enduring any sort of hardship for the sake of his family's welfare (Graves, p. 5). Mrs Macmillan always found time during her never-ending schedule of household chores to nurture their intellectual turn of mind. As Alexander later pointed out, Mrs Macmillan passed on the gifts that fitted them very well for the book business: the habit of reading (even as children they read voraciously) and the sensibility needed to appreciate good literature (Hughes, p. 5; Graves, p. 19).

Daniel left school so that he could help support the young family, becoming (1 January 1824) apprentice to Maxwell Dick, bookseller and bookbinder of Irvine. Here, he learned a variety of useful skills, including binding and selling books (Hughes, p. 5). He earned 1s. 6d. (equivalent to £2.49 in 1997) a week for the first year; he earned 1s. extra a week for the remaining six years of his apprenticeship (Hughes, p. 5). During this period, he read voraciously to fill the gaps in his formal education.

Eager to know everything about books, Daniel moved (1831) to Stirling. Malcolm (his older brother) had found him employment as a bookseller's assistant (Hughes, p. 10). Within the year, however, Daniel moved to Glasgow, where he found work at Mr Atkinson's book shop, hoping that in time he might become a partner (Morgan, C., p. 11). However, in December 1832, he became ill with tuberculosis (Cohen and Gandolfo, p. 3). He returned to Irvine, where his mother nursed him back to health.

When he recovered, early in 1833, Daniel set out to make his fortune in London. By June, he was working for Simpkin and Marshall, the publishers, at a salary of £60 a year (equivalent to £2,316 in 1997), but he found the long hours intolerable. On Saturday, for example, he worked through until six Sunday morning (Morgan, C., p. 16).

About this time, a Mr Johnson of Cambridge offered Daniel a position as shopman at £30 a year, together with board with his family (Hughes, p. 46). Altogether, he spent three key years at Cambridge. Throughout the week, he worked from 7:30 am to 7:00 pm. During this period, he improved his knowledge of the book business and expanded his circle of acquaintances. In December 1833, he joined the Baptist community, thus gaining a niche in Cambridge society and also clearing away what he called his Calvinistic cobwebs (Hughes, p. 57; Morgan, C., pp. 18-19). By all accounts, the intelligentsia visited Mr Johnson's shop in increasing numbers, because they found this wise young Scot good company. The reputation he earned at this period of his apprenticeship stood him in good stead when he established his own business ten years later (Morgan, C., p. 18).

Toward the end of 1836, Daniel accepted an offer to work for Messrs Seeley of Fleet Street, London, at a salary rising from £60 to £130 a year (equivalent to £2,259.60 to £4,895.80 in 1997). He stayed with Seeley's for six years, settled at last and with good prospects. Bouts of illness in 1839 and 1841 forced him to return to Scotland, giving him time to think about his future (Hughes, p. 61). When his older brother William died in 1840, Daniel became the head of the Macmillan family.

Alexander worked rather hard as a youth, but he prospered little. Like his brother, he attended Irvine High School, but unable to go to university he followed Daniel's example in filling the gaps in his formal education by reading widely. For two years, he taught colliery lads in village schools; during the last year of this period of his life (1838-39), he took care of 130 children of the poorest families in the mining district (Macmillan, 1908: xvii). Realizing that teaching was not his major strength, he turned his attention to other professions. For a time, he served as an assistant in a chemist's shop in Glasgow. Later, he tried to become a sailor, signing on as a member of the crew on a ship bound for the United States. This journey put an end to his romantic notion of spending his life as a sailor on the high seas, that is, he returned to Glasgow penniless (Morgan, C., p. 20). He worked as an usher for a time, earning 5s. a week.

Alexander's prospects improved in October 1839, when Daniel obtained a post for him at Messrs. Seeley of Fleet Street at the remarkable salary of £60 a year, namely, £2,014.20 in 1997 (Hughes, p. 68; Morgan, C., p. 20). Alexander moved to London immediately. The brothers were happy during this period, lodging together at a boarding-house at 8 Charterhouse Square (Graves, p. 21).

The turning point in their lives occurred in February 1843, when the brothers opened their own bookshop at 57 Aldersgate Street, London (Hughes, p. 115). Daniel continued working at Seeley's to ensure that the family had an income during the difficult period of establishing themselves as booksellers (Cohen and Gandolfo, p. 4).

In June, the brothers learned that a well-established bookseller in Cambridge (Mr Richard Newby) had put his business on the market. Thanks to a loan of £500 (equivalent to £20,865 in 1997) arranged by a friend, Archdeacon Julius Hare (1795-1855), they acquired Newby's business at 17 Trinity Street, Cambridge (Hughes, p. 152; Graves, p. 25). Alexander managed the Aldersgate shop for a few months, but finding this arrangement unworkable he closed it down.

Understandably, the brothers worried about their growing debts, but they managed their affairs with acumen and the business prospered. Daniel took charge of the business, and Alexander took on the role of his assistant. The firm grew slowly but steadily. Daniel was interested in bringing out scholarly editions of the works by English theologians, that is, along the lines of the works produced in Oxford (Hughes, pp. 163-5). Actually, the firm brought out 131 works (in such areas as religion, education, classics, science, and mathematics) during the years 1843-52. About three-fifths of these works related to Cambridge, in terms of author or subject matter (VanArsdel, p. 179).

In 1846, the Macmillan brothers absorbed the business of Mr Stevenson, a centrally-located firm at 1 Trinity Street, Cambridge. To finance the sale, they took on a partner, Mr Barclay, who stayed with the firm until 1880. They lived in ample quarters above the shop, taking in undergraduates to help pay for the upkeep of the place (Cohen and Gandolfo, p. 5). Robert Bowes, a nephew of the partners, joined the firm as an assistant (Morgan, C., p. 32). Writing to his patron (Hare) at this time (2 February 1847), Daniel said: 'Things go very smoothly and very prosperously with us, and my brother is a very great comfort and help to me' (Hughes, p. 170).

It became obvious to the people of Cambridge that the hard working and congenial brothers were no ordinary booksellers (Cohen and Gandolfo, p. 5). Undergraduates and Cambridge dons collected in their informal commonroom to read the newspapers and discuss the literary, religious, and social issues of the day (Graves, p. 27; Hughes, p. 208). William Wordsworth visited the shop; William Makepeace Thackeray lunched with the brothers; and Charles Kingsley showed them the MS. of *Alton Locke* (Morgan, C., pp. 29-30). Gradually, 1 Trinity Street became a social center or 'a little college' in its own right (Morgan, C., p. 30).

That the intellectual elite of Cambridge met at Macmillan's was a tribute to their genius for friendship (Graves, p. 100), their wisdom in literary matters, and their shrewdness as businessmen. It is remarkable how (as Cohen and Gandolfo point out), coming from a background of poverty,

Daniel and Alexander improved themselves beyond expectations. A victim of consumption from his 20th year, Daniel was sustained by a strong Christian piety, grounded in Calvinism, but enlarged by sympathy with the Christian Socialists of the school of F.D. Maurice (Graves, p. 44). In spite of his recurring absences, owing to his illness, Daniel dominated the business, yet he maintained the puritan belief that making a profit was inimical to the vocation of publisher. Alexander, marked by sincerity and generosity, did not share this belief; he was more dynamic and he had a keener eye for business (cf. Nowell-Smith, p. 19). By this time, the Macmillan brothers had become acquainted with the philosophical and the theological controversies of the day. They were (as I mentioned above) devoted to Maurice and Kingsley, leaders of the Christian Socialism movement. It has been said that they could hold their own in discussions with the best minds in Cambridge. The work they had undertaken may not have been easy, but they found it enormously stimulating.

It can be argued (Cohen and Gandolfo, p. 5) that the most remarkable element in this amalgam was the set of principles that guided their business affairs. To raise standards, the Messrs. Macmillan resolved to publish only those books that would last, giving all equal treatment in terms of printing and binding, and to be scrupulously fair in dealing with authors. They were far from mere businessmen; indeed, they were men on a mission. In a letter (dated 1843) to a friend and fellow bookman in Glasgow, Daniel wrote: 'You never surely thought you were working for bread! Don't you know that you are cultivating good taste among the natives of Glasgow helping to unfold a love of the beautiful among those who are slaves to the useful, or what they call the useful? I look on you as a great teacher or prophet, doing work just of the kind that God has appointed you to do' (Hughes, pp. 115-16).

Financially secure at last, the brothers considered marriage and family life. Daniel married (in September 1850) Frances Orridge, daughter of a Cambridge chemist and magistrate (Hughes, p. 190). Alexander married (in August 1851) Caroline Brimley, daughter of a local merchant and eldest sister of his friend George Brimley, librarian of Trinity College (Cohen and Gandolfo, p. 6). In time, Daniel fathered four children and Alexander five.

III VICTORIAN BOOKMAKING

By the 1850s, when Macmillan and Co. began making its mark as the publisher of 'quality' books, each a great pleasure to handle, the industrialization of bookmaking was well under way. In fact, all the arts involved in book production, including printing, papermaking, and binding, underwent important changes, which affected the external appearance of the book (Russell Taylor, p. 37). In some cases, old and new technologies overlapped, thus creating unique problems. The challenge all publishers faced was the need to balance the demands for aesthetic appeal, economy, and durability (Altick, p. 315).

Printing

Well into the second and even the third decade of the nineteenth century, anyone in Britain undertaking a publishing project had to use the equipment the earliest printers used (McLean, p. 2). According to tradition (Marshall, p. 18), new machinery and new processes were tested in the newspaper industry before they were used in the book industry. I should mention four major innovations. First, a new generation of presses was introduced. The Stanhope press, built completely of iron, was introduced in 1800. This machine (Glaister, pp. 383-4) employed the screw principle, combined with a system of leverage for impressing; two men could pull 200 impressions an hour on sheets twice as large as those used in former wooden presses. Secondly, a generation of power-driven presses was developed to meet the demand for increased productivity. The König cylinder press was introduced by *The Times* in November 1814, and the high-speed Hoe press (made in the United States) was introduced in the 1860s (Altick, pp. 306-7). This rotary sheet press became very popular for newspaper work. However, 30 or 40 years passed before power-driven presses were used to turn out enormous quantities of paper-bound books.

I should also comment on the development of graphic processes, especially photo-lithography and photo-gravure, for reproducing illustrations, and the invention of mechanical typesetting, two major innovations which were pioneered in the United States. In the early part of the nineteenth century, the process of reproducing illustrations was dominated by wood engraving (Marshall, p. 25), a process which had become quite sophisticated. Wood engraving is executed on boxwood, by working across the grain, thus allowing for more details to be printed than the older method of woodcut. As Alan Marshall points out, newspaper people were finding this process slow and cumbersome.

Ironically, as the medium of photography spread, newspaper people found themselves copying news photographs and then printing them as wood engravings (Marshall, p. 25). The way to reduce this duplication of effort was to develop a process based on the principles of photography.

As luck would have it, another new printing process (lithography) developed along a parallel path. Before the invention of lithography, all printing had been done on relief surfaces. Lithography used a flat surface (stone or metal), the surface qualities of which could be exploited by striking a critical balance between ink and water.

Photo-lithography and later photo-gravure represented variations on this process, enabling printers to reproduce images quickly and accurately. Reproducing illustrations has always been a vital feature of books and periodicals geared to mass audiences. *Harper's* in New York began using half-tone blocks in 1884 and the *Strand* in London began using line block and half-tone block engravings in 1891 (McLean, p. 227).

Early into the century, bookmakers realized that setting type by hand was a serious problem: this activity was labor-intensive, slow, and costly (Marshall, p. 22). Printers developed a variety of mechanical composing machines during the 1830s. By 1900, newspapers throughout the country were using several makes of type-assembling machines, which assembled ready cast type and assisted type-casting machines, thus avoiding the redistribution of type after printing (Marshall, p. 23). The machines which made a huge impact were the Linotype and the Monotype. Linotype, a machine that makes slugs, each doing the work of a line of hand-set type, and Monotype, a machine for casting and setting type for printing, were put into general use in 1890 and 1900 respectively. True, mechanical composition did not affect the 'look' of pages immediately, but it helped in the introduction of new type faces, over and above the 'modern' type which was normally used (McLean, p. 228).

Papermaking

Understandably, the increase in book production generated a serious problem, namely, keeping up with the demand for paper. Until the turn of the century, paper was made by hand, using rag as the raw material. Of course, the process was slow and rag was in limited supply. The standard paper-making machine was invented in France before 1789; a version of this machine was developed in Britain around 1806. It could make a continuous roll of paper faster and in larger sizes than had previously been possible. By 1830, machine-made paper was generally available in Britain. By the 1840s, British mills were using over 400 of these (Fourdrinier) machines (Marshall, p. 15). The problem of the chronic shortage of rag was eased in the 1870s, when wood pulp replaced rag as the chief raw material.

Binding

At the beginning of the nineteenth century, binders used equipment dating back three centuries. 'Binding' meant binding by hand, singly or in small batches, according to the requirements of the individual customer or bookseller (Ball, p. 2). I should mention two classes of innovations. The first, introduced early in the 1820s, radically altered the physical appearance of books for the next century. Previously, binders had prepared books in a variety of ways: they covered them in a number of leather styles; 'boards,' a simple covering of paper and boards; quires, gatherings left unfolded, to be bound later (this practice continued in the 1840s); and binding in successive parts (Ball, p. 6). Early in the 1820s, a London binder introduced cloth as a covering. No first- or second-hand account of this remarkable innovation has survived (Ball, p. 11). The advantage of cloth was that it offered a style intermediate between the intended permanence of leather and the intended transience of boards (Ball, p. 14). Gold blocking was applied to cloth covering about 1832. The application of gold blocking to cloth – which increased the acceptability of cloth as a material, and opened the way to the decoration of covers economically – became the standard. This meant that publishers could manufacture covers in large quantities (identical in appearance) and that they could apply them to a whole or a part of an issue when required.

The second class of innovations, the shift from hand operations to hand-fed machine operations, increased productivity enormously. A variety of guillotines and board-cutting machines were developed during the period from the late 1830s to the early 1850s. Power-driven machines were introduced during the 1850s and the 1860s. Two further innovations were important: the sewing machine, which started to have an impact during the 1880s, and case-making machines, which were introduced during the 1890s.

Commercial Bookmaking

Not surprisingly, as bookmaking technology improved, the quality of the materials used decreased (Ball, pp. 17-22). The quality of the millboards dropped, with the original hand-made product giving way to machine-made. About 1850, Douglas Ball claims, panel board, a papier mâché board, was introduced. Lighter than millboard, it created problems when it came to gluing and covering. Strawboards were introduced in the 1860s.

Richard Altick notes (p. 307) that, because of relatively low manufacturing costs, the average price of books declined. From the 1860s, 6d. (just under £1 in 1997) was a common price for a book printed in rather small type, usually in double columns, and bound in paper. In the late 1870s, several of Dickens' early books, printed from plates acquired from Chapman and Hall, appeared at 6d. in Routledge's Caxton Novels, a series which included about 800 titles. In the 1880s, two great publishing houses (Cassell and Routledge) brought the price of the rival National and World libraries down to 3d. in paper and 6d. in cloth (Altick, p. 309). Needless to say, price-cutting was accompanied by corner-cutting. In many instances, cheapness meant shoddiness. Often, books advertised as the 'works' of a great author were nothing but haphazard selections. A cheap series would seldom have the benefit of editorial supervision. Ordinary commercial book printing (McLean, p. 230) deteriorated during the 1870s and the 1880s, thanks to the new possibilities for using cheap methods and materials. Ruari McLean points out that the first edition of *Kidnapped*, printed and published (1886) by Cassell, may be cited as an example of the average of the period: several battered letters can be seen on the title page and the 'modern' type (in which the book is set) is very worn throughout. According to McLean (p. 230), the typography lacks style altogether.

In a similar vein, Altick notes that, all too often, the physical format of books was ugly as well as flimsy. The paper was the cheapest available; the wrappers soon became soiled and dog-eared; the sewing gave way; worst of all, the type was small and worn. These defects were typical of every kind of cheap book, not just reprints of the 'classics.' Whatever aesthetic pleasure readers derived from these books was confined to the text itself (Altick, p. 311).

The Revival of Fine Printing

On the one hand, the techniques of book production changed slowly during the nineteenth century; on the other, the very nature of the book itself changed quickly (McLean, p. 3). By the 1880s, it could be argued, British bookmaking had virtually exhausted itself, because publishers focused on producing cheap reading material (Comparato, p. 60). However, a handful of writers and artists, including Dante Gabriel Rossetti, James McNeill Whistler, and Oscar Wilde, small presses, including the Daniel Press, the Chiswick Press, and the Kelmscott Press, and small publishers, including the Bodley Head, rejected the commercialism that governed book production, and in doing so they inaugurated a new era in book design, its goal being to bring all the elements of the book into some kind of harmony (cf. Nelson, p. 48).

The most conspicuous of all those writers and artists engaged in revitalizing cover design (Ball, p. 91), Rossetti designed bindings that contrasted markedly with the general style of the period (McLean, p. 222). He took his cue from William Blake, whom he had 'rediscovered' in the late 1840s. For Rossetti, Blake represented the 'ideal' artist who controlled the creation as well as the presentation of his work (cf. Russell Taylor, p. 25). Blake produced – as poet, artist, and printer – works like *Songs of Innocence and Experience* (1794), for example, which contains not only one of the most celebrated poems, 'The Tyger,' but also some of the most remarkable illustrations. In this respect, Blake combined all his talents and produced the truly 'handmade' book (Nelson, p. 48).

We get a clearer sense of Rossetti's contribution to book design if we pause for a moment and consider the role he played in the arts and crafts movement. First, Rossetti quickly became the leading figure of the Pre-Raphaelite Brotherhood (1848-53), that company of angry young men who dedicated themselves to the reform and renewal of art. The members of this group, which included William Holman Hunt and John Everett Millais, believed that art in Britain 'had declined into a state of aesthetic and spiritual triviality' (Taylor, B., p. 8). Secondly, he gathered around him (in 1857) another group of men, Morris (see below) among them, in order to decorate the Debating Chamber of the new Oxford Union, and in working on this project he made a deep impression on a group who were to be a most powerful force in architecture, design, and craftsmanship in Britain and in Europe (Taylor, B., pp. 10-11). Morris, for one, emerged from this project as an important poet and designer. Thirdly, in a similar vein, he produced a number of designs for Morris and Co., the manufacturing and decorating firm Morris founded (1861) for the purpose of revitalising Victorian taste.

The quality of Rossetti's work, like Blake's, derives from the inseparability of his talents: in many ways, his pictures tend to be poems in paint and his poems (because of their intense pictorial details) tend to be pictures. What is central to his contribution to book production (Barber and Grieve offer a more detailed analysis of his work) is his conception of the book not as a collection of parts, such as type, paper, text, illustrations, and binding, but as a 'whole,' an aesthetic object (see Nelson, p. 49). Beginning in 1862, Rossetti designed entirely fresh book covers, which showed his complete disregard for the conventions his contemporaries observed (Ball, p. 37), and over the years he illustrated many volumes. He produced cover designs for Christina Rossetti's *Goblin Market* (1862), William Michael Rossetti's blank-verse translation (1865) of Part I (Hell) of Dante's *The Divine Comedy*, Christina Rossetti's *The Prince's Progress* (1866), William Michael Rossetti's *Fine Art, chiefly Contemporary* (1867), and Christina Rossetti's *A Pageant* (1881), *Poems* (1891), and *New Poems*, ed. William Michael Rossetti (1896), which were published by Macmillan and Co. *The Prince's Progress* includes Rossetti's illustrations.

I should mention three technical points here. First, Rossetti viewed the cover of a book as a continuum of three elements (front cover, spine, and back cover), aware that each must be satisfactory when examined on its own (Ball, p. 91). Secondly, he produced designs that tend to be simple and asymmetrical, deriving perhaps from Japanese art, which (as Ball rightly observes) exerted a great influence on the cover designs that appeared during the 1870s and the 1880s. Thirdly, he exhibited a sensitivity to such matters as color and texture, which must have made him the bane (Ball, p. 37) of publisher and binder.

It can be argued (McLean, pp. 164-6) that, in terms of book design, amateurs, not professionals, generated the new ideas. One of the first to point the way was the Daniel Press. In fact, Falconer Madan has argued (p. 47), this private press was the first attempt to raise the standard of Victorian printing, a project Morris carried on with higher artistic and professional idealism when he established the Kelmscott Press.

The Rev. Charles Henry Olive Daniel (1836-1919) set up and carried on the Daniel Press, first (1845-59) at Frome and later (1874-1919) at Oxford. The Daniel Press was the first of the private presses to get under way during the Victorian period and it was the last to close down. During his Frome period, Daniel printed a variety of religious and literary documents, such as poems and leaflets, first on a toy press and then on a small Albion press. During the intervening years, he studied for a degree at Worcester College, Oxford, and then lectured in classics at King's College, London. Daniel frequented the Oxford Union about the time the Pre-Raphaelites were painting scenes from *Morte d'Arthur* on the ceiling (Madan, p.2). After his sojourn in London, he returned to Oxford, where he served as Fellow (1863) and later (1903) Provost of Worcester College.

When his Proctorship at Worcester College was over (1874), Daniel picked up the thread of his early interests, collected the small hand-press from Frome, and started afresh, with a much wider outlook on the world of literature, as well as more experience and more technical skill (Madan, p. 49). In 1877, Daniel revived Fell's old-faced type, which had lain forgotten in the archives at the Clarendon Press. Madan (p. 47) claims that this innovation, together with the fine typography, setting, and style of *Rachel's Garland* (1881), printed on the second Frome press (used since 1850) in that type, may be regarded as the first true sign of the revival of fine printing in Britain. Altogether, 36 copies of this book were issued, bound in stiff white vellum, bevelled, with gold tooling and doublure consisting chiefly of straight lines.

Daniel indulged in no lofty artistic aims; he just wanted 'to please and interest friends by presenting them with old and new literature of a high order, as elegant in form as it was in kind' (Madan, p. 44). Using an old press and working with old type, printing on hand-made paper, he produced much good literature from a variety of periods, each volume displaying his trademark: sparseness, elegance, and simplicity. His books, which evoke the personal touch of the early master printers, cry out to be held and read.

Always the 'professional amateur,' Daniel championed the work of many writers, some neglected and others up-and-coming. He printed nine books for Robert Bridges, the future Poet Laureate, starting with *Prometheus the Firegiver* (1883), the poet's first book, and *Poems* (1884), his second. He printed 'with loving care' Pater's imaginary portrait entitled *The Child in the House,* in an edition of 250 copies. This edition, printed on French hand-made paper and covered in pale bluish-grey paper, sold for 6s. (equivalent to £15.44 in 1997) on 12 June 1894 at a Venetian Fête in aid of St. Thomas's Parish.

James Nelson (p. 37) remarks that the Bodley Head (see below) embodied the aims of the revival of fine printing, so often associated with the founding of Morris' Kelmscott Press. It is easy to see (Nelson adds) that, beginning with its first publication, *Volumes in Folio* (1889), the Bodley Head books marked 'a departure from the tasteless, often vulgar bindings, designless title pages, and ugly typography of the books supplied by the large commercial firms' (p. 38).

Ironically, the most influential of all the amateur bookmakers showed little interest in book design as a young man. As an undergraduate, Morris had at least one occasion to consider the ins and outs of printing. I refer to the journal he and his friends ran during the year 1856, the *Oxford and Cambridge Magazine;* Morris, Edward Burne-Jones, and Rossetti used this magazine as a vehicle for promoting the visual arts. Interestingly enough, Morris (who financed most of this enterprise) entrusted the printing to Whittingham the younger at the Chiswick Press, another major champion of artistic book design (McLean, p. 5).

The Chiswick Press dated from 1811, when Charles Whittingham the elder (1767-1840) set up a printing business in Chiswick. Here, he became known as an innovator in printing techniques, particularly the making of wood engravings, at that time a rather difficult task. As well, he was one of the first printers to use machine-made paper. According to McLean, Whittingham the elder published (from 1814) one of the earliest series of pocket books issued in uniform binding (p. 5). The Chiswick Press was already a great name in printing when the founder's nephew, Charles Whittingham the younger (1795-1876), became (1824) his uncle's partner. Whittingham the younger (well known for the excellence of his typography) inherited the business in 1840. The latter might have gone down in history as an excellent printer, had he not met (1828) William Pickering (1796-1854), bookseller and publisher.

In business since 1820, Pickering focused on cheap novels, reprints, and classics. His *tour de force* was the series called Diamond Classics, so named for their 4.5 diamond-size type, at 16 lines to the inch. Novelty, not legibility, was the selling feature (Comparato, p. 44). These books (among the smallest ever produced) could be read 'with great discomfort' under a magnifying glass.

According to at least one account, it was Pickering's binder, Archibald Leighton II (d. 1841), who inaugurated (1825) the practice of covering books in cloth (McLean, p. 6). He bound the first books in cloth manufactured for the purpose, a stiffened dyed calico impervious to the glue required to stick it to the boards; as well, he started the practice of sticking paper labels bearing the titles on the spines. By 1832, as one commentator points out, Leighton was not only embossing cloth with die-stamped patterns, but also stamping or blocking cloth with gold-leaf, having discarded the printed label he had found necessary at first (Comparato, pp. 45-6). Leighton and Co. (run by Archibald's son) also pioneered the use of power for all binding operations.

Kindred spirits on the subject of designing attractive books, Whittingham and Pickering formed (in 1829) a partnership which proved to be unique in the history of nineteenth-century book design and production (Berry and Poole, pp. 218-19). They produced books which neither could have produced alone, books which became the greatest (and most accessible) masterpieces of British book design (McLean, p. 5). They focused on careful setting and fine presswork and introduced decorative elements based largely on the fine initials and border-pieces of sixteenth-century French and Italian printers. These were drawn by Whittingham's daughter Charlotte and engraved by Mary Byfield; they gave Chiswick Press its distinctive character (Berry and Poole, p. 219).

During the 1840s, Pickering revived the use of old-face types, particularly Caslon, thus breaking an established practice of half a century in the use of modern faces (Berry and Poole, p. 219; McLean, p. 12). The Caslon type remained relatively unused until Emery Walker (1851-1933), a typography expert, and Morris revived it. Geoffrey Glaister (p. 60) points out that William Caslon (1692-1766), an eminent type founder, cut his version of old-face letters between 1720 and 1726 expressly for the printer William Bowyer. Pickering used Caslon type because it looked old-fashioned in the best sense of the word.

In addition, the Chiswick Press introduced the reproduction of illustrations in color from wood blocks. In 1843, with Henry Cole (the author) and Joseph Cundall (the publisher), Whittingham produced *The Home Treasury of Books, Pictures, Toys, etc.* Purporting to cultivate the tastes of children, this series of small books at low prices was illustrated by many famous artists and printed in colour from engraved wood blocks.

Pickering died in 1854 and Whittingham retired in 1860, and for a time their passing marked a decline in the firm's press work. However, Charles Thomas Jacobi (b. 1853), who assumed control of the Chiswick Press in 1882, revived good printing at the Chiswick Press. Jacobi was no innovator; however, he had a strong sense of style in printing and maintained the firm's reputation for taste and excellence (Berry and Poole, p. 219; Nelson, p. 39). He became a leading authority on printing, recommending modern-face type for publications like newspapers and magazines and old-face type (or revived old-style) for publication of a higher character, namely, *belles lettres*. These and other views are set out in his (1891) monograph on the art of printing, which he printed at the Chiswick Press for the Bodley Head.

To return to Morris: when the time came to publish his first books, *The Defence of Guenevere and Other Poems* (1858) and *The Life and Death of Jason* (1867), he had the printing done at the Chiswick Press. Both volumes were very well designed (McLean, p. 233). When Morris planned (1867-71) to produce a fine edition of *The Earthly Paradise,* in double-column folio, including pictures by Burne-Jones, he again contacted the Chiswick Press. Specimen pages were set up, some in Caslon type and others in Basel type (Sparling, p. 4). For some reason, however, this project was abandoned.

So far, the energetic Morris seemed content to have his books printed in the ordinary way, 'without any special attention to matters of type or arrangement of page' (Mackail, ii, 213). Soon, he started to give the matter some thought, thanks to conversations he had with Walker. Morris had met Walker in 1884 and they quickly became close friends. Two matters connected with the London Arts and Crafts Exhibition of 1888 convinced him that he should see what he could do about printing books. The first was the display of the best of commercial printing of the time, which he regarded as a great disappointment. He concluded that not one of his own publications warranted inclusion in such an exhibition.

The second matter was the lecture on typography Walker promised to give (15 November 1888) as part of the exhibition. Walker planned to show slides, and in talking about what illustrations might be included they embarked on an intensive study of old models and book-printing techniques (Sparling, pp. 8-9). Very quickly, the early printed books Morris had collected and prized for their woodcuts took on new value as experiments in type (Mackail, pp. ii, 213).

At first, Morris considered the difficulties connected with producing his own type. In consultation with Walker, he settled on a Basel roman type, an adaptation of an early sixteenth-century type, which had been cut by Whittingham in the 1850s (Thompson, p. 141). He got the Chiswick Press to use this type to print *The House of the Wolfings* (1888). By the end of 1889, he decided to set up his own printing press at Kelmscott, Hammersmith.

Morris turned to a number of experts for assistance. At times, Edward T. Prince worked as type-cutter; Thomas Binning, as compositor; Burne-Jones as illustrator; and William Hooper and R. Catterson-Smith as engravers (Sparling, p. 36; Thompson, p. 143). With Walker's help, Morris designed three types, taking his inspiration from the roman types of the fifteenth century: the Golden (1890), based on the types of Jenson and Rubens; the Gothic Troy (1891); and the Chaucer (1892).

With regard to his materials, Morris turned to Joseph Batchelor of Kent, who supplied the hand-made paper; Henry Baud of Middlesex, who prepared the vellum; and the Jaenecke firm of Hanover, who produced the inks, red as well as black.

By spring 1891, then, the Kelmscott Press was ready to print. The first book printed (in Golden type) was an historical romance called *The Story of the Glittering Plain* (1891), a story which had already appeared (as Nos. 81-84) in the *English Illustrated Magazine*. Chapter headings were re-arranged and small corrections were made to the text. A trial page, the first printed at the Press, was struck off on 31 January 1891. *Glittering Plain* was issued (8 May 1891) in an edition of 200 copies; paper copies sold for two guineas and vellum copies sold for six. Colin Franklin (p. 9) among others has argued that the revival of printing started when Morris printed this volume.

As bibliographers like to point out, the beauty of Kelmscott books lies in the harmony of type and decoration, the spacing of words and lines, the positioning of the text on the page, the careful choice of paper and ink, and the excellent presswork, which was achieved with a simple Albion hand press (Berry and Poole, p. 262). Clearly, Morris treated the book as an integral whole, in keeping with the medieval scribes, who produced manuscripts of great beauty (Comparato, p. 62). During the course of its life, the Kelmscott Press printed 153 titles, in editions ranging from 200 to 500. Some sold for 2s. 6d., but the majority sold for more than a guinea (equivalent to £50.66 in 1997).

The consensus among experts is that *The Works of Geoffrey Chaucer* (1896) in folio format, edited by F.S. Ellis, represents the crowning achievement of the Kelmscott Press. Morris spent no less than 21 months printing this volume, using Chaucer type, save for the headings to the longer poems, where he used Troye type, and red and black ink. Altogether, 425 copies on paper sold at 20 pounds each (equivalent to £1,064.80 in 1997) and 13 on vellum sold at 120 guineas each (equivalent to £6,703.20 in 1997). This magnificent volume features a woodcut title-page, together with 14 borders, 18 different frames around the illustrations, and 26 large initial words designed by Morris and engraved by Hooper among others, not to mention 87 woodcut illustrations, designed by Burne-Jones and engraved by Hooper. Altogether, 48 copies were bound in white pigskin at the Doves Bindery. This volume truly evokes that feeling of craftsmanship associated with early printing at its best.

The Kelmscott Press marked an end as well as a beginning (McLean, p. 227). The great importance of Morris' work lies not so much in his style (his books are hard to read) as in the example he provided (Thompson, p. 144). He showed bookmakers that printing could be a fine art.

At this point, I must mention Whistler's contribution, because his book work forms part of an entirely different movement in book design (McLean, p. 166), one sharing features with the best of the Bodley Head books (see below). This expatriate American painter had his own ideas about such matters as layout, as is evident from a glance at his masterpiece of self-advertisement, *The Gentle Art of Making Enemies* (1892). On the one hand, Whistler owes a great deal to Wilde, to ideas germinating in Paris and Holland; on the other, Wilde owed much to Whistler, with regard to creating an aesthetically pleasing setting for his own writings (Nelson, p. 53). Concern for the total book shaped the work of Whistler and Wilde, just as it formed the work of Rossetti and Pater. As McLean (p. 51) rightly observes, a simplicity of design, together with a certain elegance, sets Whistler's work apart from the ordinary books of the day.

The story behind *The Gentle Art* (the Pennells, pp. 285-91) begins in London, early in 1889. Sheridan Ford, an American expatriate who wrote for the *New York Herald* among other publications, got the idea for the book while sifting through newspaper files, which contained the record of Whistler's quarrels with his contemporaries. It struck him that the correspondence should be preserved. Whistler approved of the idea, so long as Ford took on the task of collecting and editing the letters for publication. The artist himself examined boxes of clippings, often altering the text of a letter that had appeared in print, so as to sharpen a barb or to improve his own position in a controversy (Weintraub, p. 338). The type was set up for *The Correspondence of James McNeill Whistler*, the original title, but the author cancelled the agreement he had made with Ford, paid him £10 (equivalent to £482.50 in 1997) by way of compensation, and advised him to proceed no further in the matter. Ford took the MS. to Antwerp; here, an English printer put the work into type and printed 2,000 copies. When Whistler's solicitor got an order to confiscate the copies printed and the type, Ford went to Ghent; here, another English printer put the work into type and printed 4,000 copies. In October 1881, Whistler's solicitor took the matter to the Belgian courts, which banned any distribution of the book.

At this point, the artist decided to create his own edition. Whistler and William Heinemann (his publisher) planned the work together. The former visited the latter almost every day to go over details. Whistler also visited the Ballantyne Press, which was entrusted with the printing. He chose the type, spaced the text, designed an asymmetrical title page, and drew butterflies (his famous butterfly signature) for each entry (each conveys a particular meaning). As well, he designed a prefatory (or publisher's) note, which explained that, due to 'a continued attempt to issue a spurious and garbled version of Mr Whistler's writings,' the publisher obtained the artist's permission to issue the present volume, printed under the latter's close supervision. He included (in the next six pages) extracts from the London and Paris press outlining the 'extraordinary piratical plot' to publish Mr Whistler's writings without his consent. The title-page followed: THE GENTLE ART / OF / MAKING ENEMIES / AS PLEASINGLY EXEMPLIFIED / IN MANY INSTANCES, WHEREIN THE SERIOUS ONES / OF THIS EARTH, CAREFULLY EXASPERATED, HAVE / BEEN SPURRED ON TO UNSEEMLINESS / AND INDISCRETION, WHILE OVERCOME BY AN / UNDUE SENSE OF RIGHT. The dedication conveys the same sentiments: 'To the rare Few, who, early in Life, have rid Themselves of the Friendship of the many, these pathetic Papers are inscribed.'

In many ways, *The Gentle Art* represents (Weintraub, p. 341) Whistler's 'artistic autobiography and testament.' For example, it condenses the famous Ruskin-Whistler trial (1878), together with newspaper encounters with the critics, among them Wilde. During the Art Nouveau Movement, *The Gentle Art* served as a model of book design – because of its meticulous and wholly idiosyncratic disposition of black and white on a page (Russell Taylor, p. 52). First, Whistler did not illustrate the book; instead, he made patterns with the print itself, so that the text appears as a dark island in a sea of white. Secondly, he experimented with asymmetrical arrangements, so that the basic block of the text is never placed squarely in the middle of the page. He placed annotations in small print, not in their conventional position at the bottom of the page but above and beside the main text, and generally he suppressed page numbers and running titles. In this way, Whistler showed book designers that striking effects could be produced with the simplest means, such as ordinary type, regular paper, inexpensive lettering, and simple binding. The result was one the ordinary book buyer might actually read, over and above admiring its physical appearance (Russell Taylor, p. 52; Weintraub, p. 341).

For his part, Morris bequeathed to bookmakers in Britain and the United States a passion for fine printing (Olmert, p. 228). As I have indicated, the revival of fine printing extended from 1891 to 1918. In Britain, it was led by a number of small private presses, including the Vale Press and the Doves Press. In the United States, the revival of fine printing was led by small presses like the Merrymount Press and the Riverside Press. Of course, the big commercial publishing houses of Boston, Chicago, and New York modified their practices in light of these developments. As well, several new publishing firms were founded in Britain during the 1890s, such as J.M. Dent, Methuen, the Bodley Head, and William Heinemann, in addition to Macmillan and Co., with a view to producing affordable, well designed books.

I conclude this brief survey with a few words about the Bodley Head, the small publishing firm which provided a model for the big commercial publishers (Nelson, p. 76). John Lane (1854-1925), for many years a railway clerk, persuaded Elkin Mathews (1851-1921), an Exeter shop keeper, to move his book shop to London. Mathews (Nelson points out) provided Lane with an opportunity to get his toe in the door of a good book-selling business and to expand it into a small publishing firm. At any rate, in Vigo Street they opened (1887) the Bodley Head, which quickly became (Nelson, p. 151) a meeting place for all the poets and the artists who comprised the *fin de siècle,* including Walter Crane, Ernest Dowson, John Gray, Selwyn Image, Lionel Johnson, Ernest Rhys, William Rothenstein, Arthur Symons, and Oscar Wilde. The name had great appeal because it suggested (for one thing) the famous library. From the very outset, business prospered: Mathews concentrated on the firm's antiquarian interests and Lane sought out prospective authors. At the same time, he was looking for the type of book that might serve as a model for future publications (Nelson, p. 13).

Lane's first 'find' proved to be significant. In Richard Le Gallienne (1866-1947), Lane found not only a budding poet and a promising belletrist, but a future colleague. Le Gallienne not only shared with the partners a passion for rare and beautiful books of the past, but also his knowledge of the production of fine books than they did (Nelson, p. 16). As well, he was far more a part of the aesthetic milieu of the late 1880s than they were. As of January 1892, when Lane officially entered the firm, the team was assembled and ready to work. Mathews was the executive who approved the contracts, signed the cheques, and dispatched the official letters; Lane sought out new talent and promoted the firm's activities, and Le Gallienne served as chief reader and literary adviser (Nelson, p. 30).

Quite deliberately, Mathews and Lane concentrated on the *belles-lettres* market, with a view to exploiting the growing demand for limited editions of (say) poetry tastefully produced. As Nelson (pp. 79-80) observes, the vogue during the 1890s had been to collect limited editions of modern writers, such as Andrew Lang, Robert Louis Stevenson, and Austin Dobson.

The Bodley Head succeeded as a publisher of limited editions because Mathews, Lane, and Le Gallienne had the aesthetic sense to regard the book as a whole and the business acumen to employ designers, such as Charles Ricketts, Charles Jacobi, Laurence Housman, Selwyn Image, and Aubrey Beardsley, who could arrange the elements, such as layout, typography, paper, and binding. In addition, they ensured that all their books were printed (on hand-made paper) by the best printers, including those at the Chiswick Press and at T. and A. Constable of Edinburgh, and that they were bound by the best of binders, including Leighton Son and Hodge of London. The most distinctive Bodley Head title-pages (Nelson, p. 67) were produced by the artists who played the most significant roles in the *art nouveau* book, namely, Ricketts and Beardsley.

In this regard, the Bodley Head embodied the ideals so often associated (Nelson, pp. 36-7) with the founding of the Kelmscott Press and set out by Jacobi in *On the Making and Issuing Books* (1891). The cost of book production during the 1890s was so low that they could not only print editions of 350 copies (compared to the 750 or 1,000 Victorian publishers usually issued) and make a profit, but also could do so charging on average 5d. (equivalent to 99p in 1997) per copy (Nelson, p. 84). Apparently, the first edition of a book rarely exceeded 500 copies.

Characteristically, the Bodley Head book was simply beautiful, achieving that sparseness, elegance, and simplicity in its format so characteristic of Whistler's books. Two examples will have to suffice.

First, Le Gallienne's *Volumes in Folio* (1889) was the first volume to bear the Bodley Head imprint. It was printed by the Chiswick Press and issued in an edition of 250 copies (signed by the author). In physical appearance and in its subject matter, then, *Volumes in Folio* is meant to appeal to the collector interested in antiquarian books (Nelson, p. 22): its (antique) boards are covered with blue-grey paper; it is printed by the Chiswick Press on Van Gelder hand-made paper; its ridged spine is bound in imitation vellum; and its title-page is tastefully designed in red and black ink. Nelson (p. 23) observes that this volumes assumes the air of something rare and precious, an object for only the 'few.'

Secondly, Wilde's *Poems* was the first volume to carry the joint imprint of Elkin Mathews and John Lane. This volume was issued in 1892 in an edition of 220 copies (the author signed each copy). Ricketts designed the title-page and the binding. Actually, this up-and-coming young artist had already collaborated with Charles Shannon (Nelson, p. 41) in bringing out the first number of the *Dial* (Summer 1889), one of the most beautiful of the journals of the Aesthetic Movement, and some of Wilde's other books, designed the title page and the binding, and he had already produced three books for Wilde: *The Picture of Dorian Gray*, *Intentions*, and *Lord Arthur Savile's Crime*, which appeared in 1891.

The aesthetic appeal of these volumes depends upon the tasteful arrangement of the most economical of materials. At the Bodley Head, this meant striving for the solidity of the page; using good paper, which enhances the beauty and the durability of the work; making sure that ornamentation forms part of the page; and selecting well-designed type.

IV THE HOUSE OF MACMILLAN

Daniel and Alexander enjoyed working in the retail book business, but they felt that their true vocation lay in publishing (Morgan, C., pp. 22-4; Cohen and Gandolfo, p. 6). As one biographer pointed out, 'they worked together in perfect balance, full of knowledge of their trade and of the love of books. The old principle of unity between book-selling and publishing had one of its greatest exemplars in them' (Morgan, C., p. 31). Remarkably, then, the people who came to the shop to buy books stayed in the publishing house to write them (Morgan, C., p. 34).

At first, the Macmillan brothers focused on theological, educational, and scientific works (Graves, p. 56). The year 1852 proved to be very good: they published F.D. Maurice's *Prophets and Kings*, Charles Kingsley's *Phaeton*, and Isaac Todhunter's *Differential Calculus*, books which turned out to be solid investments (Morgan, C., p. 39). In 1855, they published Kingsley's *Westward Ho!* and in 1857 they published Thomas Hughes's *Tom Brown's School Days*, which passed through five editions before the end of the year. These publications set the firm on a secure course and enabled the brothers to establish artistic and financial independence (Cohen and Gandolfo, p. 6).

While the business prospered, however, the Macmillans had to contend with ill health. Daniel suffered from recurring bouts of tuberculosis, and Alexander from sciatica (Graves, p. 29). Often, the former sojourned in the south of England, taking a variety of 'cures' (Hughes, pp. 277-8). Daniel died of tuberculosis on 27 June 1857, knowing that the publishing house would survive him and that his brother-partner would look after his family (Cohen and Gandolfo, p. 6).

As early as 1852, the Macmillans discussed the possibility of setting up a London office (Graves, p. 70; Hughes, p. 217; VanArsdel, p. 180). This dream became a reality in 1858, when Robert Bowes was put in charge of the office at 23 Henrietta Street, Covent Garden; however, the headquarters of the firm remained at Cambridge for another five years. Both branches followed the 'Macmillan' publishing principles, such as being careful about money, choosing books which would last, and being scrupulously fair with authors.

For the next five years, it was Alexander's habit on Thursday to take the train to London, staying for the night. Here, he kept open house for authors and prospective authors, as well as friends, anyone in fact who cared to join him in a modest meal and to take part in easy discussion (Macmillan, G., p. xxx; Graves, p. 120; Morgan, C., pp. 50-1). These meetings, known as 'Tobacco Parliaments,' were crucial to the development of the publishing business (Graves, p. 115). He was never conspicuous as the host: apparently, he had the ability to dissolve into the company assembled (Morgan, C., p. 50). To his credit, Alexander realized from the start that publishing was a personal affair, and he made an effort to attract the leading figures of the age to these gatherings, including Thomas Hughes, T.H. Huxley, Charles Kingsley, F.D. Maurice, Francis Palgrave, Herbert Spencer, and Alfred Tennyson (Morgan, C., pp. 50-1; VanArsdel, p. 181).

Alexander introduced two other major changes during this period. First, he expanded the publishing enterprise by adding departments of *belles lettres* and fiction (Graves, p. 120). As Simon Nowell-Smith (1967) points out, under his management, the firm expanded from the issue of fewer than 40 titles in 1857 to more than 150 (excluding American and colonial titles) in 1889, when he retired from active publishing (p. 19). Secondly, he added a periodical to their list of projects. As far back as 1855, he wanted to produce a monthly magazine like the *Revue des Deux Mondes*, which might be called *The World of Letters: A Chronicle of Literature* (Graves, p. 70). As a result of discussions he had with his literary and business advisors, he resolved to design such a magazine, which would serialise novels prior to publication. It was thought that this arrangement would increase the sales of the magazine, as individual chapters appeared, as well as the sales of the book, because of the publicity. Not unlike *Blackwood's Magazine*, it was to feature political and religious commentary, as well as travel sketches, fiction, and poetry. However, it was to sell for only a shilling.

The first issue of *Macmillan's Magazine* appeared in November 1859, two months before its chief rival – the *Cornhill Magazine* – was launched. Its success was immediate (Graves, p. 152). Within 18 days of its release, 10,000 copies were sold. In quality, *Macmillan's Magazine* held its own among this trio. Every literary figure of any stature contributed to the magazine (Morgan, C., p. 59).

David Masson (1822-1907) served as editor from 1859-68, when he became Professor of English Literature at Edinburgh University. He was publishing the first of the six volumes of his *Life of Milton* (1859-80) when the magazine was launched.

George Grove (1812-92), musicologist, biblical scholar, civil engineer, and editor, took over from Masson, and from 1868-83 he guided the magazine through what has been regarded by some commentators as its golden years. His personableness and his inventiveness ensured that the magazine never lacked for copy. Grove is remembered for his great work, *Dictionary of Music and Musicians* (1878-89).

John Morley (see p. 7) guided the magazine through its silver period from 1883-85. His contributions and the contributions of his personal contacts, among them James Bryce, T.H. Huxley, and Mary Ward, were substantial.

The latter contributed no less than 16 articles during this period. The bias he gave to his commentary on current issues has been called 'Philosophical Radicalism.' In terms of policy, he preferred signed to unsigned articles.

Mowbray Morris (1847-1911), a workaday literary journalist and reader for Macmillan and Co., guided the magazine through its final period, from 1885-1907. This rather conservative journalist wrote a great many anonymous reviews and articles for the magazine. Unfortunately, he failed to appreciate the work of the next generation, among them Thomas Hardy and W.B. Yeats (Morgan, C., pp. 144, 219-22), and the magazine[6] fell behind the times, disappearing almost unnoticed in 1907.

During the 1860s, under Alexander's guidance, Macmillan and Co. became one of the leading publishing houses in London. I must mention two successful projects. First, the firm launched (in June 1863) *The Cambridge Shakespeare*, which would be edited with the sort of scholarship ordinarily reserved for Latin and Greek texts. Nine stately volumes were completed in three years. This was 'a great edition, rich in learning, uncommonly free from pedantry, a trifle heavy to hold, but good to read' (Morgan, C., p. 74).

Secondly, Macmillan and Co. launched the 'Golden Treasury' series, one of the most successful series ever issued by the firm (Graves, p. 170; Morgan, C., pp. 62-3). This series was inspired by Francis Palgrave's *Golden Treasury of English Songs and Lyrics* (1861), which had appeared under the Macmillan and Co. imprint. By 1889, the *Golden Treasury Series* numbered 44 titles, including such enduring works as Coventry Patmore's *Children's Garland* (1862), Matthew Arnold's selections from Wordsworth (1879) and Byron (1881), and T. Humphry Ward's *The English Poets* (1880).

The period 1863-73 was (according to George Macmillan) the most important period of Alexander's life (Graves, p. 216). During 1863, he took a house at Upper Tooting, London; accepted the appointment of Publisher to the University of Oxford, a position he held until 1880, when the delegates abandoned the system of employing a private publisher; and in July moved the firm's headquarters to London. In July 1863, the office was moved from the Henrietta Street address to 16 Bedford Street, Covent Garden. In 1873, the office moved to a larger site at 29-30 Bedford Street, Covent Garden (Graves, p. 210). Bowes returned to Cambridge to manage the retail business as an independent enterprise, which eventually became Bowes and Bowes (Morgan, C., p. 67).

In bringing these changes about, Alexander realised that he could no longer manage Macmillan and Co. by himself, and began to look for an energetic partner who could attend to the details of publishing (Morgan, C., pp. 68-9). He found this person in George Lillie Craik (1837-1905), who had studied at Glasgow University and who had then trained as an accountant.

Craik joined the firm in 1865, about the time he married Dinah Maria Muloch (1826-87), the author of *John Halifax, Gentleman* (1857) and other books for children. He became Alexander's right-hand man, managing (until his death) most of the firm's financial affairs. He had comparatively little to do with authors or with the literary sides of the business (Nowell-Smith, p. 20). This was a fortunate choice (Morgan, C., p. 69), for he was precisely the sort of person Alexander needed as an administrator, a person full of energy and character.

About this time (June 1865), Macmillan and Co. added books-for-children to the list of the subjects included in their list of publications. The Rev. Charles Lutwidge Dodgson (1832-98), the shy mathematics don at Christ Church, Oxford, had made arrangements with Clarendon Press to produce *Alice in Wonderland* at his own expense. Lewis Carroll took great interest in the publication details (Cohen and Gandolfo, pp. 35-41) of the coffee-table book, but when the first presentation copies were circulated he changed his mind. Dissatisfied with the reproduction of the drawings, he and the illustrator, John Tenniel (1820-1914), cancelled the edition altogether. Lewis Carroll prepared another edition for Macmillan and Co. the following year. By 1867, this volume (illustrated) had earned a profit of £250 on an original investment of £350 (equivalent to £9,190 and £12,866 in 1997).

On 10 August 1867, Alexander sailed to New York, with a view to opening an American branch. To this point, the sale of his books in the United States had been handicapped by high tariffs and the absence of international copyright (Morgan, C., p. 83). To retain his share of the market, then, Alexander needed manufacturing and distribution facilities. In this undertaking, he was motivated by his dream of building the firm into a 'great international publishing house' (Graves, p. 275). With these considerations in mind, he visited Boston, Philadelphia, Toronto, and Washington.

This plan materialized in 1869, when Macmillan and Co. sent George Edward Brett (1827-90), an experienced London bookseller, to manage the operation at 63 Bleecker Street, New York. The business expanded rapidly. George's son, George Platt Brett, who was only 16, joined (1874) the staff as a travelling salesman. When Brett senior died in 1890, Brett junior took over.

At this time, the American Macmillan and Co. was set up, composed of members of the London firm, with Brett as resident partner. A further change was made in 1896, when Alexander died. Macmillan and Co. were reorganized: the English firm became a limited concern, Macmillan and Co., Ltd., and the American branch was incorporated as Macmillan Co., a separate entity with Brett as President. The American firm became a publishing house in its own right, and it was Brett's policy to encourage each department to be autonomous, to challenge if not surpass competitors in its own speciality.

During the 1870s, Macmillan and Co. consolidated its position as a major publishing house. In 1874, the firm published J.R. Green's *Short History of the English People*, which became a university text. Green planned this work as a history of England's political, social, religious, and intellectual growth, rather than a chronology of major conflicts, and this approach caught the public's interest. Surprisingly, 35,000 copies of the book sold in 18 months.

In 1877, the firm agreed to publish the work of Henry James. The firm published *French Poets and Novelists* (a collection of essays) and *The Europeans* in 1878. Although James was never a profitable author for the firm, Macmillan and Co. published most of his books up to 1899, including the definitive New York editions of his novels (Morgan, C., p. 110).

Also in 1878, Macmillan and Co. launched its most successful series, the English Men of Letters, edited by Morley, one of the firm's most valued readers and advisers. The winning formula, as Morley predicted, lay in matching subject and writer, so that any given volume offered specialist and non-specialist readers a sound introduction and a point of departure respectively. In this way, these remarkable volumes, including *Hawthorne* (1879) by Henry James; *Hume* (1879) by T.H. Huxley; *Johnson* (1878), *Pope* (1880), and *Swift* (1882) by Leslie Stephen; *Thackeray* (1879) by Anthony Trollope; and *Wordsworth* (1881) by F.W.H. Myers, remained 'standard' texts for many years (see VanArsdel, p. 186).

By the end of the 1880s, however, Alexander had ceased to be the major force behind the firm (Morgan, C., p. 101). He had remarried in 1872 (his first wife had died in 1871) and almost imperceptibly his and his brother's sons had entered the firm as partners. Thus, the basis of control gradually shifted.

George Macmillan (1855-1936), Alexander's second son, entered the firm (1874), fresh from Eton, becoming a full partner in January 1879. George concentrated on music, the classics, and natural history (Morgan, C., pp. 166-8). He encouraged such important works as the *Journal of Hellenic Studies* (1880).

Frederick Macmillan (1851-1936), the eldest son of Daniel, went straight from public school into publishing. He learned the whole range of the book-trade from Bowes (his cousin); acquired a general knowledge of printing at the University of Oxford Press; and worked through all the departments of the Bedford Street office. As well, he spent five years in the firm's New York office. He married Georgina Elizabeth, daughter of Thomas Warrin (d. 1943), of Newton, Long Island. Frederick returned to England in 1876 as a full partner (Graves, p. 54). He took a keen interest in the New York branch of the business, which in 1890 became an independent firm under the name of the Macmillan Co., with the London partners as directors. A man of genuine taste and sound judgment, he was seldom misled by the prejudices of his 'readers.' In selecting MSS for publication, he was inclined to shy away from extremes, whether of emotion or manner. He had a pleasant personality, and enjoyed the friendship of many distinguished writers. Equipped with a first-hand knowledge of all the technicalities of his profession, Frederick followed his uncle's lead in building up a world-wide organisation with branches in, for example, Canada, Australia, and India.

Moreover, Frederick was deeply interested in trade practices outside the firm (Nowell-Smith, p. 20), and led the campaign for the Net Book Agreement. For many years, the custom for booksellers had been to sell their wares not at the price fixed by publishers but at a discount fixed by individual sellers. Frederick began his campaign by writing to the *Bookseller*, which printed (6 March 1890) his letter outlining his remedy. Here, he suggested two classes of books (cf. Morgan, C., pp. 178-9), whereby the price of Net Books (books sold at the published price without discount) would be set by the publisher and the price of Subject Books (books sold at discount) would be set at the bookseller's discretion. According to one source, Macmillan and Co. began to distribute 'net books'; between July and December 1890, they launched sixteen titles on a net basis, and by 1894 the firm had circulated more than a hundred net books a year (quoted in Cohen and Gandolfo, p. 25). In January 1899, the Publishers' Association finally sent the Associated Booksellers a proposal acceptable to all (VanArsdel, p. 189).

Frederick served as president of the Publishers Association during the period 1900-02 and 1911-13 and played a leading role in framing the Copyright Act of 1911 (see p. 75n).

Malcolm Macmillan (1852-89), Alexander's eldest son and godchild of Kingsley (Graves, p. 54), trained in the firm but, owing to ill health, played little part in its activities. He studied at Balliol College, Oxford, during the period 1875-79, but ill-health interrupted his studies, and as a result he took his B.A. in 1884. Although unable to settle into the routine of the publishing business, he was deeply interested in literature and art. In 1887, he travelled abroad, visiting Greece, Cyprus, and Egypt. Malcolm disappeared in July 1889 while climbing Mount Olympus (Macmillan, G., p. 239, and Morgan, C., p. 137). According to reports, Alexander never got over his mysterious death (Graves, p. 315).

Maurice Crawford Macmillan (1853-1936), the second son of Daniel Macmillan, entered the firm as a full partner in 1883, taking charge of the firm's educational department. Maurice had distinguished himself as a classical scholar at Christ's College, Cambridge, obtaining a first class in classics in 1875. He had served as classical master at St. Paul's School from 1877-83. Initially, Maurice focused on education, and during the period 1884-85 he toured schools and universities throughout Australia and India. In this undertaking, he was taking on the job of putting into practice some of the ideas that had been stirring in Alexander's mind for 40 years, taking up the position (in 1893) as an educational agent for India and opening (in 1901) a branch of the firm in Bombay (Morgan, C., p. 187).

Not surprisingly, Macmillan and Co. grew into an important international publishing house, representing many of the major writers of the day. In 1897, the firm moved to a new building, especially designed, in St Martin's Street, between Leicester Square and the National Gallery. The following year, the firm purchased Bentley and Son, of 8 New Burlington Street, a flourishing publishing house.

V PATER'S LITERARY CAREER

Early in June 1872, Pater visited Alexander Macmillan in London, hoping to persuade Macmillan and Co. to publish a collection of his 'studies' on the Renaissance. On 29 June, he sent Alexander a prospectus, together with six essays (one in manuscript form), saying that the book would include ten essays, five of which had not been published before (p. 67). He may well have included three unpublished essays. Alexander read the essays with interest, and a few days later he proposed an octavo volume[7] and terms of 'half profits.' According to this arrangement, standard for a book of this kind, the publisher risked the cost of publishing and in turn shared the profits with the author. Pater accepted this proposal, but when he studied the proofs, he thought they were unsuitable for the book he had in mind. He explained that some were so short and that all of them were so slight that they were suitable only for a volume selling for about 5d. (equivalent to £9.19 in 1997).

Above all, Pater was concerned about the book's physical appearance. First, he made a case for printing the book in octavo size, promising (p. 68) to state his reasons when he next visited Macmillan. This matter was settled easily enough. Secondly, he made a number of suggestions about the paper and the binding. In his letter of 2 November 1872, for example, Pater wrote that he liked 'the look of the page, but not altogether the paper.' He suggested that the book be bound in the old-fashioned pasteboard covers of greyish-blue and that the title be printed on a paper back of olive green (see p. 69). Macmillan objected quite strongly to this suggestion, arguing that booksellers would be reluctant to stock such a book, and pressed for the conventional binding, that is, cloth and gilt lettering. Pater wanted to give his book the 'artistic appearance' such a work required, and attempted (p. 70) to meet Macmillan's objections in his letter of 11 November. Macmillan continued to argue for cloth binding, and on the following day sent by mail a sample book in cloth binding with imitation 'wirewove paper' in 'mock rib' in order to persuade Pater (p. 71). These samples convinced him that he could achieve the effect he wanted via modern materials.

The Renaissance (1873)

In due course, *Studies in the History of the Renaissance* was printed on ribbed paper, which has an uneven, corrugated surface, because it has passed through ridged rollers, bound in dark blue-green cloth binding (with lettering in gold on the back), and issued on 1 March 1873 with chocolate end papers in an edition of 1,250 copies, a printing run commensurate with its appeal, priced at 7s. 6d. (equivalent to £13.50 in 1997). During Pater's lifetime, the book went through four editions.

The Renaissance can be described (Small, 1991a) as the work of a young man eager to make his mark. Always the iconoclast, Pater not only challenges individual judgments that his distinguished elders take as settled, but also modifies the aesthetics that make their judgments possible. First, he formulates (in the chapter on Luca della Robbia) a romantic or expressive theory of art. In this project, he challenges Ruskin, who in Volume I (1843) of *Modern Painters* for example speaks of art as 'a noble and expressive language.' Here, Ruskin stresses the didactic function of art, arguing that the painter gathers and arranges the facts of nature (natural objects for Ruskin symbolise the divinity of God) so as to induce 'noble emotions' in the spectators. Pater too regards art as a form of personal expression, but he stresses it as the expression of the painter's personality. He argues that the charm of della Robbia's work is its expressiveness, in that the artist has objectified his thoughts and feelings via unique images. If a work of art is to have an aesthetic as distinct from an historical value (Ruskin's sense of the transcription of natural facts), it must exhibit (Pater concludes) something individual, the impress of the artist's temper and personality. This expression of individuality is what makes art worth having at all.

Secondly, Pater offers 'aesthetic criticism' as a way of liberating the appreciation of art from moral considerations. In order to invigorate the appreciation of art, thus making it more meaningful, he turns his attention from the work itself to the work in relation to the artist behind it, calling for an explanation of the process by which it was produced. In this project, he takes as his point of departure Arnold, who had spelled out the function of criticism in the first series (1865) of *Essays in criticism*. There, Arnold wrote: The goal in all branches of knowledge is 'to see the object as in itself it really is.' In the 'Preface' to his own volume, Pater agrees with Arnold, so far as criticism goes, but adds: In 'aesthetic criticism the first step is to know one's own impression as it really is, to discriminate it, to realise it distinctly.' In this respect, he shifts critical attention to the circumstances which mould the artist's genius, as well as the force of the artist's personality which resists these circumstances. Accordingly, the 'aesthetic critic' regards beautiful objects as powers or forces which produce unique, pleasurable sensations, and feels compelled to analyze, to reduce these powers to their basic elements, to indicate the sources of that impression. In order to isolate, to communicate this essence, the critic must possess (first of all) 'a certain kind of temperament, the power of being deeply moved by the presence of beautiful objects,' as well as an historical sense, or sense of tradition, because 'every intellectual product must be judged from the point of view of the age and the people in which it was produced.' Reconstructing the chief elements of the artist's genius entails a psychological analysis of the artist's temperament as it is manifested in the work. According to Pater, the 'formula' for da Vinci, for example, is 'curiosity and the desire of beauty.'

As we have seen, in the 'Conclusion,' Pater offers readers nothing less than a manifesto. Our one chance, he writes, is to expand those brief intervals we call life, to get 'as many pulsations as possible' into the few moments we have. What makes life as intense and as complete as possible (the aim of culture) is 'the love of art for its own sake.'

The middle period: 1874-78

The Renaissance excited as much censure as praise (see Seiler, 1980: 47-112). Some reviewers, like Morley, writing in the *Fortnightly Review* (April 1873), found the essays pleasant and instructive reading; others, including Mrs (Margaret) Oliphant (1828-97), critic and novelist, who in *Blackwood's Magazine* (November 1873), described them as 'pretentious' and 'artificial.'

Specialists took a dim view of the book as historical scholarship. One reviewer, writing in the *Spectator* (14 June 1873), observed that 'after most carefully perusing Mr Pater's book, we find ourselves gravely doubting whether he has rightly apprehended the Renaissance at all' (p. 765). Writing in the *Westminster Review* (April 1873), Mrs Pattison, née Emila Frances Strong (1840-1904), historian of French art, protested that Pater's book is 'in no wise a contribution to the history of the Renaissance,' attacking its title and lack of 'scientific' method. Sidney Colvin (1845-1927), critic of art and literature, writing in the *Pall Mall Gazette* (1 March 1873), observed that the choice of subjects was in fact too fragmentary for the purpose of a complete history (p. 11).

Likewise, connoisseurs of art took a dim view of the book as art criticism. Reviewers liked the essays on Leonardo, Michelangelo, Botticelli, and Winckelmann, but viewed Pater's 'aesthetic criticism' with suspicion. For example, Sarah Wister (1835-1908), pianist and linguist, writing in the *North American Review* (July 1875), questioned Pater's theory that 'incompleteness' served as an equivalent for colour in Michelangelo's sculpture.

Understandably, the *carpe diem* theme of the 'Conclusion' provoked heated opposition, from Oxford conservatives especially. Almost immediately, the chaplain of BNC, John Wordsworth (1843-1911), grand-nephew of the poet, complained (17 March 1873) to Pater about the scandal his philosophy of hedonism had caused (Evans, pp. 12-14). Like many people, Wordsworth objected to Pater's theory 'that no fixed principles either of religion or morality can be regarded as certain, that the only thing worth living for is momentary enjoyment.' Then, F.W. Farrar (1831-1903), Fellow of Trinity College, Cambridge, and Dean (1895-1903) of Canterbury, preached (11 May 1873) a sermon before the University of Cambridge, attacking as 'wretched' and 'base' this ideal of crowning life 'with the greatest number of pleasurable sensations.' Adding insult to injury, Pater's former tutor, the Rev. W. Wolfe Capes, now 'select preacher' to the University of Oxford, delivered (23 November 1873) the University Sermon, denouncing the self-indulgence and the tendency to impiety in the so-called 'humanitarian' culture. Much of the phrasing (cf. Richards, p. 9) in the sermon suggests that he had Pater in mind.

At this juncture, the point to make is that the Establishment, via Jowett, now Master (1870-93) of Balliol College and perhaps the most powerful 'academic' at Oxford, conveyed its displeasure in February 1874, when Pater angled for but missed the Junior Proctorship, which had fallen to BNC (Evans, p. 13n). Apparently, the office was as good as his. For decades, commentators have explained that Jowett had taken 'up a line of definite opposition to Pater,' identifying him with 'the advanced aesthetic school, or [had] supposed that at all events his teaching was adapted to strengthen a species of Hedonism or modern paganism' (Benson, pp. 54-5, and Wright, T., i, 255-6). Brake (1981) and Inman (1991) offer the following explanation. Early in 1874, some letters Pater had written to William Money Hardinge, a Balliol undergraduate, came into the possession of Jowett; disturbed by signs suggesting that the 'greatest evil of Greek life' was developing between Hardinge and Pater, he threatened to make the letters public should the latter ever think of standing for University office (see Seiler, 1987: 253-61). Very likely, Inman (1991) adds, Jowett mentioned Pater's 'unnatural' inclinations to the authorities at BNC just when they were considering the matter (pp. 34-5). On the very day Hardinge (as advised by Jowett) left Oxford, 25 February 1874, BNC nominated Wordsworth as University Proctor.

About 12 years passed before Pater published another book. Some commentators (cf. Gosse) have explained this period of silence in terms of the slowness of Pater's method of composition; others (cf. Benson) have explained these so-called silent years in terms of Pater's fulfilling his College duties. Actually, as Lawrence Evans (1970) points out, these were years of 'much experimentation, in which he made several false starts in several very different directions' (p. xxvii). Pater made every effort to ensure that, in the future, the reception of his works would be favourable; this meant exploring new themes; answering his critics and revising his work incessantly, so as to clarify his meaning and to remove grounds for possible offence; and soliciting reviews from influential writers.

At first, he contemplated (November 1874) writing a book on Shakespeare, an orthodox subject that might enable him to restore his somewhat tarnished reputation. He 'leaked' word of his plan to the *Academy* (7 November 1874), which announced that Pater intended 'to continue his short aesthetic studies of Shakespeare's plays in the *Fortnightly*, the present month's one on *Measure for Measure* being the first of a series that will some day make a book' (vi, 506). A short while later, the *Academy* (12 December 1874) stated that his next 'study' for the *Fortnightly Review* would be on *Love's Labour's Lost* (vi, 630). Pater abandoned this project some time in 1875.

About this time, he considered writing a series of studies of Greek myth and art. Within three years, he had written two two-part essays: 'The Myth of Demeter and Persephone,' which he delivered (in 1875) as a lecture, and 'A Study of Dionysus.' Later, he published the first part of the lecture in the *Fortnightly Review* (January 1876), and the second in the *Fortnightly Review* (February 1876). Pater revised this essay with a view (see Letters 42 and 47) to publishing it, together with 'A Study of Dionysus.' He once described this project[8] as one of the most difficult pieces of work he had ever undertaken (cf. Benson, p. 71).

Pater suffered another chastening, this time during the period from June to December, 1876, when Chapters I-III of Book I of William Hurrell Mallock's (1849-1923) satire, *The New Republic*, appeared (anonymously) in *Belgravia*. Mallock (1920) explains that he had gone up to Balliol College in 1869, but had become disillusioned with Oxford liberalism and its representatives, especially Jowett (pp. 65-6). In *The New Republic*, his satirical defense of old and traditional beliefs against the encroachments of various types of liberalism, he parodies the opinions and the manners of a number of the famous personalities, including Ruskin, Jowett, and Arnold. Pater comes off badly as Mr Rose the arch-aesthete, who speaks of two subjects in an undertone, 'self-indulgence and art.' As Inman (1990) points out, Mallock captures the Jowett-Pater antipathy perfectly (p. 233). At one point in the story, Mr. Rose expounds his views on 'art for art's sake' to the other guests, and Dr Jenkinson replies: 'All this is very poor stuff – *very* poor stuff.'

The first major opportunity he had to clarify his meaning and to remove grounds for further misunderstanding or offence presented itself in November 1876, when Macmillan suggested (p. 74) that Pater pursue his plan to issue a new and revised edition of *The Renaissance*. Of course, Pater agreed to this proposal, saying that he wanted to add some new material and to make a number of alterations. He considered (Hill, pp. 282-3) a number of important changes, which included (a) giving the book a new title, *The Renaissance: Studies in Art and Poetry*; (b) toning down expressions of aestheticism, (c) excising passages plainly provocative or critical of religion; (d) modernising the spelling, especially of such names as Mirandula, Michael Angelo, and Lionardo; and (e) suppressing the 'Conclusion' because (as he would argue later) 'it might possibly mislead some of those young men into whose hands it might fall.' Many of these changes can be tied to specific criticisms, such as those saying that the title was 'misleading.' As it happened, these revisions 'leave hardly a page untouched' (Hill, p. 282).

In addition, Pater made a number of suggestions about the 'look' of the volume, in terms of paper, layout, binding, and labelling, and proposed (p. 77) an edition of 1,000 copies, instead of 1,250, as before. Macmillan preferred the larger edition, saying that 'the last 250 make a considerable difference in the money result and they are sure to sell.' Pater made up the title page himself and prepared the advertisements that would appear in the newspapers. Moreover, he devoted much emotional energy to the printing of the 'vignette,' one of his favourite drawings in the Louvre. Later, when he received his inspection copy of the book, he complained (p. 81) about a number of minor defects, but was pleased enough to write: 'I find the binding perfectly satisfactory; with print, paper and vignette, it makes a quite typical book.' The second edition was issued on 24 May 1877 in an edition of 1,250 copies.

Many of the changes Pater made to *The Renaissance* were subtle indeed. Consider the changes he made to the 'Conclusion,' which recommended 'the supreme, artistic view of life,' before he reprinted it in the third edition (1888); he restored the 'Conclusion' because he had 'dealt more fully in *Marius the Epicurean* with the thoughts suggested by it.' Strange as it may sound, he calls these changes 'slight,' and says they were made 'to bring it closer to my original meaning.' Actually, attentive readers can find at least 38 points of difference between the first and third edition printings of the essay; five are significant, while the rest are basically stylistic variations. A collation of the third and fourth edition (1893) printings of the 'Conclusion' reveals 17 variations, the majority of which involve refinement of expression.

Pater experienced another rebuff when, in January 1877, he allowed his name to stand as a candidate for the Professorship of Poetry at Oxford. It soon became apparent that he, along with J.A. Symonds (1840-93), poet, essayist, and critic, were unlikely candidates (Grosskurth, pp. 168-73), Pater for his espousal of hedonism in *The Renaissance* and Symonds for his apologia for pederasty in *Studies of the Greek Poets* (1873). John Campbell Shairp (1819-85), poet and critic, entered the contest early in March. By the middle of March, the number of candidates would have reached eight if Pater had not judiciously withdrawn his name, because conservative opinion was obviously against him. Eventually, Shairp was appointed the Oxford Professor of Poetry.

In his letter of 1 October 1878 to Macmillan, Pater proposed to publish early in the new year a volume of miscellaneous essays collected from various periodicals. This book, provisionally called *The School of Giorgione, and other Studies,* was to include essays on Giorgione, Wordsworth, Demeter and Persephone, Dionysus, Romanticism, *Love's Labour's Lost, Measure for Measure,* and Charles Lamb. The following day, Macmillan wrote to say that he would be very glad to publish this new volume of essays 'exactly uniform' with the second edition of *The Renaissance,* the edition conveying his aesthetic intentions regarding book design. Pater felt especially confident, and again approached the *Academy* and the *Athenaeum,* both of which announced (5 October 1878) that this new book could be expected early in the following year. A short while later, he (18 November 1878) wrote to say that the book was ready to be printed, but five days later he asked Macmillan to change the title to read: *Dionysus and other Studies* (p. 87). The paper was specially made and proof copies were printed later that month, but when he revised the proofs he changed his mind and decided to stop the publication of this volume altogether. Macmillan was concerned because the book had been advertised in the press. Macmillan wrote to Pater (p. 88), arguing that there was no reason for his apprehension since the volume would make a worthy successor to *The Renaissance.* Nevertheless, the type was broken[9] up at his own expense. Curiously, he advised Macmillan not to 'announce, in any way, that the book is not to be published.'

In the midst of his Greek studies, Pater discovered his *métier,* the 'imaginary portrait,' a fictional device which derived from the critical technique he had employed in his Renaissance studies. The 'imaginary' portrait gave him the measure of objectivity he needed to explore the development of artistic personality (especially his own). He published his first piece of fiction, 'Imaginary Portraits. I. The Child in the House,' in *Macmillan's Magazine* in August 1878. In a letter dated 17 April 1878, he wrote: 'I call the MS. a portrait, and mean readers, as they might do on seeing a portrait, to begin speculating – what came of him?' (p. 83). About this time, he began, but never completed, the second portrait of this series, 'An English Poet' (1878), which was published by Mrs Ottley (1931) in the *Fortnightly Review.* Pater continued to write 'imaginary portraits' until his death, 'The Child in the House' being the origin and the paradigm of his imaginative work: *Marius the Epicurean* (1885), the *Imaginary Portraits* (1887), and the fragment of *Gaston de Latour* (1897).

The later period: 1878-94

According to Inman (1990), two passions motivated Pater during this period, namely, the desire 'To maintain his hard won place at BNC and to write as no one else had ever written or ever could write' (p. l). A conservative, moralistic strain runs through his work, together with an emphasis on traditional values, including social order, sympathy and pity, religious temper, and maternity. As Inman (1990) puts it, Pater learned how to be indirect: he learned how to express his sorrow, his sense of victimization, and homoerotic longing via historical and mythical figures (pp. xxxviii, xlix, 164, 178-9).

Marius the Epicurean (1885)
Pater probably began working (Monsman, 1967) on *Marius the Epicurean* in autumn 1878. The evidence suggests that, by 1881, he was well into the project. Obviously, he wanted to clear up the confusion he had generated in the 'Conclusion' to *The Renaissance*. From late December 1882 to early January 1883, Pater visited Rome and Naples, collecting material for the book. On 22 July 1883, he wrote to his friend Violet Paget (1856-1935), essayist and novelist, who wrote under the pseudonym 'Vernon Lee,' saying that he wanted to complete the first half of this 'imaginary portrait' of a peculiar type of mind in the time of Marcus Aurelius by the end of the Long Vacation (Evans, p. 52). Pater resigned his tutorship at BNC, so that he could spend the year 1884 writing. He read her part of the novel, presumably the first two chapters, when she stayed with the Paters in June 1884. In a letter to her mother, Paget wrote that they lacked 'vitality' (Cooper Willis, p. 147).

Via the 'portrait,' Pater explores his own thoughts and feelings (Nadel, 1984) as representative of 'that perplexity or complexity of soul' that he felt characterized life in late-Victorian times. It will be remembered that, in his first published essay, he spends as much time discussing 'modernity' as he does Coleridge. Again and again, he characterizes 'modern life' in terms of a struggle between the almost mechanical play of circumstances, now atomized by empirical science, and the comparatively inexplicable force of personality which is resistant to, but also moulded by, those forces.

In setting his narrative in second-century Rome, Pater exploits[10] the resources of a long tradition, the comparison between the Antonine 'past' and the late Victorian 'present,' thereby establishing (Fletcher, 1971; Small, 1985) a context for exploring the possibility of religious belief[11] during an age of transition, the intellectual climate of which is made up of a bewildering number of intellectual and ethical systems.

In *Marius*, Pater is concerned not with the problem of knowing what constitutes the doctrines and the practices of true religion but with the state of mind that can be called 'religious faith' (Vogeler, p. 289). Like Tennyson, Pater persuades readers that new hope exists, and like John Henry Newman persuades them that a merely philosophic faith leaves people unfulfilled. He depicts Marius' quest for religious certitude via the metaphor of a spiritual pilgrimage from his disillusionment with paganism to his acceptance (if this is the right phrase) of Christianity.

The ambiguous conclusion to *Marius* always puzzles readers. Pater provides no hint that Marius will die a martyr. It can be argued (Vogeler) that, in *Marius*, we see 'a portrait of the artist as a young man' who finds 'in the Christian service of worship a satisfying expression for his highly developed aesthetic impulses' (p. 288). Indeed, Marius' sacrificial act is a poor substitute for a profession of faith. Gerald Monsman (1971) has argued that the 'fourth sort of religious phase' Pater thought possible for the modern mind is really the 'aesthetic personality' he outlined in 'Diaphaneitè' (1864). In that remarkable essay, Pater claimed that the aesthetic personality, that subtle interpenetration of intellectual, moral, and spiritual elements, was a revolutionary nature – a sufficient number of these individuals would in fact regenerate the world.

As commentators point out, reading *Marius* as a typical historical novel can be disappointing. True, the formula is familiar: Pater presents two cultures in conflict, one dying and the other being born, but the events and the figures who take part in the cultural conflict, the individuals who undergo and give expression to the impact the historical events had upon the people living through them, fail to emerge with sufficient concreteness. The characters do not engage in face-to-face interaction and, moreover, the social context develops indirectly at best, from bits and pieces of information dropped now and then: allusions, quotations, and citations. These (source) materials make up the very texture of the novel. In fact, Small (1985) suggests that readers approach the novel as a series of intertextual relationships[12] in which Pater wrestles with the dilemma of the modern agnostic and attempts to get his bearings *vis-à-vis* his earlier writing.

Characteristically, Pater tried to publish the work serially. He submitted (June 1884) the first two chapters to Morley, who had become the editor of *Macmillan's Magazine*, but the latter found them unfit for serial publication. Pater acknowledged their unsuitability, and early in July he sent them to Alexander Macmillan, with the view to having the work published in the spring of the following year. He also hoped that the book might be taken 'on slightly more favourable terms' (p. 91) than in the case of his former volume. Macmillan pointed out (11 September 1884) that Macmillan and Co. would greatly like to publish the new book, but could not offer better terms than 'equal division of profits' because of the uncertainty of the book's sales' (pp. 91-2). As an expression of his confidence in this book, however, Macmillan offered to pay him, on publication, £50 on account (equivalent to £2,205.50 in 1997), whether his share reached this amount or not. Pater accepted this offer, but asked that the book be precisely similar to the second edition of *The Renaissance* with regard to 'size, quality of paper, and binding.' *Marius* was printed in two volumes, bound in dark blue-green cloth lettered in gold on the back, as were his subsequent books (Stonehill, pp. 129-40) and issued on 4 March 1885 in an edition of 1,000 sets, priced at 21s. (equivalent to £49.13 in 1997).

Meanwhile, some weeks before publication, Pater had launched his log-rolling campaign, leaking a bound copy of the proofs of his *Marius* to a friend, William Sharp (1855-1905), poet and critic. Sharp is remembered for the 'mystical' prose and verse he wrote (from 1893) under the pseudonym 'Fiona Macleod.' As it happened, he published two 'premature' reviews: the one in the *Athenaeum* (28 February 1885), which appeared four days before the book was released, and the one in *Time* (March 1885). On the day the book appeared, Alexander wrote to Pater, saying that he regretted these early reviews. Pater's reply is missing.

Reviewers on both sides of the Atlantic greeted the publication of this unique work with great respect (see Seiler, 1980: 113-61). Writing in *Macmillan's Magazine* (May 1885), Mary Ward praised the work highly, saying that there is 'added to the charm of style, and deftly handled learning, a tenderness of feeling, a tone of reverence for human affections, and pity for the tragedy of human weakness worthy of George Eliot' (lii, 134). The reviewer for *The Times* (8 April 1885) expressed the general impression when he described the book as 'fine writing and hard reading' (p. 3).

Most readers liked the graphic descriptions of Rome, the classic banquet in honour of Apuleius at Lucian's house, the view from the house of Cecilia, the rituals of the early Christians, and Marius's visit to the Christian tombs. A number of critics remarked on the striking resemblance between Pater's Antonine Rome and Victorian England. Only Mary Ward (Fletcher, 1971) understood the true significance of this resemblance, that is, *Marius* represented a trenchant and indirect analysis of the problem of belief in Victorian England (p. 23). In her view, *Marius* expressed the reflections of 'a real mind' not of the second but of the nineteenth century. She added that the book voiced the subtleties and elusiveness of 'English feeling' at a particularly troubled time – a time when intellectuals who had repudiated orthodox Christianity constructed world views or beliefs for themselves which would satisfy their emotional cravings for the certitude of the old dispensation.

We cannot count Mary Ward among those readers who were misled by the ethical drift of the book; she contested the view that *Marius* represented a reassessment of the sceptical philosophy of life expressed in the 'Conclusion' to *The Renaissance*. She claimed that Pater still spoke of religion in terms of aesthetics and that he still sought 'exquisite moments.' After pointing out that, in the 'Conclusion,' he protested against submitting to 'some abstract morality we have not identified with ourselves,' she observed that he 'now presents obedience to this same morality as desirable, not because of any absolute virtue or authority inherent in it, but because practically obedience is a source of pleasure and quickened faculty to the individual' (lii, 137).

Because he spent so many years writing and revising the book, it is tempting to say that Pater intended *Marius* to be his *magnum opus*. Almost immediately after its publication, he began to revise *Marius* for a second edition. On 11 June 1885, Pater learned that the first edition was almost sold out. The type was reset and a different format and binding were used (Chandler, p. 24) to conceal the large number of corrections and emendations he made.[13] Actually, Macmillan and Co. (pp. 95-6) made two proposals for a less expensive edition, either in one volume on thinner paper or in two volumes uniform with the attractive Eversley Edition (p. 162) of the works of Charles Lamb. Ultimately, in June 1885, Pater chose the second suggestion, and the second edition of 2,000 sets was released on 13 November 1885.

In 1885, Pater experienced one more rebuff from the Establishment at Oxford (Levey, p. 173). After Ruskin's resignation from the Slade Professorship, Pater allowed (in July 1885) his name to go forward as a candidate, possibly feeling that he would be the ideal successor to Ruskin. As luck would have it, however, Hubert von Herkomer (1849-1914), the Bavarian-born artist, entered the contest. This associate of the Royal Academy and founder (in 1883) of the Herkomer School of Art, Bushey, Herts., won Ruskin's support – and eventually the appointment, holding it for the rest of Pater's life (Cooper Willis, pp. 178 and 192).

Perhaps in frustration, Pater moved to London, which as John Gross (1969) has argued, was the center of culture from the 1880s. In August 1885, Pater and his sisters rented the house at 12 Earl's Terrace, Kensington, opposite Holland Park. Understandably, he ventured into London society hoping to make a name for himself as 'a man of letters.' At first, he found this experiment interesting and enjoyable (Benson, p. 117): he attended many dinner-parties, where he met the celebrities of the day.

Imaginary Portraits (1887)

During the period from March 1885 to May 1887, Pater worked on a collection of 'imaginary portraits,' publishing one portrait a year in *Macmillan's Magazine*. At first, he planned to include 'The Child in the

House' in this proposed volume, but at the last moment decided that it required too many alterations and settled for the portraits of Jean Baptiste Watteau, Denys l'Auxerrois, Sebastian van Storck, and Duke Carl of Rosenmold. In these remarkable 'stories,' which are set in eighteenth-century Flanders, thirteenth-century France, seventeenth-century Holland, and eighteenth-century Germany, Pater explores moments of intellectual and cultural 'awakening,' to paraphrase Monsman (1967). The tales are all mediated, as Brake (1994) points out, by means of filters through which the narrative is conveyed (p. 46).

On 24 May 1887, *Imaginary Portraits* was issued in an edition of 1,000 copies, selling for 6s. (equivalent to £14.94 in 1997). Three years later, on 30 May 1890, Frederick (p. 105) informed him that there were fewer than forty copies left. A second edition of 1,250 copies was released in November.

The reviewers on both sides of the Atlantic warmed to Pater's third book, which stimulated only a modicum of discussion, by comparison with either of his previous books (see Seiler, 1980: 162-93). Critics generally felt that the book failed to match the first two in power and charm.

In June 1888, Pater began work on *Gaston de Latour*, the second book of his proposed trilogy (cf. Monsman, 1991, 1995). He published the first five chapters in *Macmillan's Magazine* from June to October, and the greater part of chapter vii ('The Lower Pantheism') as 'Giordano Bruno' in the *Fortnightly Review* in August 1889. He temporarily abandoned this work to complete one of the most difficult compositions he had undertaken, namely, the essay on 'Style,' which he published in the *Fortnightly Review* (December 1888). Pater never gave up hope of publishing *Gaston*, for he struggled with this work until late 1891.

Appreciations (1889)

Pater made a third attempt to publish a collection of miscellaneous essays in June 1888. He proposed that this book, provisionally entitled *On Style, with other studies in literature*, should be printed for publication before the first of November and that it should appear in all respects similar to the third edition of *The Renaissance*. He collected 11 of his essays on English literature, including the essays on Wordsworth, Coleridge, Charles Lamb, Sir Thomas Browne, D.G. Rossetti, together with three essays on Shakespeare, which had appeared in a variety of periodicals, such as the *Westminster Review*, the *Fortnightly Review*, *Macmillan's Magazine*, and *Scribner's Magazine*. He included two theoretical essays, 'Style,' the opening piece, which dates from 1888, and 'Romanticism,' the concluding piece, but here renamed 'Postscript,' which dates from 1876. In these essays, he outlines his conception of the literary critic, taking Newman (DeLaura, 1969:

329-38) and Arnold (Brake, 1994, p. 47) as his points of departure, thereby challenging two pre-eminent interpreters of British culture.

He offers readers 'appreciation,' the constructive, sympathetic reading of a text, in place of 'criticism,' the assessment (as Arnold defined the concept) of a text in terms of external criteria; and secondly, he suggests that the literary critic is better served by a sensitivity to Romanticism, an antinomian impulse, involving the addition of 'strangeness to beauty,' than by Classicism, the impulse toward order in beauty. Accordingly, in the essay on 'Style' specifically, he argues that 'imaginative prose' is the medium most responsive to the variety as well as the complexity of modern experience.

Macmillan and Co. released this collection of essays under the title of *Appreciations, with an Essay on Style* on 15 November 1889 in an edition of 1,000 copies, selling for 8s. 6d. (equivalent to £20.51 in 1997). The book sold very rapidly. On 23 December 1889, George Macmillan (p. 103) informed him that there were only 120 copies left. Macmillan felt that, although sales would slacken a little after Christmas, a reprint should be issued without delay. He lingered over the correction of the proofs, and the second edition of 1,500 copies was not released until May 1890. In July of that year, 1,000 copies were printed for release in the United States.

British and American reviewers greeted *Appreciations* with mixed feelings (see Seiler, 1980: 194-241). The writer for the *Pall Mall Gazette* (10 December 1889) expressed the consensus of opinion in Britain when he claimed that the book contained some of Pater's finest work. The writer for the *Atlantic Monthly* (March 1890) expressed the consensus of opinion in the United States when he judged *Appreciations* to be of less consequence and originality than any of his previous books (lxv, 424).

Like many critics, the writer for the *Saturday Review* (28 December 1889) hailed the title as eminently appropriate and indicative of the author's special sensibility (lxviii, 745). Writing in the *Speaker* (22 March 1890), Wilde interpreted 'appreciations' in its Latin sense, by which he meant 'an exquisite collection of exquisite essays.' For some critics, the term meant simply admiration and sympathy, but for others it defined a critical technique.

Late in 1889, Pater turned his attention to revising *Appreciations* for the second edition, which appeared in December without the essay on 'Aesthetic Poetry.' A friend, Lionel Johnson (1867-1902), poet and critic, later wrote that Pater dropped the essay because 'there were things in it; which some people, pious souls! thought profane, yes! profane' (quoted in Evans, p. xxiii). He may have been thinking of those critics who thought that he had encouraged the 'pagan spirit.'

As well, Pater intensified his log-rolling, in part because (he felt) a number of reviewers still misunderstood him. Because he had heard that Johnson was likely to write an article on the book for the *Century Guild Hobby Horse*, he wrote (24 December 1889) to a mutual friend, Herbert Horne (1864-1916), architect, art historian, and connoisseur, who edited (1887-91) the periodical. Pater extended Xmas wishes and expressed his interest in the next number of the journal (Evans, pp. 105-6). In his letter, he enclosed a clipping (of a favourable review). Presumably, Horne had mentioned that a review of *Appreciations* by Johnson would appear in the *Hobby Horse* (Evans, p. 106n). Immediately after hearing some of the details of Johnson's article from A.H. Galton (1852-1921), scholar, critic, and priest, who served as assistant-editor of the *Hobby Horse*, Pater called on Johnson at nine in the morning on 18 February 1890. He was agitated and insisted on knowing what Johnson had said in his article. Johnson wrote to Galton, who sent Pater a copy of the article (Evans, p. 108n).

Similarly, on 4 January 1890, Pater wrote to Wilde, expressing a keen interest in the *Speaker*. This review of politics, letters, science, and the arts had appeared for the first time that day (Saturday), and advance notices of the weekly had listed Wilde as a contributor. This hint did not go unheeded, for Wilde published an enthusiastic notice of *Appreciations* in the March issue.

Pater was so satisfied with the 1887 collection of 'imaginary portraits' that early in 1892 he planned to produce a second series, which would have included (Evans, p. xxxn) 'Hippolytus Veiled,' a portrait set in the time of the Albigensian persecution, and 'a modern study,' possibly 'Emerald Uthwart' (1892). On 22 January 1892, he announced that a revised version of this series was near completion and by 14 December the volume was tentatively called *Three Short Stories* (Letter 112). It would have included (Benson, p. 123) 'Hippolytus Veiled,' 'Emerald Uthwart,' and 'Apollo in Picardy.' This volume was 'cancelled.' Pater died with four published portraits still uncollected: 'The Child in the House,' 'Hippolytus Veiled,' 'Emerald Uthwart,' and 'Apollo in Picardy,' and unpublished fragments of at least four more: 'An English Poet,' 'Gaudioso, the Second,' 'Il Sartore,' and 'Tibalt the Albigense' (see Evans, p. xxx).

Plato and Platonism (1893)

In December 1890, Pater began writing the lectures[14] on Plato and Platonism that he published under that title three years later. He delivered a series of lectures on the topic, beginning on 21 January 1891. Typically, he attempted to secure a wider audience by publishing the chapters separately as articles. On 21 December 1891, he sent 'The Genius of Plato' (ch. vi) to Percy William Bunting (1836-1911), social reformer, who edited (1882-1911) the

Contemporary Review. In his letter, he remarked: 'I have treated the subject in as popular a manner as I could' (Evans, p. 124). Bunting liked the article, and published it in the February 1892 issue. During 1892, Pater sent four more: 'Plato and the Doctrine of Motion' (ch. i), 'Plato and the Doctrine of Rest' (ch. ii), 'Plato and the Doctrine of Music' (ch. iii), and 'Lacedaemon' (ch. viii). The first appeared in *Macmillan's Magazine* (May 1892) and the last in the *Contemporary Review* (June 1892). Bunting and his colleague, William Canton (1845-1926), author and editor, pointed out that these lectures required alterations and subdivision of the text into paragraphs. Although Bunting found 'The Doctrine of Plato' (ch. vii) particularly interesting, Pater decided (1 November 1892) that it was too long and unsuitable for publication. He believed that, if the lecture appeared as an article, it might prejudice his proposed volume with 'average readers.' Macmillan and Co. accepted *Plato and Platonism*, and on 13 December 1892 drew up a contract, awarding him an additional bonus of 10 per cent of the American sales. The book was issued on 10 February 1893 in an edition of 2,000 copies, selling for 8s. 6d. (equivalent to £21.17 in 1997).

Pater intended these lectures to 'interest' a larger number of students of philosophy than his Oxford undergraduates, but, as many commentators pointed out, what results is not philosophy or metaphysics as one understands those terms. Ostensibly, his goal is to show how, as a philosopher, Plato emerged from his cultural environment, namely, his precursors: Pythagoras, Parmenides, and Heraclitus. The objective of criticism generally (he argues) is to determine where 'environment' leaves off and personality (genius) begins. Almost imperceptibly, as Denis Donoghue (pp. 250-3) puts it, Pater glides over Plato's metaphysics and his politics, in order to get to his aesthetics, with a view to showing how Plato anticipates modern thought. In the end, this portrait of Plato, like his portrait of Wordsworth, resembles Pater himself, namely, a relativist.

This book, arguably Pater's most impressive work, but the least known (Ward, A., 1966: 177), can be read as Pater's 'final, most elaborate, but still characteristically hesitant and irresolute, iteration' of the question he first raised (imperfectly) in *The Renaissance*: how to reconcile the religion of antiquity with the religion of Christ (Knoepflmacher, pp. 152-3). From this perspective, we might say that Pater's quest resembles Marius' quest: how to achieve a synthesis of opposites. He exploits the conflict between science and religion, and like Arnold attempts to establish a tradition outside doctrinal Christianity, while avoiding the former's biblical exegesis. In Chapter VIII, Pater formulates a kind of Hellenistic Christianity, called 'a religion of sanity,' and he sees the stern and disciplined ecclesiastical art, architecture, and liturgical ritual of the Catholic Church (particularly of the Middle Ages) as a remnant of the Greek love of form. As well, Pater rejects his earlier enthusiasm for 'a universal pagan sentiment,' an argument he made in *The Renaissance*, but his answer to the problem of unbelief remains (as Knoepflmacher observes) rather hesitant. DeLaura (1969: 296) agrees with this reading, but he questions the importance Pater attaches to the work, namely, as an ambitious synthesis of all the assumptions that underlie his scattered essays and works of fiction.

All the same, Pater was rather anxious about the critical response to *Plato and Platonism*. Dugald Sutherland MacColl (1859-1948), art critic for the *Spectator*, tells (1931) the following story, which evokes the intensity of his concern:

> *Plato* appeared, and one morning I was called from a scandalously late bath by a visitor. It was Pater with a copy in his hand. He gave me this, and explained that he was concerned about its reception by the reviewers. Could I arrange to deal with it in the *Spectator*? I stammered my astonishment that he should care what any reviewer said, and urged the difficulty of invading Mr Hutton's domain. It would fall, I was certain, into more competent hands, but I would find some less preoccupied corner to say my modest word. Evidently he was conscious, even in 1893, of disapproval and suspicion. (iv, 760)

MacColl had met Pater while he was an undergraduate (1881-84) at Lincoln College, Oxford, and had attended Pater's lectures on Plato's *Republic*, possibly in spring 1882. He co-founded and co-edited the *Oxford Magazine*, and solicited at least one contribution from his teacher, namely, his unsigned favourable review of *Love in Idleness* (1883), which appeared in the April-May issue of the magazine (Evans, pp. 49n, 64n).

Again, British and American reviewers applauded the publication of the book, thereby confirming Pater's established literary reputation (see Seiler, 1980: 242-77). Commentators were especially enthusiastic about the chapters on 'Plato and the Doctrine of Motion' (ch. i), 'The Genius of Plato' (ch. vi), and 'Lacedaemon' (ch. viii). Many critics regarded the sixth chapter as particularly 'sympathetic,' in terms of its representation of 'a living Plato' and in its unravelling of 'a complicated and fascinating personality.' Most reviewers, however, hailed the chapter on Lacedaemon as the most original part of the book.

However, most commentators felt obliged to qualify their praise by isolating a few minor points for censure. The writer for the *Saturday Review* regretted that Pater took for granted 'a very considerable knowledge of philosophy and history' and avoided such academic problems as determining the chronology of the 'Dialogues.' Not surprisingly, Lewis Campbell (1830-1908), classics scholar and biographer of Jowett, identified the largest number of minor 'oversights.' Campbell pointed out that much of the 'matter' of the book had been common property for about 40 years; that it was incorrect to infer from isolated passages in the first book of the *Republic* that 'Art is to be for Art's sake alone, and not for the sake of life'; that the assessment of Plato's attitude towards mysticism was inadequate; that Lacedaemon may not have been the deep and wide dividing line between Dorian and Ionian characteristics; that Pater used some Greek expressions incorrectly; that Pater may have over-estimated the Puritanism of the *Republic*; and, finally, that he failed to capture Plato's spontaneity.

According to one biographer (Wright, T., ii, 165), Jowett congratulated Pater on the publication of this book, content to let bygones be bygones. Their reconciliation – and Pater's acceptance as a serious scholar by the Establishment at Oxford – was thus brought about.

The evidence suggests that, eventually, Pater grew weary of London, and without fanfare he and his sisters returned (13 August 1893) to Oxford, renting the house at 64 St. Giles. In December 1893, he was confined to his rooms with bronchitis. By 4 January 1894, he felt better, but not entirely fit, and he completed the essay on Notre-Dame d'Amiens, which appeared in the March issue of the *Nineteenth Century*. On 13 April 1894, he was awarded an honourary LL.D. by the University of Glasgow. In May, he felt unwell again, and in June gout prevented him from walking round Oxford. After this, he was confined to his bed with rheumatic fever, and was nursed by Hester and Clara, together with Charlotte Green (1842-1929), Symonds' sister. Pater began to recover, and he made plans (Evans, p. 156n) to deliver a lecture on Peter Paul Rubens at the Sixth Summer Session of the University Extension, Oxford. While working on 'Pascal' (1895), he caught a chill which turned to pleurisy. He died suddenly and unexpectedly of a heart attack on 30 July 1894.

Posthumous Publications

Soon after Pater's death, Clara resigned her position at Somerville College and with Hester moved to London, renting a small house in Kensington, 6 Canning Place, off Gloucester Road (Levey, p. 151). For a number of years, until serious illness incapacitated her, Clara tutored privately, Virginia Woolf[15] being her most famous pupil. Ultimately, as Mary Ward (1918) puts it, the sisters devoted themselves to preserving their brother's literary reputation. This meant authorizing the publication of (a) previously uncollected papers, in MS. or otherwise; (b) reprints (whole or in part) of popular works; (c) translations of popular works; and (c) private documents (letters) in biographies. Throughout this project, they and their literary advisers were guided by the concern to print nothing that might injure Pater's literary reputation, attending to such matters as printing and binding along the way.

New Publications

In his letter of 16 August 1894, George Macmillan invited (p. 116) Hester and Clara to consider the possibility of 'collecting unpublished papers whether in MS. or otherwise,' with a view to publishing them. Clearly, Macmillan and Co. wanted to exploit Pater's books before the copyright expired, thereby stimulating an interest in his other books. Hester and Clara pursued this offer, and in the following years Macmillan and Co. published three posthumous works. Shadwell, Pater's close friend and literary executor, with the able assistance of Johnson, another close friend, prepared *Greek Studies* for release on 11 January 1895 in an edition of 2,000 copies; *Miscellaneous Studies* for release on 18 October 1895 in an edition of 1,500 copies; and *Gaston de Latour* for release on 6 October 1896 in an edition of 1,500 copies. Shadwell wrote a short Preface for each book, inserting in the second a chronology of Pater's writings. He hoped that these volumes would bolster Pater's reputation, by dispelling the popular belief that he was merely a master of style.

Another very close friend, Edmund Gosse (1848-1928), poet, critic, biographer, and civil servant, edited *Essays from 'The Guardian'*, which he printed (1896) for private circulation. Gosse served as assistant librarian of the British Museum, translator of the Board of Trade, and Librarian to the House of Lords. As well, he was chief reviewer for *The Times* for the period 1914-25, but is now remembered for his childhood recollections, *Father and Son* (1907).

Reprints

Late in 1900, Frederick Macmillan proposed publishing Pater's works in the handsome and profitable *Edition de luxe*. This sort of limited edition was printed on high-grade paper, using special cast type, and expensively bound. Frederick advised (p. 122) Hester that such an edition would be 'at once bought up by collectors.' She welcomed this proposal, but was greatly disappointed to learn that Macmillan and Co. would not alter the terms. On 4 September 1900, 775 sets of the *Edition de luxe* were issued; 1,000 copies of *Essays from 'The Guardian'*, printed from the private edition of 1896, were included.

In 1910, Frederick planned a new (and uniform) edition of Pater's works, along the lines several large booksellers had suggested. The kind of edition suggested, namely, the Library Edition, featured an elegant binding, with strengthened joints and covers, so that it appeared much more attractive than the usual trade edition, in which sets of books were sometimes bound. Frederick explained (p. 134) that the stock of *The Renaissance* was low and it would have to be reprinted in a few weeks. Moreover, he pointed out, another edition would have to be printed in a year or two because the copyright expired in 1915. Hester agreed to this suggestion and 1,250 sets of the Library Edition were issued late in 1910.

Finally, Frederick suggested (in 1912) publishing a series of books to be printed in the 'Riccardi' type (p. 140), thereby appealing to collectors of 'bibliographic toys.' Hester agreed to this proposal, and in March of that year Macmillan and Co. published *Marius the Epicurean* in a limited edition of 1,000 sets, selling for 12s. 6d. each (equivalent to £26.81 in 1997). In return, Hester was awarded 'an outright payment of £250' (equivalent to £10,722.50 in 1997).

Sales

Pater's books were reprinted frequently in the period 1901-10. Three were popular; *Marius* sold well in England (5,100 copies were released, as compared to 2,500 in the United States), while *The Renaissance* and *Appreciations* sold well in the United States (4,600 and 4,000 copies were issued, as compared to 3,750 and 2,750 in England).

Just what these figures meant to Hester and Clara in terms of their income is uncertain. Our point of departure for this kind of speculation has to be the letter George Macmillan wrote (p. 116) to the Pater sisters shortly after the funeral, estimating that, for probate purposes, Macmillan and Co. would send them the sum of £175 (equivalent to £9,007.25 in 1997), over and above the share due to the sale of his books for the fiscal year 1894-95. Based on an examination of the sums the Pater sisters earned according to the half-share system from the sale of their brother's books for the fiscal years 1907-08, 1909-10, 1910-11, and 1911-12, that is, £419.19.8, £100, £378.13.6, and £250 respectively (equivalent to £19,639.20, £4,541.00, £17,056.00, and £11,027.50 respectively in 1997), my guess is that Hester and Clara (and Hester by herself after 1910) had trouble making ends meet, for as late as 1912 Hester still tried to turn her brother's unpublished work into cash.

VI CONCLUDING REMARKS

By the middle of the 1870s, Pater had earned a distinct place for himself in the world of English letters, but he never achieved the academic recognition he had hoped for. He made Oxford the center of his life, but those in authority, from Jowett downwards, took little notice of him as a scholar or an administrator (Fletcher, 1971: 6). True, he was a conscientious if not a conspicuously successful teacher, and he served on the obligatory committees, but he failed to impress his colleagues as a committee man (see Seiler, 1987: 57-60). In this regard, Pater failed to exert an influence commensurate with his abilities. His weakness[16] in Latin and Greek, and his habit of misquoting from the Bible, were well known to colleagues and students alike (Wright, T., i, 236). As some reviewers of *The Renaissance* pointed out, novice readers should not turn to Pater's work expecting to find information, because he had little interest in established facts and informed opinions as such (cf. Donoghue, 1995). He faced the dilemma the imaginative scholar today faces (Fletcher, 1984), namely, trying to find a suitable place for himself or herself in the academy. We read Pater as a mixture of critic, journalist, and novelist, not to mention classics teacher, realizing that his work survives at the margins of many genres. At the outset of his career, he took up as his speciality the culture of the Renaissance, with an emphasis on painting, literature, and architecture; seeking a way to redeem his somewhat tarnished reputation as a scholar, he turned to literary criticism, with a focus on English and German Romanticism and French aestheticism; for a time, he thought he might make his mark with his Greek studies, focusing on pre-Socratic philosophy, mythology, rhetoric, and sculpture; but from 1878 he concentrated on ruminative fiction, via the 'imaginary portrait,' thereby combining biography and autobiography. Throughout his career, he contested the rules of orthodox literary production (cf. Brake and Small, 1991a: xvi), formulating (DeLaura, 1991) a 'subversive' (modern) sensibility, which only now, more than a century later, is being appreciated. In this regard, Pater succeeded in exerting an influence on subsequent ages. For this aesthete, life as well as art became a ritual, requiring no less than total discipline. This included exercising control over the shape as well as the content of his writings.

NOTES

1. As Small (1991a) observes, it is tempting to conceptualize Pater's relationship with (intellectual) authority simply in terms of his reaction to the sexual politics of the period. It makes sense to construe Pater's insistence upon the autonomy as well as the sovereignty of 'taste' in aesthetic matters in terms of a thinly disguised claim for freedom of the individual. This has meant helping readers understand Pater's 'subversive' homoerotic sensibility. Cf. Dowling (1986, 1994), Williams (1989), Dellamora (1990, 1994), Loesberg (1991), Adams (1995), Sussman (1995), and Morgan (1996). After all, hostility towards Pater intensified over the years, especially during the period 1874-77, and some of the personal attacks may well have been disguised as a critique of a literary or an artistic position. However, conceptualizing Pater's troubles exclusively in these terms deflects attention from other concerns, thereby obscuring the attitudes themselves. In this reconstruction of Pater's career, I conceptualize Pater's relationship to (intellectual) authority in terms of his reactions to the academic politics of the time. As Small argues (1991a: 1-30 and 91-111), the changes critical discourse experienced during the final stages of the nineteenth century coincided with the professionalisation as well as the institutionalization of knowledge, which took place (mainly) in the universities, namely, Oxford and Cambridge. Whereas Pater located authority for 'assessing' a work (say) within the individual, many of his colleagues, including Jowett, located authority in the institution or the discipline, based on scholarly consensus (see note 4 below). Like Small, I would suggest that, in many instances, including the Preface to *The Renaissance*, Pater employed a critical discourse which looked back to the critical writing of the 1850s. Taken together, these approaches explain the forces that shaped Pater's life and career.

2. Brake (1991, 1994) argues that Pater's work should be read in terms of such discourses as journalism. From this perspective, we see Pater in a new light. An informal survey will show that Pater wrote for many journals: the *Westminster Review*, 1866-68; the *Fortnightly Review*, 1869-92; the *Academy*, 1875; *Macmillan's Magazine*, 1876-92; the *Eclectic Magazine*, 1885-92; *Littell's Living Age*, 1886-94; *the Athenaeum*, 1889; the *Nineteenth Century*, 1889-94: *Scribner's Magazine*, 1889; the *New Review*, 1890-92; the *Bookman*, 1891; and the *Contemporary Review*, 1892-94.

3. For studies of Pater as educator, see d'Hangest, i, 75-82, 206-11, and 289, and ii, 13-16; Monsman (1977), pp. 36-9 and 139-40; Richards (1986); and Shuter (1988).

4. The University Commission of 1854 ushered in an era of competition based on a wide variety of rigorous examinations. One question that went unsettled for many years was the question of what constituted the 'ideal' mode of scholarship. Two tendencies vied for preeminence: (a) Mark Pattison, the Rector of Lincoln College (from 1861) and a teacher of great genius (Faber, pp. 166-67), was the leading representative of the mode of inquiry which ultimately gained the upper hand: his extensive knowledge, his grasp of first principles, and his command of clear expression gave him an influence far beyond his immediate circle. Pattison identified (b) John Conington, Professor of Latin (from 1854) at Oxford, as the example of the spirit he deprecated. Pattison upheld the 'scientific' ideal of scholarship, whereas Conington upheld the ideal of 'refined taste,' whereby the critical faculty, together with the command of Latin and Greek, served as the best evidence of scholarship (Jackson, pp. 24-9).

5. Of course, 'salary' is the modern locution. In the years before the first University Commission, which was appointed in 1850, BNC Fellows received food and accommodation, a basic stipend, and a share of the various benefactions, rents, and other profits the College earned, the size of the share being determined by their seniority. The Bursar and the Dean earned a bit more, because additional payments were attached to their offices. Understandably, the Principal received a larger share of these payments, and he might also have a number of outside incomes. Fellows might also hold benefices, University Lectureships (say), and they would take on private tuition in order to increase their income. BNC paid fellows twice a year, in June (Lady Day) and in December (Michaelmas). Usually, payments were made by cheque, with perhaps £50 or so in cash or Banker's Order.

6. For a detailed study of *Macmillan's Magazine,* see Gurr, pp. 37-55.

7. Tebbel discusses this matter in his four-volume study. See also Thompson.

8. As Shuter (1989) has pointed out, in this essay Pater revises the view of Greek art and religion that he had advanced in 'Winckelmann' (p. 514). Three commentaries on 'Demeter and Persephone' warrant mention here. First, DeLaura (1969) reads the essay as a re-thinking of Arnold's view of the classical/medieval antagonism, formulated in the essay on Coleridge and then expanded in the essay on Winckelmann (pp. 245-9). Secondly, Dowling (1988) reads the essay as Pater's attempt to combine 'the seemingly unpromising materials of the new 'human sciences' of mythology, anthropology,

and archaeology with the modified familiar essay for which he had already made uniquely his own.' Thirdly, Inman (1990) argues that he wanted his critics to see that he possessed too much religious spirit to pose a danger to his students; that he firmly supported the institution of the family; and that he was no shallow aesthete (pp. 384-5).

9. According to Brake (1994), the widely reported debate about aestheticism put Pater on his guard. A case in point is the review-article, 'The Greek Spirit in Modern Literature,' which Richard St. John Tyrwhitt published in the *Contemporary Review* 29 (March 1877): 552-66. Basing his critique on *Arnold's Poems* (1853), *Essays in Criticism* (1865), and *Culture and Anarchy* (1869), and on Symonds's *Studies of the Greek Poets* (1876), Tyrwhitt lamented the fact that the term 'Hellenism' had undergone a change in meaning, slipping from an 'intellectual habit of mind,' as Arnold first used it, to 'a standard of the artistic wing of atheism,' as Symonds now uses it. As Inman (1990) points out, Tyrwhitt assumes that Arnold would not be prepared to accept Walt Whitman as his guide to things Greek (p. 356). Tyrwhitt would have been pleased to see Arnold prepare some kind of rebuke, regarding the 'phallic ecstasy' and the 'palpitations' male beauty excited in these new Hellenists.

Inman (1990) suggests that he was reluctant to publish the book before he was ready to 'set up' the essay on 'The *Bacchanals* of Euripides,' which he eventually published in *Macmillan's Magazine* 60 (May 1889): 63-72. She adds (pp. 357-8) that, since he began preparing (in late 1877 or early 1878) on early Greek sculpture, Pater may have postponed the publication of the book, hoping to include other essays on Greek art.

10. A case can be made for saying that the 'germ' for *Marius* can be found in Arnold's inaugural lecture 'On the Modern Element in Literature' (1857), which was later published in *Macmillan's Magazine* (February 1869), and his essay on 'Marcus Aurelius,' which was later published in *Victoria Magazine* (November 1863). By the early 1880s, a number of writers interested in Stoicism had utilized this analogy, including W.W. Story, 'A Conversation with Marcus Aurelius,' the *Fortnightly Review* 19 (February 1873): 178-96; Frederick Pollock, 'Marcus Aurelius and the Stoic Philosophy,' *Mind* 4 (January 1879): 47-68; W.W. Capes, *Stoicism* (1880); William Wallace, *Epicureanism* (1880); and Frederic W.H. Myers, 'Marcus Aurelius Antoninus,' the *Fortnightly Review* 37 (May 1882): 564-86.

11. It is possible to catch a glimpse of Pater's motives for shaping his narrative the way he does in the letter he wrote (22 July 1883) to Paget.

Here, Pater (Evans, pp. 51-2) says that he regards completing the book as 'a sort of duty' and that 'there is a fourth sort of religious phase possible for the modern mind, over and above those presented in your late admirable paper in the *Contemporary*, the conditions of which phase it is the main object of my design to convey.'

In 'The Responsibilities of Unbelief,' Paget (1883) depicts three 'intellectuals' in a conversation, trying to formulate three distinct positions regarding the modern question of unbelief. Rheinhardt, the 'optimistic Voltairean' and intellectual epicure, has trouble understanding how religion can be a reality to anyone; Vere, the aesthetic pessimist, claims that it does not matter what a person believes, so long as this belief satisfies his or her soul; and Baldwin, the positivist and 'militant, humanitarian atheist,' argues that every individual is required to formulate a theory of conduct, based on sound principles.

Marius resembles Baldwin in many respects, especially in terms of his search for just the right 'principle of conduct.' One can see that both are rather serious, solitary individuals, instinctively religious; both seek to reconcile the evil they see in the world around them with the desire to do good. Baldwin forces himself to doubt, to examine all the more, whereas Marius translates his doubt into action, thereby (symbolically) embracing Christianity.

12. Small (1985) identifies three levels of intertextuality in *Marius*. Pater engages (a) the past and historical representation. Readers need to understand the classical referents, such as the geography of Rome, especially its urban geography, together the literary culture of Greece and Rome (p. xi). (b) contemporary historiography and those nineteenth-century appropriations of the *Meditations*. And (c) Pater's on-going revisions/his attempt to come to terms with his earlier writing. Taken together, these three levels of intertextuality have a enormous implications for features like allusions, quotations, and citations.

13. In is interesting to note that these alterations, a little more than 100 in number (primarily in word order and punctuation), are insignificant in comparison with the changes he made for the third edition (2,000 sets were released on 4 June 1892). He considered this revision so important that he spent four more years on the book. Apparently, this edition (Chandler, p. 10) contains over 6,000 textual variations from the previous editions: the great majority of the alterations are made within the context of the original sentence in meaning and shape.

14. E.B. Titchener (1867-1927), experimental psychologist, tells (1894) us that he was 'one of the scant half-dozen Brasenose undergraduates who heard Pater's lectures on Plato and Platonism . . . on their first delivery (ii, 201). Titchener recalls being summoned to Pater's rooms and finding the lecturer sitting at the side of the open hearth, before a little table, on which 'lay a neat pile of small oblong slips of paper.' As it happened, each slip of paper expressed some aspect of the subject at hand. Pater shuffled the slips this way and that, like a pack of cards, and he decided the final arrangement only after much testing and re-testing. For a short time, Titchener taught biology at Oxford, but in the autumn of 1892 he became assistant professor of psychology at Cornell University. He is remembered for *Experimental Psychology* (1901-05). See Shuter (1989), pp. 500-25, for a discussion of how Pater's 'reshuffled text' was understood by its author.

Arthur Waugh (1866-1943), writer, editor, and publisher, reports (1893) that, when Pater delivered his Plato lectures in 1890, at noon on Wednesdays, beginning 21 January 1890, the audience grew so large that he moved the class from the BNC lecture room to one of the larger public halls of the University. Waugh served as London Correspondent to the *Critic* from 1893-97.

15. Virginia (Stephen) Woolf took private lessons in Latin and Greek from two classical scholars: Clara Pater, from 1899 to 1901; and Janet Case (1862-1937), from 1901. Virginia Woolf (1928) left at least one 'telling' portrait of Clara, namely, in the short-story 'Slater's Pins have no Points.'

16. One theme running through the first biographies is the judgment that Pater was no scholar, that is, as Oxford understood the word: cf. Benson, pp. 22-3, and Wright, T., i, 236. The latter wrote that Pater's weakness in Latin and Greek and his habit of misquoting from the Bible 'were well known not only among the dons of Brasenose and other colleges, but also among his own pupils.' For decades, commentators have dismissed his use of other writers' work as dishonest, unoriginal, or inaccurate. Cf. Ricks (1977). Today, studies of his complex use and misuse of his sources are apt to argue that he concealed his sources, so as to suggest knowledge he did not possess, and reshaped evidence, so as to offer as 'developed' ideas which were in fact taking shape, such as 'romantic' and 'classic.' Cf. Inman (1981, 1990), DeLaura (1991), Small (1991), Brake (1994), Bullen (1995), and Shuter (1995).

NOTE ON THE TEXT

The letters that make up this volume can be found in the Macmillan Archive, arguably the most important publishing archive in the world. John Handford (personal communication) points out that the idea of making this material available to scholars dates from 1965, when Macmillan and Co. moved from St Martin's Street to Little Essex Street, London. Both buildings had cavernous and windowless basements, but in the new one priority had to be given to storing vehicles rather than thousands of ancient documents. Thus, in 1967, the correspondence, together with the papers, e.g., reports, totalling 1,250 volumes, were moved to the British Museum, to the Department of Manuscripts to be precise, which now forms part of the British Library. About 1060 volumes are devoted to correspondence. In 1990, the British Library acquired an additional 800 volumes, together with boxes of assorted financial and administrative materials, bringing the coverage in some sections to 1970 volumes (James, pp. 67-8). The earliest items include the letter Daniel Macmillan wrote (1833) to his childhood friend David Watt, the missionary, and the letters Charles Kingsley and George Grove wrote to the firm in 1849 and 1852 respectively. The collection of autograph letters (making up the Letter Books) begins to take shape in 1854, and runs up to 1940. After Daniel's untimely death in 1857, Alexander Macmillan moved the firm's headquarters from Cambridge to London. The 459 volumes of 'official' correspondence provides scholars with a valuable record of publishing activity.

Of course, many of the letters Daniel and Alexander wrote in the very early days have already appeared in print (Blake-Hill, p. 74). The following writers used the archive in preparing their work: Thomas Hughes, author of *Memoir of Daniel Macmillan* (1883); George A. Macmillan, editor of his father's letters, *Letters of Alexander Macmillan* (1908); C.L. Graves, author of the *Life and Letters of Alexander Macmillan* (1910); Charles Morgan, author of the centenary volume, *The House of Macmillan, 1843-1943* (1943); and Simon Nowell-Smith, editor of *Letters to Macmillan* (1967).

The first section of the Macmillan Archive comprises 125 volumes of letters from publishers, printers, literary agents, solicitors, and so on. The second section comprises 342 volumes of special correspondence with authors – novelists, poets, dramatists, historians, literary scholars, critics, and so on. The authors represented in this section include F.D. Maurice, Archdeacon Hare, Charles Kingsley, Thomas Hughes, Charlotte M. Yonge, Thomas Hardy, Henry James, Rudyard Kipling, and H.G. Wells. The literary critics represented in this section include Walter Pater, George Saintsbury, and A.C. Bradley. Then, 28 volumes of 'general correspondence' follow, covering the period 1855 to 1943. The outgoing letters, in 565 volumes, cover the period 1854 to 1940, and consist of pressed and carbon copies. Many are extremely fragile (Blake-Hill, pp. 76-7), especially those of the earliest years. Because these volumes were bound before they arrived, the original arrangement of these letters has been preserved, so that a complete division of outgoing and incoming letters exists. Each volume has its own index. The Editions Books in 22 volumes, covering the period 1892 to 1939 provide valuable material for the bibliographer. These documents provide the most exhaustive information – the number of copies ordered, the name of the printer, the type of paper ordered and date, details of dust-covers, and so on.

Altogether, 189 letters make up the file we could call the Pater-Macmillan letters. I base my text on the autograph letters, i.e., as they appear in the Letter Books or on transcriptions of the manuscripts. Although some of the letters printed here have appeared in one form or another, I have used the original as my text. I include these letters to offer the reader the complete Pater-Macmillan correspondence. I have tried to keep my editorial principles as simple as possible, and throughout I use the procedures listed below, except where I indicate otherwise. Finally, for convenience, I print my Explanatory Notes in one section at the back of the volume, on pp. 147-79. I identify the titles used throughout the work on pp. 185-94.

1. I indicate the source of each letter and where appropriate information about where it has been printed before: on p. 70, for example, I indicate that Pater's letter dated 11 November [1872] appears in Morgan (pp. 105 and 106) and in Evans, pp. 9-10.

2. In dating the letters, especially Pater's, I have taken my cue from previous editors who have printed these materials, principally Lawrence Evans, and from the Indexes to the Letter Books, supplying this information in square brackets.

3. I normalize the position as well as the structure of the letters, situating date, address, and closing in the same place. As well, I place all postscripts after the closing, regardless of their position in the manuscript.

4. I have taken very few liberties with the text, but I silently spell out abbreviations ('wh' for 'which') and insert material in square brackets, i.e.,

offering a reading of an illegible handwritten passage, and correct slips of the pen, for the sake of readability. I also normalize the placing of punctuation and quotation marks at the end of quotations.

5. When not specified, the place of publication of all books mentioned should be understood as London.

THE LETTERS

1 Walter Pater to Alexander Macmillan, 29 June [1872]

Text: Morgan, p. 104. Printed in Evans, pp. 7-8.

Brasenose College, /Oxford. /June 29.

Dear Sir,

I send you by this post the papers of which I spoke when I called on you in London and must apologise for not having sent them before.

The paper in MS. has not been published hitherto, that on Winckelmann appeared in the *Westminster Review* and the other four in the *Fortnightly*. I enclose a table of the proposed series which I hope to complete by the end of the long Vacation, with a short Preface. I think in the form in which I should like the essays to appear they would make a book of about 300 pages. Of the ten essays five only will have appeared before. With many thanks for the kindness with which you have consented to consider my proposal,

I am, dear Sir,

Yours faithfully,
W.H. Pater.

2 Alexander Macmillan to Walter Pater, 2 July 1872

MS.: British Library.

W.H. Pater Esq., /Brasenose College, /Oxford. /July 2.

Dear Sir,

I have been reading your essays on art subjects with very considerable interest, and shall feel pleasure and honour in publishing them. I am also so far encouraged to hope that it may also be profitable to at least some small extent that I am willing to risk the cost of publishing your volume, sharing equally with profits, if they should accrue, and bearing loss, should an inappreciative public leave us with loss. I thought of a handsome 8vo volume. As soon as you decide that these terms will satisfy you and you are ready to print we can consult on the points of style etc.

Yours sincerely,
A. Macmillan.

3 Walter Pater to Alexander Macmillan, 21 September [1872]

MS.: British Library. Printed in Evans, p. 8.

Brasenose College, /Oxford. /Sept. 21.

Dear Sir,

I have received a printed specimen of the essays, but regret to say not in the form which I think most suitable for the book. Some of the essays are so short, and all of them in some ways so slight, that I think the only suitable form would be a small volume, costing about five shillings; and I should like to make some suggestions on the binding and some other points.

I will use the copy now sent for corrections, which will save the printers some trouble. I expect to get the remaining essays finished very soon – in two or three weeks – and hope then to have the pleasure of calling on you with them, if you will make an appointment with me for the purpose.

Believe me

Very faithfully yours,
W.H. Pater.

4 Alexander Macmillan to Walter Pater, 24 September 1872

MS.: British Library.
W.H. Pater Esq., /Brasenose College, /Oxford.

Sept. 24.

My dear Sir,

I shall be glad to see you about the form and binding of your essays any day you can fix. I am here generally from 10:00 until 5:00, except on Saturday, when I leave about 2:00. I shall be glad to meet your wishes as far as possible, but my experience leads me to think that an 8vo volume is most suitable for such a book as yours. But I will give you my reasons when we meet. Of course I am very anxious that your book should be a success in our hands.

Yours very truly,
A. Macmillan.

5 G.L. Craik to Walter Pater, 28 October 1872

MS.: British Library.
W.H. Pater Esq.

Oct. 28.

Dear Sir,

In Mr. Macmillan's absence I am answering your letter. The essay you refer to was printed, but in compliance with your wishes it shall be cancelled. This however reduces the book to 210 pages, a smaller book than might have been advisable. I suppose you have no other matter that can be added?

Yours very truly,
G. Lillie Craik.

6 G.L. Craik to Walter Pater, 30 October 1872

MS.: British Library.
W.H. Pater Esq.

Oct. 30.

Dear Sir,

The essay [will be] sent to you in order that you [can] embody parts of it in the Preface. It will be necessary for you to revise the proofs in small instalments in order that the Postscript of the book may be printed [well] before the rest is in type. In this way a smaller quantity of type is employed. It is in every way a convenience.

Yours faithfully,
G. Lillie Craik.

7 Walter Pater to Alexander Macmillan, 2 November [1872]

MS.: British Library. Extracts are printed in Morgan, p. 105. Printed in full in Evans, p. 9.

Brasenose College, /Oxford. /Nov. 2.

Dear Mr. Macmillan,

I have not yet received the Preface and the rejected essay, which were to be returned to me for the alteration of the former. I should be glad to have them as soon as possible; and I hope to send you in a day or two an additional essay, to form the conclusion of the series.

I like the look of the page very much, but not altogether the paper. It has occurred to me that the old-fashioned binding in paste-board with paper back and printed title, usual, I think, about thirty years ago, but not yet quite gone out of use, would be an economical and very pretty binding for my book. It would, I am sure, be much approved of by many persons of taste, among whom the sale of my book would probably in the first instance be. I have just had in my hands an old book so bound, the paste-board covers of a greyish-blue, and the paper back olive green; nothing could be prettier or more simple; and I should be very glad if you could indulge me in this particular.

I do not know whether without adding to the expense of publication, the present paper might be changed for paper with rough edges and showing the water-mark; but suppose not.

I will send you on Monday the proofs I have already received with corrections, and remain

Very sincerely yours,
W.H. Pater.

8 Alexander Macmillan to Walter Pater, 7 November 1872

MS.: British Library.
W.H. Pater Esq.

Nov. 7.

Dear Mr. Pater,

I wished to have seen you when I was in Oxford yesterday, but our train was an hour late, so that I was little more than in time for Mr. Combe's funeral. I meant to speak to you about the binding, which you wish: paper boards and labels. This will be a serious drawback to book sellers keeping it in stock, as these kinds of covers are so apt to get soiled and spoiled. Besides, I don't like it anyway. It is like a recurrence to the *fig-leaf*. The cloth in gilt is infinitely more useful and surely not less beautiful. Please don't wish for it.

The alterations in the chaptering will I fear cause a good deal of additional expense, as I suspect the cut [alters] the paging, but the type itself will be distributed. Perhaps you might go to the Press and see how this can best be adjusted. Mr. Wheeler will give you every attention.

Yours very truly,
A. Macmillan.

9 Walter Pater to Alexander Macmillan, 11 November [1872]

MS.: British Library. Extracts are printed in Morgan, pp. 105 and 106. Printed in full in Evans, pp. 9-10.

Brasenose College, /Oxford. /Nov. 11.

Dear Mr. Macmillan,

I was disappointed at the contents of your letter, as the cover I wish for had occurred to me as a way of giving my book the artistic appearance which I am sure is necessary for it, without the expense and trouble of an unusual form of binding. I fancy that if I saw you I could persuade you to think the old-fashioned binding in boards as pretty as it seems to me. The objection as to its liability to be soiled might be met by the paper wrapper for packing, now not uncommon. Something not quite in the ordinary way is, I must repeat, very necessary in a volume the contents of which are so unpretending as in mine, and which is intended in the first instance for a comparatively small section of readers. For a book on art to be bound quite in the ordinary way is, it seems to me, behind the times; and the difficulty of getting a book bound in cloth so as to be at all artistic, and indeed not quite the other way, is very great. I prefer in all cases the paper label, as the lettering is necessarily clumsy on cloth binding, especially when as in this case the volume is a thin one.

I have been to the Press and find that the paging may be set right with little trouble, and spoke to Mr. Hall, in the absence of Mr. Wheeler, about the paper. I should like, with your permission, to select the kind of paper I think the nicest, providing it is not more expensive than that ordinarily used.

Believe me

Very sincerely yours,
W.H. Pater.

10 Alexander Macmillan to Walter Pater, 12 November 1872

MS.: British Library. Printed by Macmillan, pp. 266-7.
W.H. Pater Esq.

Nov. 12.

Dear Mr. Pater,

I don't think you would convince me that paper covers are more beautiful than cloth, and they certainly are very much less useful. I am speaking with recent experience when I say that it would interfere with the sale of the book, as booksellers won't keep them, even with the paper cover. My friend Mr. MacLehose of Glasgow published *Olrig Grange* in this fashion at first and has been obliged to abandon it for cloth. He still uses paper labels and gives a duplicate label to be stuck on when the old gets dirty! This is droll to say the least of it. The bookseller or possessor has to remove the old one and get paste, which he possibly has not at hand, and repaste the clean one on.

The use of inferior unuseful materials cannot be needful to the realisation of any art which is of much value, at least I cannot see how. Gold lettering on cloth was an immense advance on the old paper boards and was welcomed as such. I remember the period of change. I still possess books which are done up in smooth cloth with paper label and value them historically, just as I would value Adam's fig-leaf, if I could find it.

But I will most gladly cede my tastes to yours as far as possible. I send you by this post a book in a style of binding which I devised for the author and which he liked. His tastes were 'artistic.' He is an intimate friend of Mr. Burne Jones and others who think in that line. Also, the paper of the book is made to imitate the old wire wove paper which can only now be got in this mock rib, which is really rather pleasant to my own eye. If you like the paper, let me know at once, as it will have to be made on purpose. Perhaps we can meditate on the binding a little further.

Yours very truly,
A. Macmillan.

11 Walter Pater to Alexander Macmillan, 13 November [1872]

MS.: British Library. Text printed in Morgan, p. 106, and in Evans, pp. 10-11.

Brasenose College, /Oxford. /Nov. 13.

Dear Mr. Macmillan,

The volume you send seems to me a beautiful specimen of printing, and I should much like to have the same sort of paper. I like the black cloth cover, and think, with some modifications, about which I will write shortly, it will do very well for my book.

Believe me,

Yours very truly,
W.H. Pater.

12 Alexander Macmillan to Walter Pater, 29 November 1872

MS.: British Library.
W.H. Pater Esq.

Nov. 29.

Dear Mr. Pater,

I accepted the black [vignette] as a not unusual or unbeautiful variety on a title page, but have no special enthusiasm for it and very gladly accept your decision on the subject.

Yours very truly,
A. Macmillan.

13 Macmillan and Co. to Walter Pater, 3 January [1873]

MS.: British Library.
W.H. Pater Esq.

Jan. 3.

Dear Sir,

We enclose a form of agreement for your *Studies in the Renaissance*. The copy we have signed is for you to keep, the other is for you to sign and return to us.

Yours faithfully,
Macmillan and Co.

14 Alexander Macmillan to Walter Pater, 12 February 1873

MS.: British Library.
W.H. Pater Esq., /Brasenose College, /Oxford.

Feb. 12.

My dear Mr. Pater,

We have been stifled in the issue of your book by being unable to get a further supply of the cloth you approved of, as I also did. It was ordered by our binder five weeks since in advance, and the maker cannot supply it, or promise when. Might we use our own design in the proper colour? We have some more, but the bulk of the edition will be in a somewhat different colour, which I hope you will like. [It won't] do to delay longer. Sidney Colvin writes me that his paper is ready and waiting.

Yours very sincerely,
Alex Macmillan.

15 Walter Pater to Alexander Macmillan, 18 February [1873]

MS.: British Library. Printed in Evans, p. 12.

Brasenose College, /Oxford. /Feb. 18.

Dear Mr. Macmillan,

I was sorry to hear of the change in the binding, not only as undesirable in itself, but as not likely to be a change for the better. I should have preferred a quite different colour *of the same* character rather than any ordinary green cloth. However, I think you were quite right not to delay the book longer. How many copies are there altogether in the original binding? I still require four copies of the book, one of which might be in the new colour.

Very sincerely yours,
W.H. Pater.

16 Alexander Macmillan to Walter Pater, 19 February 1873

MS.: British Library.
W.H. Pater Esq., /Brasenose College, /Oxford.

Feb. 19.

Dear Mr. Pater,

I am glad to tell you that just after I had written my last letter to you our binder sent down word to say that at last the proper cloth had come, so that the whole edition can be bound in its own cloth.

So the matter is now settled as we had originally agreed.

Yours very truly,
Alex Macmillan.

17 Alexander Macmillan to Walter Pater, 13 November 1876

MS.: British Library.
W.H. Pater Esq., /Brasenose College. /Oxford

Nov. 13.

Dear Mr. Pater,

About a new edition of your essays? You spoke of altering some and adding some. I think a new revised edition might do.

Yours very truly,
Alex Macmillan.

18 Walter Pater to Alexander Macmillan, 15 November [1876]

MS.: British Library. Printed in Evans, pp. 17-18

Brasenose College, /Oxford. /Nov. 15.

Dear Mr. Macmillan,

I shall be very glad to have a new and revised edition of my essays, adding a small quantity of new matter, and making a good many alterations, so that the book would be of the size of the present. I should like the new edition to be as perfect as possible, as regards paper etc. with an engraved vignette, as I once suggested to you. I hope to be in London about Xmas, and will call on you on the subject. It might be ready by about March or April. Should you wish to put it in a list of books, I think the title ought to be as follows. *The Renaissance, a Series of Studies in Art and Poetry, A new edition, etc.* Also, perhaps the price might be raised.

With many thanks, I am

Very sincerely yours,
W.H. Pater.

19 Alexander Macmillan to Walter Pater, 30 November 1876

MS.: British Library.
W.H. Pater Esq.

Nov. 30.

Dear Mr. Pater,

I am not sure whether I told you not to speak about a new edition of your book, as if a [word] gets abroad of one, it is likely to paralyse the sale of the present one.

I shall be very glad to see you when you are in town. [Then] we can discuss the details you mention.

Yours very sincerely,
Alex Macmillan.

20 Walter Pater to Alexander Macmillan, 30 January [1877]

MS.: British Library. Printed in Evans, pp. 18-19.

Bradmore Road, /Oxford. /Jan. 30.

Dear Mr. Macmillan,

I had hoped to have written to you before now, but have been much occupied with an examination since the beginning of term. Of the two specimen papers, I enclose the one I think preferable. I should like the line under the heading, and the number of the essay omitted. The page might, I think, be shortened by one line. This would increase, instead of slightly diminishing, the number of pages in the first edition, besides improving the look of the page, which to my eye is the better for a broad space at the foot. I shall be quite ready to send to you, or take to the press here, the corrected copy, as soon as I have heard from you, and will send you, as soon as I can, the corrected title and notices of the press, for advertisement.

I shall look out for the proof of the vignette, and specimens of binding, and I think the title on the back would perhaps be neatest in print on white paper.

The engraving from *Theologia Germanica* arrived quite safe. Many thanks for that and cheque.

Believe me

Very sincerely yours,
W.H. Pater.

21 Alexander Macmillan to Walter Pater, 1 February 1877

MS.: British Library.
W.H. Pater Esq., /Bradmore Road, /Oxford.

Feb. 1.

Dear Mr. Pater,

I have instructed the printer to go on [printing] with a page such as you decide on. We are also ordering the paper and our burden is looking after the cloth and I hope we will succeed. Mr. Jeens too is at work on the little vignette but you will hardly see a proof for six weeks or so.

Yours very sincerely,
Alex Macmillan.

22 *Alexander Macmillan to Walter Pater, 14 February 1877*

MS.: British Library.
W.H. Pater Esq., /Bradmore Road, /Oxford.

Feb. 14.

Dear Mr. Pater,

After many trials the enclosed are the results of what can be done in the way of reproducing your colour. The lightest is the nearest, but the *texture* makes such a difference in the effect to the eye that I cannot say whether the result might not be nearer your wishes if we might put a graining on the cloth instead of leaving it smooth.

When you are next in town we can talk it over.

Yours very truly,
Alex Macmillan.

23 *Walter Pater to Alexander Macmillan, 24 February [1877]*

MS.: British Library. Printed in Evans, pp. 19-20.

Bradmore Road, /Oxford. /Feb. 24.

Dear Mr. Macmillan,

I have nearly finished correcting the proofs, so that they might begin printing in about a week from this time, if the paper can be sent. I like one of the specimens of binding, but think perhaps one of those you have in use already, e.g., Green's *Stray Studies*, might do still better. I hope to be in town at the beginning of the vacation and will call on you about it. Meantime could you ascertain from Mr. Jeens the exact size of the vignette, as the title-page must be made up accordingly?

Very sincerely yours,
W.H. Pater.

How many copies are to be printed? I should propose 1,000 instead of 1,250, as before.

P.S. I am anxious that the new edition should appear as soon as possible, and I will write myself to Mr. Jeens about the size of the vignette, which will be more direct and save you the trouble.

24 Alexander Macmillan to Walter Pater, 26 February 1877

MS.: British Library.
W.H. Pater Esq., /22 Bradmore Road, /Oxford.

Feb. 26.

Dear Mr. Pater,

As the paper we are to use is an unusual size we have to order it to be made, and the exact quantity needed. We are writing to the Press to ask how many pages exactly the book now comes to. When we know this we will order paper and get it in a week or ten days. I think I would prefer to print 1250 copies. The last 250 make a considerable difference in the money result and they are sure to sell. Could you kindly send me back the specimens of cloth as we want them for another book? I shall be glad if you adopt the colour of Green's *Stray Studies*, which I think very good. I also am writing to Mr. Jeens to say that it is important to get the vignette early.

Yours very sincerely,
Alex Macmillan.

25 Walter Pater to Alexander Macmillan, 6 March [1877]

MS.: British Library. Printed in Evans, p. 20.

Bradmore Road, /Oxford. /Mar. 6.

My dear Mr. Macmillan,

My book will be ready for printing in a few days. But Mr. Jeens has not yet answered my letter. Could you ascertain, and let me know, the exact size of the vignette, as it is impossible to make up the title-page properly without knowing that.

Very sincerely yours,
W.H. Pater.

26 Alexander Macmillan to Walter Pater, 7 March 1877

MS.: British Library.
W.H. Pater Esq., /Bradmore Road, /Oxford.

Mar. 7.

Dear Mr. Pater,

The paper is ordered for your book, and as soon as the printer has it he can begin printing. This we [hope] will be in a few days.

Mr. Jeens has been seriously ill, dangerously I fear. But he is sticking to his work, and when I saw him on Saturday he hoped to be able to answer your letter yesterday. As the title page is the last thing printed in a book I don't like to hurry him, as he had hoped to get the plate done in a fortnight or so.

When do you come to town? I want to show you an actual book bound in the cloth that was made after your colour. You could hardly judge of it from the bits you saw. I cannot well send the book by post.

Yours very truly,
Alex Macmillan.

27 Walter Pater to Alexander Macmillan, 10 March [1877]

MS.: British Library. Printed in Evans, p. 21.

Bradmore Road, /Oxford. /Mar. 10.

Dear Mr. Macmillan,

I hope to be in London the week after next and will make an appointment to see you. As I am anxious for the book to appear as soon as possible, perhaps you would give the printers a hint to that effect. I enclose the exact form of an advertisement which I should be glad to have inserted, as soon as possible, in your list of forthcoming books, in the *Pall Mall Gazette* for instance, with an extract which I have copied accurately from John Morley's article on my essays in the *Fortnightly Review* for April, 1873. I will bring you, when I come to see you, some other press notices for a longer advertisement.

Believe me

Very sincerely yours,
W.H. Pater.

I hope to finish and print before long, my essays on Demeter and Dionysus, and should like to talk to you about the same.

28 Alexander Macmillan to Walter Pater, 12 March 1877

MS.: British Library.
W.H. Pater Esq., /Bradmore Road, /Oxford.

Mar. 12.

Dear Mr. Pater,

An advertisement such as you send with the long extract would cost about 25/- if properly displayed in the *Pall Mall Gazette*. This I don't think we should spend before the book is published. We can announce the coming of the edition in the gossip of the *Athenaeum* and the *Academy* of this week and this would attract notice. Don't you think that the *subject* of the vignette should be given? I remember that it is a head by Leonardo and is in the Louvre, but I can't recall the subject. Can you tell me by return of post?

I shall be very glad to see you when you come to town, and shall be delighted to negotiate with [you] for the essays on Demeter and Dionysus.

Yours very truly,
A. Macmillan.

29 Walter Pater to Alexander Macmillan, 13 March [1877]

MS.: British Library. Printed in Evans, pp. 21-22.

Bradmore Road, /Oxford. /Mar. 13.

Dear Mr. Macmillan,

I daresay you are right: but I am anxious that the book should be thoroughly advertised when it does appear. The subject of the vignette has no recognised name, being only a small drawing. The words of the advertisement might run: 'with a vignette after Leonardo da Vinci, engraved by Jeens,' and in any gossip on the subject it might be described as being from a favourite drawing by Leonardo da Vinci in the Louvre.

Unless I hear from you to the contrary I hope to call on you Tuesday next.

Very sincerely yours,
W.H. Pater.

30 Alexander Macmillan to Walter Pater, 14 March 1877

MS.: British Library.
W.H. Pater Esq.

Mar. 14.

Dear Mr. Pater,

If you can fix what hours on Tuesday – between 11:00 and 4:00 – you will call I will be careful to be in and free.

Yours very truly,
Alex Macmillan.

31 Walter Pater to Alexander Macmillan, 31 March [1877]

MS.: British Library. Printed in Evans, p. 22.

Bradmore Road, /Oxford. /Mar. 31.

Dear Mr. Macmillan,

I have received the proof of the vignette, and think it the most exquisite thing I have seen for a long time – a perfect reproduction of the beauty of the original, and absolutely satisfactory in the exactness and delicacy of its execution. My sincere thanks to Mr. Jeens. I should like to see an impression in red, that I may judge the colour. I suppose it ought to have a morsel of tissue paper inserted to cover it; and lest the monogram should rub it, that must be removed to some other place in the volume. I enclose a pattern for the lettering of the back; I think the letters ought to be perfectly plain, but as thin and delicate as possible.

I think you told me you had thoughts of publishing a translation of Schnaase's *History of Sculpture*. In that case I daresay you are already provided with a translator. If not I should venture to recommend one of my sisters, to whom I fancy I could give some real assistance in the work.

Very sincerely yours,
W.H. Pater.

32 Walter Pater to Alexander Macmillan, 9 April [1877]

MS.: British Library. Printed in Evans, pp. 22-3.

Bradmore Road, /Oxford. /Apr. 9.

Dear Mr. Macmillan,

I return by this post the proof of the vignette which I think on the whole the best in colour. I think it very beautiful. The others I should like to keep as specimens, unless they are wanted. The purple ones seem to me wonderful reproductions of some tints used by Bartolozzi and that set, though perhaps the engraving seems to lose some of its delicacy in them.

Very sincerely yours,
W.H. Pater.

33 Alexander Macmillan to Walter Pater, 10 April 1877

MS.: British Library.
W.H. Pater Esq., /Bradmore Road, /Oxford.

Apr. 10.

Dear Mr. Pater,

The colour you chose is what we had liked, so we gladly adopt it. By all means keep the specimens.

Jeens' account of how he did this work is curious. He found it impossible to copy the photo, or indeed do any work on the steel while looking at it. The spots and blotches perplexed him, so he just 'learnt it by heart' and said all off without ever looking at the photo again.

Very sincerely yours,
Alex Macmillan.

34 Walter Pater to Alexander Macmillan, 26 April [1877]

MS.: British Library. Printed in Evans, pp. 23-4.

Bradmore Road, /Oxford. /Apr. 26.

Dear Mr. Macmillan,

I find the binding perfectly satisfactory; with print, paper and vignette, it makes a quite typical book. But there are some points to notice. The title-page is insecurely fixed. [It] came out, as you can see, without pulling. There is a curious irregularity in the folding of the sheets, which makes the margins unequal, and produces an odd appearance on the upper edge of the volume. Please to notice also the irregularity of pp. viii and ix, and that the whole of the Preface is printed on a different level from the rest of the book. I trust this is an accident of this particular copy. Alas! also, for the hands of bookbinders, which are apt to tarnish a little title-page, and the last page of all, where you will notice also an irregularity similiar to that of p. ix. On the title-page, it seems to me that the letters are not bitten in enough. I thought the vignette was to be pasted on, though perhaps it is well enough as it is.

It looks very beautiful. I think it was a pity the attribution to Leonardo da Vinci was omitted, and that Jeens' own name might have been much more distinctly visible. Also, in this copy, the vignette is printed awry, and not, as it ought to be, exactly midway between the printing immediately above and below it.

Please don't forget my suggestions about advertising; and I should be glad if the book could be got out as soon as possible, and also if you will kindly send me, when it is ready, the number of copies for presentation you usually allow.

I am working at the other volume proposed, and am

Very sincerely yours,
W.H. Pater.

35 Alexander Macmillan to Walter Pater, 30 May 1877

MS.: British Library.

May 30.

Dear Mr. Pater,

We are sending you six copies of your book by rail today. People seem to like the look of the book very much. I do think it fulfils your ideal of being 'dainty.'

My daughter greatly enjoyed your kind hospitality and that of your sisters. I do hope they will come and see us on your return to England.

Yours very sincerely,
Alex Macmillan.

36 Walter Pater to Alexander Macmillan, 23 January [1878]

MS.: British Library. Printed in Evans, p. 27.

22 Bradmore Road, /Oxford. /Jan. 23.

My dear Mr. Macmillan,

I beg to acknowledge a cheque for £4.17.8, with many thanks. I had hoped to be able to call on you before this, having never thanked you for your kind invitation to myself and my sisters, of which we hope to avail ourselves some time in the warmer weather.

I suppose Malcolm will be resident again this term, and hope he will give me a call.

With very kind regards, I remain

Sincerely yours,
W.H. Pater.

37 Walter Pater to Alexander Macmillan, 31 January [1878]

MS.: British Library. Printed in Evans, pp. 28-9.

22 Bradmore Road, /Oxford. /Jan. 31.

Dear Mr. Macmillan,

A second copy of *Mirage* has just reached me. I read the first with very great pleasure, and acknowledged it in a letter which I hope reached you, for the writer. If this second copy was sent by mistake I will return it; but, not hearing from you, shall hand it on, some time, to a friend.

Very sincerely yours,
W.H. Pater.

38 George Macmillan to Walter Pater, 1 February 1878

MS.: British Library. W.H. Pater.

Feb. 1.

Dear Mr. Pater,

In answer to your letter of this morning my father asks me to say that the second copy of *Mirage* was sent by mistake. If you have no special object in view for it he would be glad if you would send it with his kind regards to Mrs. Humphry Ward.

I am

Yours very truly,
George A. Macmillan.

39 Walter Pater to George Grove, 17 April [1878]

MS.: British Library. Printed in Evans, pp. 29-30.
George Grove Esq.

22 Bradmore Road, /Oxford. /Apr. 17.

Dear Mr. Grove,

I send you by this post a MS. entitled 'The House and the Child,' and should be pleased if you should like to have it for *Macmillan's Magazine*. It is not, as you might perhaps fancy, the first part of a work of fiction, but is meant to be complete in itself; though the first of a series, as I hope, with some kind of sequence in them, and which I should be glad to send *you*. I call the MS. a portrait, and mean readers, as they might do on seeing a portrait, to begin speculating: what came of him?

Very sincerely yours,
W.H. Pater.

40 Walter Pater to George Grove, 12 May [1878]

MS.: British Library. Printed in Evans, p. 30

22 Bradmore Road, /Oxford. /May 12.

Dear Mr. Grove,

I have just sent the corrected proofs of my article to the printers and told them I should like to have a revise. Also, I should prefer the article to appear without signature.

Yours very truly,
W.H. Pater.

41 Walter Pater to George Grove, 11 June [1878]

MS.: British Library. Printed in Evans, p. 31.

George Grove Esq.

22 Bradmore Road, /Oxford. /June 11.

Dear Mr. Grove,

I have sent the corrected revise of my paper for *Macmillan's Magazine* back to Messrs. Clay and Sons, and have restored the signature, as you proposed.

With many thanks for your letters, I remain

Very sincerely yours,
W.H. Pater.

42 Walter Pater to Alexander Macmillan, 1 October [1878]

MS.: British Library. Printed in Evans, p. 32.

22 Bradmore Road, /Oxford. /Oct. 1.

Dear Mr. Macmillan,

I propose to print a volume of essays from the *Fortnightly* etc. and should be glad if you would take it on the same terms as my former volume, to the second edition of which I should like it to correspond in type etc. It might appear at the beginning of next year; and I will, if you like, call on you, at the beginning of November about it. Meantime perhaps it might be got into type. I propose to call it

The School of Giorgione, and other studies

and give, opposite, a list of contents. I think it would be a volume of about 300 pages.

Very sincerely yours,
W.H. Pater.

Contents:
The School of Giorgione
Wordsworth
The Myth of Demeter:
1. The Homeric Hymn
2. Demeter and Persephone
The Myth of Dionysus:
1. The spiritual form of fire and and dew
2. The Bacchanals of Euripides
Romanticism
On 'Love's Labour [sic] Lost'
On 'Measure for Measure'
The Character of the Humourist: Charles Lamb

43 Alexander Macmillan to Walter Pater, 2 October 1878

MS.: British Library.
W.H. Pater Esq., /22 Bradmore Road, /Oxford.

Oct. 2.

Dear Mr. Pater,

We shall be very glad to undertake the publication of your new volume of essays on the same terms as we did your studies in the Renaissance.

We will print it as before at the Clarendon Press and we are writing to the printers there to say that you are ready to supply them with copy as soon as they like to begin and that it is to be printed exactly uniform with the second edition of your *Studies.*

We will send a paragraph to the *Athenaeum* and *Academy* saying that it is coming and giving them the title as you give it.

I shall be very glad to see you when you come to London.

Very sincerely yours,
Alex Macmillan.

44 Alexander Macmillan to Walter Pater, 30 October 1878

MS.: British Library.
W.H. Pater, /22 Bradmore Road, /Oxford.

Oct. 30.

Dear Mr. Pater,

I shall be very glad to see you on Saturday about noon. The press has not given us the exact number of pages so that we may order the paper which is rather peculiar, but we are writing them today.

Very sincerely yours,
Alex Macmillan.

45 Walter Pater to Alexander Macmillan, 13 November [1878]

MS.: British Library. Printed in Evans, p. 33.

22 Bradmore Road, /Oxford. /Nov. 13.

Dear Mr. Macmillan,

Accept my best thanks for the beautiful copy of Milton, and for the *Europeans*, which I am reading slowly, as it deserves, with immense enjoyment of its delicate beauty. It makes most other literature seem rather vulgar.

Will you kindly give directions that the paper should be sent as soon as possible to the Oxford Press, for my essays, as they are now ready to begin printing. I suppose there will be no delay in the binding; and will send, in a few days, a note about the advertisements for the end of the volume.

Very sincerely yours,
W.H. Pater.

46 Alexander Macmillan to Walter Pater, 16 November 1878

MS.: British Library.
Walter Pater Esq.

Nov. 16.

Dear Mr. Pater,

The paper for your book had to be specially made. It was ordered as soon as we had a clear idea of the size of the book. We expect it in the printers' hands early next week. We will do all we can to get your book out early. Have you given the printers your title-page yet? They will send us a proof of it and from this we fix the latter on the outside. When we get this we can have all ready so that the binding causes no delay.

With kind regards

Very sincerely yours,
Alex Macmillan.

47 Walter Pater to Alexander Macmillan, 18 November [1878]

MS.: British Library. Printed in Evans, pp. 33-4.

22 Bradmore Road, /Oxford. /Nov. 18.

Dear Mr. Macmillan,

I enclose a selection of 'Opinions of the Press,' which I should like to appear as an advertisement, at the end of my new volume. They might, I think, occupy two pages, in the order which I have given; and be followed by the advertisements of 'Belles Lettres,' which appear in *Mirage* etc., of course, omitting from the latter, the advertisement of my book, now there. Would you let me have a proof of the 'Opinions,' I enclose?

Many thanks for your letter. I will take the title-page etc. to the Press, almost immediately.

I should like the lettering on the back to be precisely as before, in type and arrangement, with, at the top,

Dionysus and other Studies.

Believe me,

Very sincerely yours,
W.H. Pater.

48 Walter Pater to Alexander Macmillam, 30 November [1878]

MS.: British Library. Printed in Evans, p. 34.

22 Bradmore Road, /Oxford. /Nov. 30.

Dear Mr. Macmillan,

I find more and more, as I revise the proofs of my essays, so many inadequacies that I feel compelled, very reluctantly, to give up the publication of them for the present. You will of course let me know all the cost of setting up in type, for which of course I will immediately repay you. The paper which I fancy has not yet arrived, may, I suppose, be used for some other book. I hope you will forgive me all the trouble I have given you. But, sincerely, I think it would be a mistake to publish the essays in their present form; some day they may take a better and more complete form. Please send me a line of assent at once.

With many apologies,

Very sincerely yours,
W.H. Pater.

P.S. Please do not announce, in any way, that the book is not to be published.

49 Alexander Macmillan to Walter Pater, 2 December 1878

MS.: British Library.
W.H. Pater Esq., /22 Bradmore Road, /Oxford.

Dec. 2.

Dear Mr. Pater,

Please don't! At least wait a little till we have gone carefully over the proofs. There is no reason so far as I have seen for your apprehension. I think this will be a quite worthy successor of your *Renaissance*. The paper is in the printers' hands, but of course we could arrange that. But it would be awkward to answer the many questions that would come to us as 'Why is Pater's book not forthcoming'? Let us wait a little at best.

Yours very sincerely,
Alex Macmillan.

50 Walter Pater to George Grove, 4 December [1878]

MS.: British Library. Printed in Evans, p. 35.

22 Bradmore Road, /Oxford. /Dec. 4.

Dear Mr. Grove,

I am glad to hear of your safe return. Many thanks for your letter. I fear I shall not be able to send you another instalment just yet, as I have found it necessary to take up again, some work I thought I had finished, of another sort.

I heard a conversation among some musical people the other night about your *Musical Dictionary*, which made me put your article on Beethoven down among things to be read.

Very truly yours,
W.H. Pater.

51 Alexander Macmillan to Walter Pater, 5 December 1878

MS.: British Library.
W.H. Pater Esq., /22 Bradmore Road, /Oxford.

Dec. 5.

Dear Mr. Pater,

I have had a note from the Clarendon Press, and £35 would cover the printers' expenses. We had sent down paper which cost us £39 and part of which they had 'wetted ready for working' before you called. The paper is peculiar and was made specially for this book, but we will most likely be able to use it somehow. If I find we incur any loss I will tell you hereafter.

Would you like the type taken down at once?

I am rather sorry about the matter, but you clearly are the final judge and I submit.

Very sincerely yours,
Alex Macmillan.

52 Walter Pater to Alexander Macmillan, 9 December [1878]

MS.: British Library. Printed in Evans, pp. 35-6.
Alex Macmillan Esq., /Bedford St., /Covent Garden, /London W.C.

22 Bradmore Road, /Oxford. /Dec. 9.

Dear Mr. Macmillan,

I enclose a cheque for £35. You will let me know if you incur any expense about the paper. I am sorry to have given you so much trouble for nothing.

Very sincerely yours,
W.H. Pater.

P.S. I should like the type to be broken up.

53 Alexander Macmillan to Walter Pater, 11 December 1878

MS.: British Library.
W.H. Pater Esq., /Bradmore Road, /Oxford.

Dec. 11.

My dear Mr. Pater,

I enclose receipt for the printing expenses of the discarded *Dionysus*. I cannot but feel he is rather hardly treated by his father, but of course the father in this case is the judge, a Brutus come to judgment and execution too. The paper question must stand over for a time. If we sustain any loss over it we will let you know by and by. It is a peculiar paper and we will have a look about to see how we can use it. If we can without actual loss we will leave you free.

Very sincerely yours,
Alex Macmillan.

We are ordering the type to be taken down.

54 Walter Pater to Alexander Macmillan, 4 June [1879]

MS.: British Library. Printed in Evans, pp. 36-7.
A. Macmillan Esq.

Brasenose College, /Oxford. /June 4.

Dear Mr. Macmillan,

A friend of mine, E.S. Dodgson of New College, is anxious to make and publish a translation of Dante's *Convito,* and I believe he has written to you on the subject. He is very enthusiastic about Dante and I think really knows a good deal about him. There seems to be so wide an interest felt just now on the subject of Dante that I should think a well-made translation of the *Convito* might sell fairly well. If you should feel inclined to encourage my young friend, would you propose that he should write a short introduction, explaining the place of the *Convito* in Dante's writings, and also that the translation should be as carefully finished as possible, without haste?

Very sincerely yours,
W.H. Pater.

55 Alexander Macmillan to Walter Pater, 5 June 1879

MS.: British Library.
W.H. Pater Esq., /Brasenose College, /Oxford.

June 5.

Dear Mr. Pater,

I am afraid I must say that a translation of Dante's *Cantos* by itself would have little chance of success. If it were possible to get a complete translation of all the minor works, and make them range with such a translation of the *Commedia* as Dr. John Carlyle has partly done it might be worth considering. The *New Life* has been excellently well done by C.E. Norton ranging with Longfellow's translation, and the poems from it and the *Convito* were done by Lyell to range with Cary's and Miss Rossetti in her *Shadow of Dante* gives a good deal from both the *Convito* and the *Vita Nuova.* If Mr. Dodgson happened to be in London I should like to see and talk the whole matter over with him, if he would write and make an appointment.

Very sincerely yours,
Alex Macmillan.

56 Alexander Macmillan to Walter Pater, 9 June 1884

MS.: British Library.
W.H. Pater Esq., /2 Bradmore Road, /Oxford.

June 9.

Dear Mr. Pater,

The first chapters, pp. 1-31, of *Marius* have duly reached us. I hope to see Morley tomorrow or next day and will put it in his hands, and try to discuss it with him, if I find time to read it, as I hope to do, before I see him.

Ever truly yours,
Alex Macmillan.

57 Walter Pater to Alexander Macmillan, 9 September [1884]

MS.: British Library. Printed in Evans, p. 55.

2 Bradmore Road, /Oxford. /Sept. 9.

My dear Mr. Macmillan,

I was not surprised that Morley was unable to take my MS. for the magazine, its unfitness for serial publication having sometimes occurred to me, though for some reasons I should have preferred that mode. I am now thinking of offering it to a publisher with a view to its appearing in the spring. I should feel much honoured if you could take it. It would be pleasing to me in many ways, and the convenience of printing it in Oxford great. I wonder whether you could take it on slightly more favourable terms than in the case of my former volume. Excuse the plainness of my question. I had thoughts of asking Morley to consult you on the matter, but it seems unfair to poach on his already so much occupied time.

I should like the book to appear early in the new year, and would call on you about it, if necessary.

Believe me

Very sincerely yours,
W.H. Pater

58 Alexander Macmillan to Walter Pater, 11 September 1884

MS.: British Library.
W.H. Pater Esq., /2 Bradmore Road, /Oxford.

Sept. 11.

My dear Mr. Pater,

I would greatly like to publish your new book, and I am inclined to hope that its sales would be larger than the Essays, but that is uncertain, and I don't feel that we could offer any terms beyond those on which we published your Essays, that is, equal division of profits. But we are willing to pay you, on publication, the sum of £50 on account of your half share of profits, agreeing that whether your share reaches this amount or not it will still be yours.

I suspect that authors do not realize that in the case of half profits arrangements the publisher only charges the actual cost of production and advertisements. House rent, clerks' salaries, our own time, thought, correspondence: whatever they are worth are supposed to be paid out of *our* share of profits. I am fully and keenly aware [of] how little the money result ever is to writers like yourself [who] by careful elaboration of thought and skill work out results that have intellectual value. But I think we do our best for the higher literature, as distinguished from the merely popular.

With all kind regards,

Very faithfully yours,
Alex Macmillan.

We shall be glad to have your copy soon and arrange for a delicate and dainty form of book and also early publication.

59 Walter Pater to Alexander Macmillan, 14 September [1884]

MS.: British Library. Printed in Evans, pp. 55-6.

2 Bradmore Road, /Oxford. /Sept. 14.

My dear Mr. Macmillan,

Many thanks for your letter. I shall be very pleased to accept your offer, and sincerely hope you will lose nothing by it. I am not one of those (if such there be) who complain of the useful office of the Publisher; and I know not how long ago I formed the ambition that *you* should publish what I might write as I glanced over the fascinating list of your publications in the 'higher' literature, certainly, before I could afford to buy them.

The MS. will not be quite complete till the end of October, at the earliest, when it shall be duly delivered to you. I suppose three months will be sufficient for the printing, and that the book might appear in February. Three quarters of the whole are ready, and the printing might begin at once, if necessary.

I should like the volume to be, in size, quality of paper, and binding, precisely similar to the second edition of my Essays, which, though simple in form, is, I think, a model of what such a book should be, as regards that matter.

Ever

Very sincerely yours,
W.H. Pater.

60 Alexander Macmillan to Walter Pater, 31 October 1884

MS.: British Library.
Walter Pater Esq., /2 Bradmore Road, /Oxford.

Oct. 31.

My dear Mr. Pater,

I shall be very glad to see you here on Monday morning. I generally reach the office a little before 11:00 a.m.

Yours very truly,
Alex Macmillan.

61 Alexander Macmillan to Walter Pater, 20 November 1884

MS.: British Library.
Walter Pater Esq., /2 Bradmore Road, /Oxford.

Nov. 20.

My dear Mr. Pater,

We are writing to the Press telling them that we are anxious that your book should be hastened on. But you are on the spot and please add personal emphasis to our communication.

We do not order paper till we have received the first sheet marked finally for press. Will you kindly give them your information and when they send it to us we will return it with our instructions as to number and paper, at once.

Very sincerely yours,
Alex Macmillan.

62 Alexander Macmillan to Walter Pater, 17 December 1884

MS.: British Library.
Walter Pater Esq., /2 Bradmore Road, /Oxford.

Dec. 17.

Dear Mr. Pater,

The paper for your book is ordered and will be in the printers' hands early in January. We are working for publication about the end of January, so as to be ready for the Lent Term and the London post-Christmas Season. I have read the proof copy. It seems to me excellent and rare. Perhaps too fine for a wide popularity. We'll see. But we are hopeful of adequate sales for a book treating out of the way material. Malcolm has read it with great interest.

Very sincerely yours,
Alex Macmillan.

63 Alexander Macmillan to Walter Pater, 6 February 1885

MS.: British Library.
Walter Pater Esq., /2 Bradmore Road, /Oxford.

Feb. 6.

Dear Mr. Pater,

We had a dummy copy of your book put into cloth to show the general effect of the binding. We are sending it by today's post. We are writing to urge the printers to get on with the book. Nothing could be gained by binding volume one separately. Our binder could bind a thousand volumes as quickly as one hundred.

Very sincerely yours,
Alex Macmillan.

64 Alexander Macmillan to Walter Pater, 16 February 1885

MS.: British Library.
Walter Pater Esq., /2 Bradmore Road, /Oxford.

Feb. 16.

My dear Mr. Pater,

We will attend to your wish that the boards are not too heavy. Your presentation list will be attended to. We hope to publish about [the] 20th.

Very sincerely yours,
Alex Macmillan.

65 Alexander Macmillan to Walter Pater, 4 March 1885

MS.: British Library.
Walter Pater Esq., /2 Bradmore Road, /Oxford.

Mar. 4.

My dear Mr. Pater,

Marius is in the hands of the trade today. Our first subscription was not large. But that does not count for much. The reviews, and especially the cultivated readers, tell the most.

The premature notice in the *Athenaeum* and in *Time* is rather unfortunate.

We take pains that all papers have their copies for review as nearly as possible at the same time. We certainly sent early copies to neither the *Athenaeum* nor the *Time*. How did they get them?

It probably won't matter much, but the other papers, if they notice it, will certainly feel irritated.

I hope the look of the book pleases you.

Very sincerely yours,
Alex Macmillan.

66 Alexander Macmillan to Walter Pater, 16 March 1885

MS.: British Library.
Walter Pater Esq., /2 Bradmore Road, /Oxford.

Mar. 16.

My dear Mr. Pater,

We have already made our extract from the *Saturday Review*. It is shorter than yours and we think not less effective, and it will cost less. But if you much prefer your own we will use it.

We are sending the book to Professor Nettleship.

Very truly yours,
Alex Macmillan.

67 Macmillan and Co. to Walter Pater, 11 June [1885]

MS.: British Library.
Walter Pater Esq. /2 Bradmore Road. /Oxford.

June 11.

Dear Sir,

We are pleased to be able to report that the first edition of *Marius the Epicurean* is all but exhausted. Our idea about a second edition is that it should be not cheap, but at a rather lower price than the present one. It might be printed in the same type as at present on a paper of the same size but thinner, and published in one volume, or it might be printed in two pretty little volumes like the second edition of *John Inglesant*, the so-called 'Eversley Edition' of Kingsley's novels and several other books we have published recently. The advantage of the former plan would be that the book would be uniform with your *Renaissance* but we think the two volumes would be prettier. We shall be glad to know your views on the subject and also whether you will have any corrections or alterations to make before reprinting.

We are

Yours truly,
Macmillans.

68 Walter Pater to Alexander Macmillan, 16 June [1885]

MS.: British Library. Printed in Evans, pp. 61-2.
Alex Macmillan Esq., /for Messers. Macmillan and Co.

2 Bradmore Road, /Oxford. /June 16.

Dear Mr. Macmillan,

I am pleased to hear that the first edition of *Marius* is all but exhausted, and should be glad to proceed with the second edition. There are many minute corrections to make, but I could send away the first sheets, thus corrected, at once to the printers. Two volumes would, I think, be best, of the size of the 'Eversley' Kingsley. If the present paging were exactly followed, we should have two volumes of about 250 pages, with a fair margin, if type of the size of Kingsley were used. I think a volume of that size should be not stumpy; so that a thinner kind of paper than before might be used – the nicest paper you have in use, not above the average price.

Might it be printed by Clark or your London printers? I think the Oxford printing, as exemplified in the first edition, far from what it might be. Of course I could correct the proofs by post, either sheet by sheet, or all together, according to the convenience of the printers.

As to binding, I feel uncertain. I think it should be something quite distinct from that of the larger edition. It has occurred to me that cloth binding of the colour enclosed, with yellowish white vellum back, would look well. I suppose it would be impracticable to bind in oriental silk of that colour, which can be obtained at very moderate cost. What do you think of the old-fashioned binding in boards? or wholly in thin vellum?

What do you think the price of the book should be: about 12 shillings?

With many thanks, I remain

Very sincerely yours,
Walter Pater.

P.T.O. I think the paper on which *Miss Bretherton* is printed is good, for ordinary paper. Do you ever use paper like the morsel enclosed?

69 Frederick Macmillan to Walter Pater, 16 September 1885

MS.: British Library.

Sept. 16.

Dear Mr. Pater,

I send the 'dummy' copy of *Marius* by this post so that you may see how the label on the back will look. The printers have omitted 'Vol. I' but that can easily be put right.

I am

Yours truly,
Frederick Macmillan.

70 Frederick Macmillan to Walter Pater, 5 November 1885

MS.: British Museum.

Nov. 5.

Dear Mr. Pater,

We shall publish the second edition of *Marius* on Friday week. We were delayed very much by the paper which had to be made in Holland and it seemed impossible to get the phlegmatic Dutchmen to hurry themselves.

You shall have a copy as soon as possible. I am,

Yours very truly,
Frederick Macmillan.

71 Frederick Macmillan to Walter Pater, 25 November 1885

MS.: British Library.

Nov. 25.

Dear Mr. Pater,

I am glad you like the appearance of the second edition of *Marius*. I am sending you by this post a copy of an edition that we have printed for America. It will not be on sale in this country.

I am glad to find that Mr. Knowles has secured a charming paper from you for the next number of *Macmillan's Magazine*. I hope that you will find it possible to be a frequent contributor.

Believe me

Yours sincerely,
Frederick Macmillan.

72 Frederick Macmillan to Walter Pater, 12 April [1887]

MS.: British Library.
Walter Pater Esq., /12 Earl's Terrace, /Kensington, /London W.

Apr. 12.

Dear Mr. Pater,

We found that there was no paper of the necessary size and quality for your book to be bought ready made and I have therefore ordered a supply which will be in the printers' hands by the middle of next week without fail. You will not have been able to correct the proof sheets before then so no time will be lost.

I am

Yours very truly,
Frederick Macmillan.

73 Frederick Macmillan to Walter Pater, 15 April [1887]

MS.: British Library.
Walter Pater Esq.

Apr. 15.

Dear Mr. Pater,

I enclose a specimen of the type we propose to use for your new book. It will make 180 pages like this.

I also send a proof of the advertisement that has been set up for the May number of *Macmillan's Magazine*. It is very ugly and will have to be altered: if the extracts from the reviews could be cut down it would be easier to make the advertisement look well. At present it is too crowded.

Believe me

Yours very truly,
Frederick Macmillan.

74 Frederick Macmillan to Walter Pater, 15 November [1887]

MS.: British Library.

Nov. 15.

Dear Mr. Pater,

I am forwarding the revised copy of your *Renaissance* to Clark and I will also send you proofs forthwith. You have not forgotten, I hope, that the Americans are expecting a photograph of you.

Believe me

Yours very truly,
Frederick Macmillan.

75 Walter Pater to Messrs. R. and R. Clark, 1 December 1887

MS.: Brasenose College. Printed in Evans, p. 78.

Brasenose College, /Oxford. /Dec. 1.

Dear Sir,

I send you by this post some more copy of *The Renaissance*. I find your compositor has a way of forcing (I think) every chapter to end at the end of a page, which seems to me not desirable; and although some new matter has been added, he has gained by about four pages on the original copy, which, as the book is not a long one, is disadvantageous. Please note that the added chapter on 'The School of Giorgione' is to be printed *between* those of 'Leonardo da Vinci' and 'Joachim du Bellay.'

Very truly yours,
Walter Pater.

After Saturday, until further notice, my address will be
12 Earl's Terrace, /Kensington, /London W.

76 Frederick Macmillan to Walter Pater, 18 January 1888

MS.: British Library.
Walter Pater Esq.

Jan. 18.

Dear Mr. Pater,

The paper on which the last edition of your *Studies in the Renaissance* was printed was a rather expensive one, and we cannot get a paper not unlike it in appearance but a good deal cheaper which I cannot half think would do so well. I send you a book printed on this cheap paper that you may judge of its appearance. It would have to be made in a different size and rather thicker for your book but the quality would be the same. The difference in cost will amount to about £15 on the edition. Please let me know what you think about it.

Yours very truly,
Frederick Macmillan.

77 Frederick Macmillan to Walter Pater, 12 March 1888

MS.: British Library.
Walter Pater Esq.

Mar. 12.

Dear Mr. Pater,

A proof of the steel plate of the title of your *Renaissance* printed in purple ink was sent to Earl's Terrace last week for your approval. As we have heard nothing from you I presume you must be at Oxford. We shall be glad to know as soon as possible whether the colour is as you wish in order that the printing may proceed.

I am

Yours very truly,
Frederick Macmillan.

78 Frederick Macmillan to Walter Pater, 27 March 1888 MS.: British Library.

Walter Pater Esq.

Mar. 27.

Dear Mr. Pater,

We sent you another proof of the vignette for *The Renaissance* which I hope you like better than the first. I am afraid it still has something of the roughness of which you complained: this seems to be the fault of the coloured ink.

I am

Yours very truly,
Frederick Macmillan.

79 Frederick Macmillan to Walter Pater, 30 August 1888

MS.: British Library.
Walter Pater Esq.

Aug. 30.

Dear Mr. Pater,

I am sorry to say that I have not been able to send you a copy of the

American edition of *The Renaissance.* We sent the whole edition to America with the exception of half a dozen which are imperfect. These are being put right and you shall have one of them in a few days.

I am

Yours very truly,
Frederick Macmillan.

80 George Macmillan to Walter Pater, 3 January [1889]

MS.: British Library.

Jan. 3.

W.H. Pater Esq., /12 Earl's Terrace, /Kensington, /London.

Dear Mr. Pater,

The post office people in Paris cannot find Mr. [Samazin] at the address you gave me: 11 Rue Troyan. Can you find out where he is? The books meanwhile lie at his disposal in Paris.

I am

Yours very truly,
George A. Macmillan.

81 Walter Pater to Messrs. R. and R. Clark, [20 June 1889]

MS.: Brasenose College. Printed in Evans, p. 97.

Messrs. R. and R. Clark, /42 Hanover St., /Edinburgh.

12 Earl's Terrace, /Kensington, /London W.

Dear Sir,

Messrs. Macmillan propose that you should print a book of mine, for publication by November 1st, to be entitled

On Style, with other Studies in Literature.

The volume is to be precisely similar, in all respects, to the edition of *The Renaissance,* printed by you, in 1888. I am anxious to finish the correction of proofs, and to get the whole ready for press, by August 8th; soon after which I propose to leave England for some weeks. I send, by this post, the first portion of the copy, and will send the remainder in good time. Please send me the proofs at the address above.

Opposite is the list of contents.

Truly yours,
Walter Pater.

82 Frederick Macmillan to Walter Pater, 16 September 1889

MS.: British Library.
Walter Pater Esq.

Sept. 16.

Dear Mr. Pater,

Clark says that he sent you proofs of the whole of your new book on August 12th with some queries and that they have not been returned for press. I expect that you are away. Perhaps you will kindly send Clark his proofs as soon as you get back. The paper is all ready and it will take a very short time to work it.

I am

Yours very truly,
Frederick Macmillan.

83 Frederick Macmillan to Walter Pater, 30 September 1889

MS.: British Library.
Walter Pater Esq.

Sept. 30.

Dear Mr. Pater,

I enclose the annual statement of account and at the same time I send you final memoranda of agreement as arranged. Kindly sign and return one copy of the latter.

I am

Yours very truly,
Frederick Macmillan.

84 Frederick Macmillan to Walter Pater, 18 October 1889

MS.: British Library.
Walter Pater Esq.

Oct. 18.

Dear Mr. Pater,

I understand from Clark that he is still waiting for the return 'for press' of the title page to your new book. I shall be glad if you can send this back as we should like to publish it before the work on Childrens' books etc. begins. When bookshops become crowded with 'Christmas books' serious literature is apt to receive shabby treatment.

I am

Yours very truly,
Frederick Macmillan.

85 Frederick Macmillan to Walter Pater, 1 November 1889

MS.: British Library.
Walter Pater Esq.

Nov. 1.

Dear Mr. Pater,

Appreciations which is now ready for publication contains 264 pages and makes a goodly volume. I think the price might be 7/6or 8/6. *Imaginary Portraits* which is 6/contains 186 pages. What are your views?

I am

Yours very truly,
Frederick Macmillan.

86 Maurice Macmillan to Walter Pater, 17 December 1889

MS.: British Library.
Walter Pater Esq., /12 Earl's Terrace, /Kensington, /London W.

Dec. 17.

Dear W. Pater,

The words marked by you in the *Athenaeum* notice shall be used in our advertisements of *Appreciations* where it is possible.

I am

Yours very truly,
Maurice Macmillan.

P.S. I return your copy of the review.

87 George Macmillan to Walter Pater, 23 December 1889

MS.: British Library.
Walter Pater Esq., /12 Earl's Terrace, /Kensington, /London W.

Dec. 23.

Dear Mr. Pater,

We have only 120 copies left of *Appreciations* and though no doubt the demand will slacken a little after Christmas, we certainly ought to begin upon the reprint without undue delay. Will you therefore let us have by the end of the week a note of any corrections you may wish to make? It would be quite safe to print 1,250 copies or even 1,500 if you can make up your mind to it. The rapidity of the sale is very encouraging.

I am

Yours very truly,
George A. Macmillan.

88 George Macmillan to Walter Pater, 7 February 1890

MS.: British Library.
W.H. Pater Esq., /12 Earl's Terrace, /Kensington, /London W.

Feb. 7.

Dear Mr. Pater,

Messrs. Clark inform us that you have not yet sent them a corrected copy of *Appreciations*. Please do so as soon as possible. The book is quite out of print and the delay cannot fail to be injurious.

I was so glad to hear from Miss Pater that you thought well of my friend Mr. Francis Lucas' poems.

I am

Yours very truly,
George A. Macmillan.

89 George Macmillan to Walter Pater, 3 March 1890

MS.: British Library. Walter Pater, / 12 Earl's Terrace, / Kensington, / London W.

Mar. 3.

Dear Mr. Pater,

re. *Appreciations*

I have just come across this card which I ought to have sent you when it first came. I suppose I laid it aside with the at that time not unnatural idea that a new edition would hardly be wanted just yet. Events happily proved otherwise. I only hope it is not too late to correct the statement if it really needs correction. You are I think in direct communication with the printers.

This needs no reply.

Yours very truly,
George A. Macmillan.

90 Frederick Macmillan to Walter Pater, 15 April 1890

MS.: British Library.
Walter Pater Esq.

Apr. 15.

Dear Mr. Pater,

I send you herewith a specimen cover for *Appreciations* giving only the first title as you suggested. I shall be glad to know by return whether you prefer this to the original arrangement as the copies of the second edition are ready for binding.

Yours very truly,
Frederick Macmillan.

91 Frederick Macmillan to Walter Pater, 30 May [1890]

MS.: British Library.

May 30.

Dear Mr. Pater,

I find that we have less than 40 copies of your *Imaginary Portraits* left. Would it not be well to be thinking about a new edition?

I am

Yours very truly,
Frederick Macmillan

92 Frederick Macmillan to Walter Pater, 1 July [1890]

MS.: British Library.
Walter Pater Esq.

July 1.

Dear Mr. Pater,

We have an order from our New York House for some copies of your *Studies in the Renaissance* and *Appreciations* and we propose, with your approval, to print 1,000 copies of each book. The price at which we shall sell them will afford a profit of something over £50 to divide. Unless you have any objections we shall proceed at once with the manufacture.

I am

Yours very truly,
Frederick Macmillan.

93 Frederick Macmillan to Walter Pater, 8 August [1890]

MS.: British Library.
Walter Pater Esq.

Aug. 8.

Dear Mr. Pater,

The manager of our American branch has written to order 1,000 copies of *Marius* uniform with the editions of *Appreciations* and *The Renaissance* which we are printing for him. Have you any objection to our getting up an edition and if not do you wish to make any alterations?

I am

Yours very truly,
Frederick Macmillan.

94 Frederick Macmillan to Walter Pater, 27 August [1890]

MS.: British Library.

Aug. 27.

Dear Mr. Pater,

I enclose an application from somebody who wants to translate *Marius* into French.

I am

Yours very truly,
Frederick Macmillan.

95 Frederick Macmillan to Walter Pater, 2 September [1890]

MS.: British Library.
Walter Pater Esq., /12 Earl's Terrace, /Kensington, /London W.

Sept. 2.

Dear Mr. Pater,

If you will kindly return M. Lepelletier's letter I will write to him to say that he is at liberty to do what he proposes on condition that he can find a French publisher who will bring out his and will pay you £15 for the right of translation. I mention that modest sum because

I don't suppose any foreign publisher will be likely to give it more. Of course whatever we get for the translation will be paid over to you.

I am busy preparing to start for America. We leave London on the 10th instant.

I am

Yours very truly,
Frederick Macmillan.

96 George Macmillan to Walter Pater, 12 November [1890]

MS.: British Library.
Walter Pater Esq., /Brasenose College, /Oxford.

Nov. 12.

Dear Mr. Pater,

Thank you for telling me that the new edition of *Imaginary Portraits* is out of your hands. We will give the printers the necessary instructions as to the number of copies etc.

Yours very truly,
George A. Macmillan.

97 Frederick Macmillan to Walter Pater, 8 December [1890]

MS.: British Library.
Walter Pater Esq.

Dec. 8.

Dear Mr. Pater,

I am glad to hear that the proofs of *Marius the Epicurean* have gone back for press. Our people in New York want the book badly.

You told me in July that you did not wish to see proofs of *Appreciations* and the new edition of that book has accordingly been printed off and dispatched to New York.

I am

Yours very truly,
Frederick Macmillan.

98 Frederick Macmillan to Walter Pater, 6 January 1892

MS.: British Library.
Walter Pater Esq., /12 Earl's Terrace, /Kensington, /London W.

Jan. 6.

Dear Pater,

The stock of the second edition of *Marius the Epicurean* is now reduced to something under 60 copies and we ought to be thinking about a third. What do you say to putting it into one volume large crown octavo uniform with your three other books? We will of course do what you like, but there seem to me to be advantages in having them all alike.

I take this opportunity of enclosing a cheque for the balance due to you in the course of this month, and wish best wishes for the New Year, remaining

Yours truly,
Frederick Macmillan.

99 Frederick Macmillan to Walter Pater, 8 January 1892

MS.: British Library.
Walter Pater Esq., /12 Earl's Terrace, /Kensington, /London W.

Jan. 8.

Dear Pater,

I see no reason why we should not return to the original form of *Marius.* I shall be pleased to see you and talk it over any day next week except Thursday.

I am

Yours very truly,
Frederick Macmillan

100 Frederick Macmillan to Walter Pater, 28 January 1892

MS.: British Library.
Walter Pater Esq., /12 Earl's Terrace, /Kensington, /London W.

Jan. 28.

Dear Pater,

The revised copy for the first volume of *Marius* has reached me this morning and the new edition shall be put in hand at once. We will follow exactly the type and style of the first edition of 1885. I think that the price might be at least 15s.

I am quite well and back at work again.

With kind regards, believe me

Yours very truly,
Frederick Macmillan.

101 Walter Pater to Frederick Macmillan, 3 April [1892]

MS.: British Library. Printed in Evans, p. 173.

12 Earl's Terrace, /Kensington, /London W. /Apr. 3.

Dear Macmillan,

I enclose a specimen of Mr. C.L. Shadwell's translation of Dante's *Purgatorio*. Anyone who compares it with the original will, I think, be surprised by its almost literal faithfulness; while it seems to me singularly rhythmical to the ear and fresh in effect. The metre, as I mentioned, is that of Marvell's Ode, of which that Ode is the only, or almost the only, example. Mr. Shadwell had reasons for thinking it more suitable for use in an English translation than the Terza Rima of the original. I think his work very interesting as an experiment in scholarship and should be glad to tell him you would publish it for him on the terms on which you publish for me.

Very sincerely yours,
Walter Pater.

102 Frederick Macmillan to Walter Pater, 8 April 1892

MS.: British Library.

Walter Pater Esq.

Apr. 8.

Dear Pater,

I write to say that we shall be happy to undertake the expense of publishing Mr. Shadwell's translation of the *Purgatorio*, dividing with him any profits that may arise from the sale. We think that it ought to be printed in a dainty little volume, and unless Mr. Shadwell and you feel strongly about it we should not advise the inclusion of the text.

I understand that the volume is to have an introduction by you. We can begin printing whenever it is convenient to Mr. Shadwell.

I am

Yours very truly,
Frederick Macmillan.

103 Frederick Macmillan to Walter Pater, 2 May 1892

MS.: British Library.

Walter Pater Esq., /Brasenose College, /Oxford. May 2.

Dear Pater,

We agree with you in thinking that 2000 copies of the new edition of *Marius* had better be printed and I am therefore ordering paper for that number.

I am

Yours very truly,
Frederick Macmillan.

104 George Macmillan to Walter Pater, 11 May 1892

MS.: British Library.

Walter Pater, /12 Earl's Terrace, /Kensington, /London W.

May 11.

Dear Pater,

We are putting in our Classical Series an annotated edition of the *Bacchae* of Euripides by Professor Tyrrell of Dublin who will at least be known to you by repute as a brilliant scholar. He wishes to reprint as a general introduction to the play your article which appeared in our magazine for May of 1889. He admires it greatly and thinks it would be invaluable for putting his younger readers at the right point of view. I quite agree with him but it is another question whether you care to allow such free use of a paper which I hope you may some day see your way to reprint with some of your other contributions to the study of Greek life and thought. I have never ceased to regret the withdrawl of that volume which was justly printed years ago, containing among other things the beautiful and suggestive essay on Demeter. Do think seriously of such a classical volume, and in the meantime tell me what to say to my friend Professor Tyrrell. I have prepared him for the possibility that you may not care to have more than a few quotations made from the paper in question.

Yours very truly,
George A. Macmillan.

105 Walter Pater to George Macmillan, 15 May [1892]

MS.: British Library. Printed in Evans, pp. 173-74.

Brasenose College, /Oxford. /May 15.

Dear Macmillan,

Your letter has been forwarded to me here. Of course I know Professor Tyrrell as a distinguished scholar and excellent writer, and feel flattered by his proposal to put my paper as an introduction to his edition of the *Bacchae*. Kindly tell him so. I will send you a corrected copy of it in a week or ten days, if that will not be too late. It pleases me much that you like those papers of mine, which I should like some day to compile in a small volume, but shall not be able to do so for some time to come. The paper on the *Bacchae* might thus also be reprinted with the rest. In any case, it would be well disposed of in Professor Tyrrell's volume; I am afraid better than it deserves.

Very sincerely yours,
Walter Pater.

106 George Macmillan to Walter Pater, 16 May 1892

MS.: British Library.
Walter Pater Esq., /Brasenose College, /Oxford.

May 16.

Dear Pater,

Many thanks for your generous compliance with Professor Tyrrell's wish. It will do quite well if the revised copy of your essay reaches me by about the end of the month. Its appearance in Tyrrell's edition of the *Bacchae* will of course not prevent its inclusion hereafter in the volume of similar essays which I am glad to know you intend some day to issue.

Yours very truly,
George A. Macmillan.

107 George Macmillan to Walter Pater, 27 May 1892

MS.: British Library.
Walter Pater Esq., /Brasenose College, /Oxford.

May 27.

Dear Pater,

Many thanks for your paper on the *Bacchae*, which I have at once sent on to Professor Tyrrell.

Yours very truly,
George A. Macmillan.

108 Frederick Macmillan to Walter Pater, 12 October 1892

MS.: British Library.
Walter Pater Esq., /Brasenose College, /Oxford.

Oct. 12.

My dear Pater,

There is one point I omitted to mention the other day when you told me about your new volume on Plato, and that is with regard to the American sale. Under the new copyright law it is necessary that in order to obtain protection a book should be printed in the United States, and it would I think be a mistake to leave your book open to the pirates. I suggest that you allow us to print and publish an edition through our New York House. The terms that we should propose for this American edition are a royalty of 10 per cent of the retail price on all copies sold.

I am

Yours very truly,
Frederick Macmillan.

109 Frederick Macmillan to Pater, 11 November 1892

MS.: British Library.
Walter Pater Esq., /Brasenose College, /Oxford.

Nov. 11.

My dear Pater,

Mr. Shadwell wishes us to ask you how many copies of his translation of Dante you will accept for yourself. Please let me know.

Yours very truly,
Frederick Macmillan.

110 Frederick Macmillan to Walter Pater, 2 December 1892

MS.: British Library.
Walter Pater Esq., /Brasenose College, /Oxford.

Dec. 2.

My dear Pater,

When do you think you will be able to send us corrected proofs of your new book from which the American edition can be printed? We ought to have them in good time, because in order to obtain copyright in the United States, the American edition must be published simultaneously with the English one, and I want to give our people there time to get it nicely printed.

I am

Yours truly,
Frederick Macmillan.

111 George Macmillan to Walter Pater, 13 December 1892

MS.: British Library.
Walter Pater Esq., /12 Earl's Terrace, /Kensington, /London W.

Dec. 13.

Dear Pater,

We are sending the order to Oxford to print 2000 copies of the book on Plato, which I think was what you arranged with my cousin. But as he is not here today I think it best to tell you this in case there should be any mistake. The paper will be sent as soon as we know the quantity required.

Yours very truly,
George A. Macmillan.

112 Frederick Macmillan to Walter Pater, 14 December 1892

MS.: British Library.
Walter Pater Esq., /12 Earl's Terrace, /Kensington, /London W.

Dec. 14.

My dear Pater,

I enclose a formal memorandum of agreement (in duplicate) for *Plato and Platonism*. Will you kindly sign and return one copy.

I suppose you will not begin printing *Three Short Stories* until this book is quite out of your hands.

Believe me

Yours very truly,
Frederick Macmillan.

113 George A. Macmillan to Walter Pater, 7 June 1893

MS.: British Library.
Walter Pater Esq., /Brasenose College, /Oxford.

June 7.

Dear Pater,

We have received from America an elaborate thesis on Plato's Theory of Education in the *Republic*. I wonder whether you would be willing to read the MS. for us and advise us as to its publication? Our usual fee for such advice is £2.2. The author, A. Guyot Cameron, is a Professor at Yale. May I send you the MS.?

Yours very truly
George A. Macmillan.

114 George A. Macmillan to Walter Pater, 12 June 1893

MS.: British Library.
W.H. Pater Esq.

June 12.

Dear Pater,

Many thanks. The MS. goes today. Your opinion will be regarded as in strict confidence.

Yours very truly,
George A. Macmillan.

115 George A. Macmillan to Walter Pater, 30 October 1893

MS.: British Library.
W.H. Pater Esq., /Brasenose College, /Oxford.

Oct. 30.

Dear Pater,

My cousin is not here today so I opened your letter. Your request for copies of *The Renaissance* shall be duly attended to when the book is ready, but the title page is not yet printed off and I enclose herewith two specimens that you may say whether you prefer the lighter or the darker impression.

With kind regards, I am

Yours very truly,
George A. Macmillan.

116 Clara Pater to George Macmillan, 13 August [1894]

MS.: British Library.

25 Horton Street, /Kensington, /London W. /Aug. 13.

Dear Mr. Macmillan,

My sister and I both thank you sincerely for your very kind letter of sympathy. It was such a sudden and unexpected shock, for we had every reason to think he would quite recover. We are quite overwhelmed with sorrow.

We have to make a statement at the Probate Office of everything that is due to my brother. Would you be so kind as to tell us the amount due to him from you from July of 1893 to July of 1894.

With kind regards to Mrs. Macmillan and yourself,

I am

Yours very truly,
Clara Pater.

117 George Macmillan to Clara Pater, 16 August 1894

MS.: British Library.

Miss Pater, /25 Horton St., /Kensington, /London W.

Aug. 16.

Dear Miss Pater,

My cousin who is in Yorkshire has sent me your letter of the 13th. I am afraid it will take a few days for us to make out with approximate correctness what sum would have been due to your brother on account of sales during the year end June 30th, but you shall have the information as soon as possible. I think you will also be asked to state the value of his books for probate purposes, so when I write I will name what seems to us a fair sum based upon the average of several years' sales.

With kind regard, I am

Yours very truly,
George A. Macmillan.

P.S. May I add that if there is an idea of collecting unpublished papers whether in MS. or otherwise it would be a great pleasure to us to publish them.

118 George Macmillan to Clara Pater, 17 August 1894

MS.: British Library.
Miss Pater, /25 Horton St., /London W.

Aug. 17.

Dear Miss Pater,

I am now able to say that the amount due for your brother's books in January next will be £110. We should estimate his interest in all the books for probate purposes and apart from the sum due at £175. The sales have been very steady for some years but it is impossible to say how long they will remain so when the influence of his personality is withdrawn.

With kind regards, I remain

Yours very truly,
George A. Macmillan.

119 Macmillan and Co. to Hester Pater, 11 September 1894

MS.: British Library.
Miss Hester M. Pater, /5 Alfred Street, /St. Giles's, /Oxford.

Sept. 11.

Madam, Mr. Frederick Macmillan will be able to see you at 3:00 o'clock tomorrow, Wednesday, as you propose.

Yours very truly,
Macmillan and Co.

120 Frederick Macmillan to Hester Pater, 12 September 1894

MS.: British Library.
Miss Pater, /5 Alfred St., /St. Giles's, /Oxford.

Sept. 12.

Dear Miss Pater,

I write to say that I shall be here tomorrow (Thursday) morning at 11:00 o'clock, and shall be very glad to see you on the object of the volume of collected papers.

I am

Yours sincerely,
Frederick Macmillan.

121 Frederick Macmillan to Hester Pater, 13 September 1894

MS. British Library.
Miss Pater, /64 St. Giles's, /Oxford.

Sept. 13.

Dear Miss Pater,

I enclose a formal memorandum of agreement for the three new volumes of collected papers. If you or your sister will kindly sign and return it I will send you a duplicate signed by ourselves.

I am

Yours truly,
Frederick Macmillan.

122 Frederick Macmillan to Hester Pater, 18 September 1894

MS.: British Library.
Miss Pater, /Oxford.

Sept. 18.

Dear Miss Pater,

Messrs. Warne and Co. the publishers of a book called *Half Hours with the Best Authors* have asked us to give them permission to make an extract of about nine pages in length from W. Pater's paper on Botticelli in the volume of *Studies in the Renaissance*. Will you please let me know whether you would like this permission to be given or refused? On the whole I think I should be inclined to allow them to make use of the extract on the premise that it could hardy injure the sale of the book and that its effect on your brother's reputation would be good rather than bad. But if you have the least feeling that you would rather not give the permission, please say so and I will refuse it.

Believe me

Yours sincerely,
Frederick Macmillan.

123 Hester Pater to Frederick Macmillan, [19 September 1894]

MS.: British Library.

11 Victoria Grove, /Gloucester Road, /London W. /Sept. 19.

Dear Mr. Macmillan,

We should like the extract from 'Botticelli' to be put into *Half Hours with the best Authors* as it seems to us as to you that it might add to our brother's reputation and a wider knowledge of his writings. We are sending the agreement and the only photograph of my brother we have. We should like to know if you think it a good enough likeness to use as a frontispiece for the book, and whether it would be reproduced satisfactorily. We are staying at the above address for another week, when we get into our house.

Believe me,

Yours sincerely,
Hester M. Pater.

P.S. We should like the original photograph returned to us after the reproduction has been made.

124 Frederick Macmillan to Hester Pater, 20 September 1894

MS.: British Library.

Miss Pater, /11 Victoria Grove, /Gloucester Road, /London W.

Sept. 20.

Dear Miss Pater,

I am obliged to you for the agreement, and enclose a duplicate signed by ourselves.

I think that the photograph of your brother will reproduce very well and that it will make an attractive frontispiece for the new volume which many of his admirers will be glad to have. We will make a photogravure plate from it and let you have it back again.

I am

Yours sincerely,
Frederick Macmillan.

125 Frederick Macmillan to Hester Pater, 28 September 1894

MS.: British Library.
Miss Pater, /11 Victoria Grove, /Gloucester Road, /London W.

Sept. 28.

Dear Miss Pater,

On looking at the enclosed I cannot say there seems to me to be too much shoulder. If, however, you think there is, will you kindly say what you would like to have omitted and we will have it done.

Believe me

Yours very truly,
Frederick Macmillan.

126 Frederick Macmillan to Hester Pater, 2 October 1894

MS.: British Library.
Miss Pater, /11 Victoria Grove, /Gloucester Road, /London W.

Oct. 2.

Dear Miss Pater,

I shall be happy to see you tomorrow (Wednesday) at 12:00 o'clock.

I am

Yours very truly,
Frederick Macmillan.

127 Frederick Macmillan to Hester Pater, 15 October 1894

MS.: British Library.
Miss Pater, /11 Victoria Grove, /Gloucester Road, /London W.

Oct. 15.

Dear Miss Pater,

I send herewith a proof of the photogravure plate which seems to me very good. I also return the original photograph.

I am

Yours very truly,
Frederick Macmillan.

128 Frederick Macmillan to Hester Pater, 17 October 1894

MS.: British Library.

Miss Pater, /6 Canning Place, /Kensington Gate, /London W. Oct. 17.

Dear Miss Pater,

We will have the portrait printed in a warm brown ink and will let you see it. I hope we shall manage to please you as I should like to use the plate which I must say seemed to me to be if anything a better likeness than the photograph from which it is taken.

I am

Yours sincerely,
Frederick Macmillan.

129 Frederick Macmillan to Hester Pater, 18 January 1897

MS.: British Library.

Miss Pater.

Jan. 18.

Dear Miss Pater,

I enclose a letter from a Belgian gentleman asking the conditions on which he may publish a French translation of *Imaginary Portraits*. As the book appeared so long ago as 1887 the right of translation which can only be reserved for ten years has almost become common property. If a translation appears before the expiration of ten years there will be a copyright in it and a question for you to consider is whether it would be best to sell the right to this gentleman for a small sum (I don't suppose he would give much) or whether it would be better to let the right of translation lapse so that it might be open to anybody to publish as many translations as he pleased. From certain points of view it might seem that it was bad for your brother's literary reputation that the foreign translation of this work should be open to everyone. Of course if you could sell the right of translation for a large sum it would be another matter. But I do not think you could get more than £10 for it.

I am

Yours very truly,
Frederick Macmillan.

130 Frederick Macmillan to Hester Pater, 31 August 1897

MS.: British Library.
Miss Pater, /6 Canning Place, /Kensington Gate, /London W.

Aug. 31.

Dear Miss Pater,

I enclose a letter from a man who wishes to know if he can purchase copies of the *Essays from 'The Guardian'*. I think you told me that you had a few copies which you would sell for two guineas. If this is the case will you kindly communicate with Mr. Allen.

I am

Yours very truly,
Frederick Macmillan.

131 George Macmillan to Hester Pater, 22 March 1898

MS.: British Library.
Miss Pater.

March 22.

Dear Miss Pater,

Have you still any copies to dispose of of your brother's *Essays from 'The Guardian'*? I ask for an old friend, Mr. Robert MacLehose, bookseller and publisher in Glasgow who is particularly anxious to secure a copy of (presumably for a customer) and is willing to pay a good price for it. Hoping you will be in a position to oblige him (and me),

I am

Yours very truly,
George A. Macmillan.

132 Maurice Macmillan to Hester Pater, 14 May 1898

MS.: British Library.
Miss Pater, /6 Canning Place, /Kensington Gate, /London W.

May 14.

Dear Miss Pater,

I enclose a letter received this morning. There are some questions in it which you perhaps might be willing to answer. I should think that the right of translation into French must have elapsed by this time. I do not know whether any translation has already been made. At any rate it is not possible to obtain any money for the right, but we or you will write to our correspondent and give him permission. I send the letter however to you on account of the personal matters which we cannot answer.

I am

Yours very truly,
Maurice Macmillan.

133 Macmillan and Co. Ltd. to Hester Pater, 2 June 1899

MS.: British Library.
Miss Pater.

June 2.

Dear Madame,

An American firm of publishers proposes to introduce into Great Britain a work which they have already issued in the United States entitled *The International Library of Famous Literature* comprised in twenty volumes, and made up of extracts from the works of various writers of all ages – amongst which is one from *Marius the Epicurean.*

We have been applied to and have given permission for the use of this extract as we cannot think that its appearance in a work of this nature, which is only to be sold in complete sets at a high price, will have any injurious effects upon the sale of Mr. Pater's book. As, however, the proprietors have made no payment for the right to use this extract we beg to enclose for the acceptance of the Misses Pater a cheque representing their share in it.

Yours faithfully,
Macmillan and Co. Ltd.

134 Frederick Macmillan to Hester Pater, 24 January 1900

MS.: British Library.
Miss Pater.

Jan. 24.

Dear Miss Pater,

You may possibly have seen the so-called *Edition de luxe* of the works of Lamb, Tennyson, and Kipling which we have published during the last two years. These books are very handsome in appearance and profitable to publish as the number of copies printed is limited and they are consequently at once bought up by collectors – people who regard books as bric-a-brac. We have been thinking of following up the books we have already published by an edition of your brother's writings in the same style, that is, if we have your approval and consent.

We should propose to put the shortest books, *Imaginary Portraits* and *Gaston de Latour*, into one volume, and the series would then be contained in eight volumes of about 300 pages each in type like that of the enclosed specimen.

I shall be glad to know what you think of the idea, and also whether you would care to add to the edition the little collection of reviews from *The Guardian* which Mr. Gosse published.

I am

Yours very truly,
Frederick Macmillan.

135 Hester Pater to Frederick Macmillan, 25 January 1900

MS.: British Library.

Jan. 25.

Dear Mr. Macmillan,

We should very much like to have the *Edition de luxe* produced and I should think your suggestion of putting *Imaginary Portraits* and *Gaston de Latour* together in one volume and so making a set of eight would be a very good arrangement. The specimen leaf enclosed we like very much, both type and paper. We have not happened to see the Lamb or Tennyson so may we call on you some day soon and see the binding? As the books have sold so well for the last few years, do you think you could see your way to allowing us a larger share of the profits in future with this new edition? With regard to the reviews from *The Guardian*, we would rather not have them included, as they were never revised or intended for further publication.

With kind regards,
Very sincerely yours,
H.M. Pater.

136 Frederick Macmillan to Hester Pater, 31 January 1900

MS.: British Library.
Miss Pater, /6 Canning Place, /Kensington Gate, /London W.

Jan. 31.

Dear Miss Pater,

I am very glad to hear that you approve of the scheme for an *Edition de luxe* of your brother's works.

I regret that we do not see our way to make any alterations in the terms upon which his books are published, but if it will be a convenience to you in any way we are quite willing to make you an offer of a lump sum of money for this particular *Edition de luxe* to be paid on publication. I am unable to say what sum we could give as we have not yet decided of how many copies the edition is to consist.

I am

Yours very truly,
Frederick Macmillan.

137 Clara Pater to Frederick Macmillan, 1 February 1900

MS.: British Library.

Feb. 1.

Dear Mr. Macmillan,

We do not at all desire the lump sum for the *Edition de luxe* suggested in your letter. We should prefer to have the same arrangement for that as for the other books.

But we have long thought that, for a writer of reputation, half profits were not permanently satisfactory terms.

Yours sincerely,
Clara A. Pater.

138 Frederick Macmillan to Hester Pater, 2 February 1900

MS.: British Library.
Miss Pater, /6 Canning Place, /Kensington Gate, /London W.

Feb. 2.

Dear Miss Pater,

If you and your sister wish it we shall be quite willing to alter the arrangement for your brother's books from half profits to a royalty of 20 (twenty) per cent of advertised price. There is perhaps some advantage in the royalty system inasmuch as the returns to the author's representatives are more regular in amount.

Kindly consider this matter at your leisure and let me know your views. If we made the alteration it might as well run from the first of July last.

I am

Yours very truly,
Frederick Macmillan.

139 Clara Pater to Frederick Macmillan, 6 February 1900

MS.: British Library.

Feb. 6.

Dear Mr. Macmillan,

We have considered your suggestion of a royalty of twenty per cent instead of half profits and we do not see that it would be any advantage to us or worthwhile to make the alteration.

When I said that the present arrangement was unsatisfactory I meant that half profits were very well to begin with, but now that my brother's books are so well known and have been selling so well for the last five years, we think it only reasonable that in the future we should have a larger proportion of the profits.

We consider that two thirds would be a satisfactory arrangement.

I am

Yours sincerely,
Clara A. Pater.

140 Frederick Macmillan to Hester Pater, 8 February 1900

MS.: British Library.
Miss Pater, /6 Canning Place, /Kensington Gate, /London W.

Feb. 8.

Dear Miss Pater,

I am sorry that we do not see our way to make any alteration in the terms on which we publish your brother's books. At the same time I should like you to understand exactly what the conditions are. As you know, the profits that we divide with you are the gross profits, that is to say, out of our share we have to pay all the expenses of selling the books, which, with the large organization that we have for such a purpose, I need not point out are very heavy. Roughly speaking, we may say that supposing the profits to be divided amount to £100, £50 of which go to you and £50 to us, our share is reduced to £25 by the cost of business expenses, that is to say, although our gross share of the profits is £50, what we actually get is only £25. Some publishers make a charge for working expenses in the general account, so that the amount to be divided is reduced thereby. This is a perfectly legitimate method of procedure, but as a matter of fact we have never done it and have always divided up the gross profits with our authors.

I am

Yours very truly,
Frederick Macmillan.

141 Frederick Macmilan to Hester Pater, 23 May 1900

MS.: British Library.
Miss Pater.

May 23.

Dear Miss Pater,

I find that the plate from which the portrait of your brother was printed for the frontispiece of *Greek Studies* is a good deal worn and that in order to get a satisfactory result we ought to have a new one for the *Edition de luxe.* Can you for this purpose send me a copy of the photograph from which the plate was made? It will of course be returned to you when done with.

I am

Yours very truly,
Frederick Macmillan.

142 Frederick Macmillan to Hester Pater, 25 May 1900

MS.: British Library.
Miss Pater, /6 Canning Place, /Kensington Gate, /London W.

May 25.

Dear Miss Pater,

I think we had certainly better have the portrait of your brother which appeared in *Greek Studes* for the *Edition de luxe,* for it is in itself an admirable one. If you would like to have some other portraits reproduced in addition to this to be used as frontispieces to the other volumes we shall be glad to engrave them if you will let us have say two others that you consider good. It would no doubt interest purchasers of the book to have portraits of him at various ages.

I am

Yours very truly,
Frederick Macmillan.

143 Frederick Macmillan to Hester Pater, 5 June 1900

MS.: British Library.
Miss Pater, /6 Canning Place, /Kensington Gate, /London W.

June 5.

Dear Miss Pater,

I am afraid that the enclosed photographs are too faint to enable us to make satisfactory plates from them and we had better therefore confine ourselves to the portrait which appeared in *Greek Studies*. We will make a new plate of this from the negative as soon as it comes from Mr. Hollyer.

I am

Yours very truly,
Frederick Macmillan.

144 Frederick Macmillan to Hester Pater, 25 February 1901

MS.: British Library.
Miss Pater, /6 Canning Place, /Kensington Gate, /London W.

Feb. 25.

Dear Miss Pater,

I aught to have written to you before this with reference to the proposed reprint of the *Essays from 'The Guardian'*. I find that if set in the type of the accompanying specimen page we might manage to make a volume of 174 pages. We should propose to issue the book independently of the *Edition de luxe* but to bind it uniform with that series so that people wishing to make their series complete could purchase it. The price would have to be less than the volumes of the *Edition de luxe*. I think it might be 7/6. If you approve we will proceed with printing so that the book may be ready to issue after the last of the *Edition de luxe* has appeared.

I am

Yours very truly,
Frederick Macmillan.

145 Clara Pater to Frederick Macmillan, 27 February 1901

MS.: British Library.
6 Canning Place, /Kensington Gate, /London W. /Feb. 27.

Dear Mr. Macmillan,

We think your proposal with regard to the issue of *Essays from 'The Guardian'* is a very good one. Certainly the price should not be more than 7/6.

May we have the original copy back again, at your convenience?

Yours very truly,
Clara Pater.

146 Frederick Macmillan to Clara Pater, 28 February 1901

MS.: British Library.

Miss Pater, /6 Canning Place, /Kensington Gate, /London W. Feb. 28.

Dear Miss Pater,

I will let you have back the copy of *Essays from 'The Guardian'* as soon as it is finished with, but we must have it for some little time to print from. I am telling the printers to be careful and not to injure it in any way.

I am

Yours very truly,
Frederick Macmillan.

147 Frederick Macmillan to Clara Pater, 7 June 1901

MS.: British Library.

Miss Pater, /6 Canning Place, /Kensington Gate, /London W.

June 7.

Dear Miss Pater,

A London bookseller who is much interested in Mr. Pater's writings has sent us the enclosed list of articles by him which he says he has been able to trace in various periodicals, and none of which are included in the recently published *Edition de luxe*. Our friend wishes to know whether it would be worth while to make up another volume containing these papers. I shall be much obliged if you will think this over and will consult somebody such as Mr. Shadwell on the subject. It may be that these articles have already been considered, and that you and Mr. Shadwell concluded that they had better not be reprinted.

I am

Yours very truly,
Frederick Macmillan.

148 Clara Pater to Frederick Macmillan, 12 June 1901

MS.: British Library.

6 Canning Place, /Kensington Gate, /London W. /June 12.

Dear Mr. Macmillan,

All the articles on the list you sent us were considered by us and Mr.

Shadwell some time back, when you may remember there was some talk of publishing all the scraps that could be traced.

We still think it best to adhere to the decision we came to then, and not publish anything more. These articles are very slight, and would not make a volume of any size: many are not signed and were never intended to be brought out.

Yours sincerely,
Clara Pater.

149 Frederick Macmillan to Clara Pater, 17 June 1901

MS.: British Library.
Miss Pater, /6 Canning Place, /Kensington Gate, /London W.

June 17.

Dear Miss Pater,

Will you kindly send me back the list of the articles by Mr. Pater which I sent you the other day as I must return it to the man from whom it came. I will explain to him that they are not to be reprinted.

I am

Yours very truly,
Frederick Macmillan.

150 Frederick Macmillan to Clara Pater, 21 September 1901

MS.: British Library.
Miss Pater.

Sept. 21.

Dear Miss Pater,

I return the copy of the original reprint of *Essays from 'The Guardian'* which you kindly lent us for our edition.

By the way, am I right in thinking that Mr. Gosse asked you for permission to print a second 100 copies and was it because of the demand of the existence of which such a request was proof that you consented to the publication of the volume by us?

I am glad to say that the publication of the volume was justified. We have already disposed of the first 1000 copies and are reprinting.

The sales of all the books during the past year have been very satisfactory as you will see from the accounts which will reach you on the first of October.

With kind regards, I am

Yours very truly,
Frederick Macmillan.

151 Clara Pater to Frederick Macmillan, 23 September 1901

MS.: British Library.

6 Canning Place, /Kensington Gate, /London W. /Sept. 23.

Dear Mr. Macmillan,

Thank you for returning the original copy of *Essays from 'The Guardian'* and also for the new edition. We are very glad to hear that you think we did well in having them published. No, it was not Mr. Gosse. It was a publisher at Oxford, whose name I forget, who asked permission to bring them out, urging that there was a great demand for them.

We are glad that the general sale of the books during the past year has been good and are anxious to see the accounts.

With kind regards

Yours very truly,
Clara A. Pater.

152 Frederick Macmillan to Clara Pater, 18 March 1903

MS.: British Library.

Miss Pater, /6 Canning Place, /Kensington Gate, /London W. Mar. 18.

Dear Miss Pater,

I have been told (though I am not at liberty to mention my informant's name) that you have been approached by someone who has asked your permission to print some letters of your brother's and to publish a biography of him. I don't know whether the information is accurate, but in case it is I think it as well to warn you to be exceedingly careful now or at any time about giving any such permission. There are many inferior book makers about, on the look out for material and it would be distressing to you and your brother's friends if by any inadvertence you were led into giving any kind of sanction to a book that might turn out very unsatisfactory. If any application of the kind is made to you I would advise you to consult Mr. Shadwell or someone like him before acceding to it.

I am

Yours very truly,
Frederick Macmillan.

153 Frederick Macmillan to Clara Pater, 11 May 1903

MS.: British Library.
Miss Pater, /6 Canning Place, /Kensington Gate, /London W.

May 11.

Dear Miss Pater,

We think there is no reason whatever why you should refuse Mr. Daniel's request for permission to print the essay on 'Aesthetic Poetry.'

I am,

Yours very truly,
Frederick Macmillan.

154 Frederick Macmillan to Clara Pater, 11 June 1903

MS.: British Library.
Miss Pater, /6 Canning Place, /Kensington Gate, /London W.

June 11.

Dear Miss Pater,

If Mrs. Robert Ottley will kindly send us the manuscript of her book when it is ready, it shall have our careful attention.

I am,

Yours very truly,
Frederick Macmillan.

155 George Macmillan to Clara Pater, 31 July 1903

MS.: British Library.
Miss Pater, /6 Canning Place, /Kensington Gate, /London W.

July 31.

Dear Miss Pater,

We have received the enclosed letter of which one passage, which I have marked with a red pencil, concerns you. We have given the printer permission to reproduce as tracts the two writings by F.D. Maurice to which he refers, but before dealing with his similar request in regard to a chapter in *Marius the Epicurean* we should be glad to have your views on the subject.

We do not think it could hurt the book, but you may nevertheless see some objection and we should of course be guided by your wishes in the matter. Please return Mr. Newman's letter.

I am,

Yours very truly,
George A. Macmillan.

156 Maurice Macmillan to Clara Pater, 12 February 1904

MS.: British Library.
Miss Pater, /6 Canning Place, /Kensington Gate, /London W.

Feb. 12.

Dear Miss Pater,

In my brother's absence I have opened your letter, and have much pleasure in sending you a copy of *Marius*.

I am,

Yours very truly,
Maurice Macmillan.

157 Frederick Macmillan to Clara Pater, 21 March 1907

MS.: British Library.

March 21.

Dear Miss Pater,

We had a visit this morning from a young American lady, Miss Ethel Randall, 5 Mecklenburg Square, who came with an introduction from D. Furnivall. She wishes to take the Ph.D at the University of Chicago and intends to offer as a thesis an essay on the Art Teaching of Mr. Pater.

Miss Randall intends to print and to publish her thesis and she also has the idea of compiling a bibliography of Mr. Pater's writings. In addition to this she would like to have permission to reprint some sixteen reviews of books which she says exist but which have never been collected. It was this last matter that she came to see us about.

I, of course, told Miss Randall that the question as to which of Mr. Pater's fugitive writings should be reprinted had been carefully considered by you and Mr. Shadwell and that it did not seem to me at all probable that you would give permission to any other person to reprint articles which you excluded from the edition of your brother's writings over which you had control. Miss Randall, however, was very anxious that the matter should be laid before you and I promised that I would write to you about it. If you will kindly instruct me as to your wishes I will communicate with Miss Randall. I should imagine that the best plan would be to say that if it is ever decided to reprint any more articles it will be done under Mr. Shadwell's editorship and in your edition.

I am,

Yours very truly,
Frederick Macmillan.

158 Frederick Macmillan to Clara Pater, 8 January 1908

MS.: British Library.
Miss Pater, /3 Radnor Cliff, /Folkestone.

Jan. 8.

Dear Miss Pater,

I enclose a cheque for the sum which is due to you in the course of the present month: £419.19.8.

I am very sorry to hear that you have been ill: you are certainly wise to escape from London where it is horribly cold and terribly dark. I think it is the darkness of the winters in London that gets on one's nerves. My wife is in Rome where she says the weather is delightful. She is going to the Riviera at the end of this month. I hope to join her there in February.

With kind regards, I am

Yours sincerely,
Frederick Macmillan.

159 Clara Pater to Frederick Macmillan, 11 January 1910

MS.: British Library.

6 Canning Place, /Kensington Gate, /London W. /Jan. 11.

Dear Sir Frederick,

I want to present a copy of *Essays from 'The Guardian'* to a friend, if you would kindly order one to be sent to me.

Kind kind regards

Yours sincerely,
C.A. Pater.

160 Macmillan and Co. to Clara Pater, 12 January 1910

MS.: British Library.
Miss C.A. Pater, /6 Canning Place, /Kensington Gate,/London W.

Jan. 12.

Dear Madam,

In the absence of Sir Frederick Macmillan in the United States, we write to acknowledge receipt of your letter of yesterday addressed to him, and to say that we have much pleasure in sending you a copy of *Essays from 'The Guardian'* by this post.

We are,

Yours faithfully,
Macmillan and Co.

161 Frederick Macmillan to Clara Pater, 2 February 1910

MS.: British Library.
Miss C.A. Pater, /6 Canning Place, /Kensington Gate,/London W.

Feb. 2.

Dear Miss Pater,

It has been suggested to us by several large booksellers that it would be a good thing to publish a new and uniform edition of your brother's books in an attractive form at 7/6 per volume. It would not be a serious undertaking as we could print from the existing stereotype plates which are in very good condition and I think that the [fillip] which the publication of such a set would probably give to the sale would have a satisfactory effect on the next annual statement of accounts. The question arises just now because the stock of *Studies in the Renaissance* is low and it will have to be reprinted in some form within the next few weeks. If you approve of my proposal, we shall publish the book in the new edition about Easter and continue to bring out a book per month until the set is complete.

We must not forget that the copyright of *The Renaissance* will expire in five years and a year or two before that takes place it will be advisable to bring out a changed edition of the whole series so as to get as much as possible from the books before they fall into the public domain, but there is no necessity to take that step yet, and in the meantime we can, I hope, make something considerable for you and ourselves out of the proposed 7/6 edition.

My wife and I have just come back from America where we went to spend Christmas. We enjoyed our holiday, but are very glad to be back again. With kind regards,

I am,

Yours very truly,
Frederick Macmillan.

162 Hester Pater to Frederick Macmillan, 3 February 1910

MS.: British Library.

6 Canning PLace, /Kensington Gate, /London W. /Feb. 3.

Dear Sir Frederick,

We think your proposal of a 7/6 edition of my brother's books a very good one and the need of the reprint of the *Studies in the Renaissance* seems a very good opportunity to make the change. We are glad that you think it will be a monetary success.

We should have called on Lady Macmillan in the autumn but my sister has been very ill for some months and has had to undergo a very serious operation in a Nursing Home this autumn so my time has been fully occupied.

With kind regards,

Yours truly,
H.M. Pater.

163 Hester Pater to Frederick Macmillan, 15 September [1910]

MS.: British Library.

17 Elm's Avenue, /Eastbourne. /Sept. 15.

Dear Sir Frederick,

Will you kindly forward the next books to Miss Strong, 39 Kensington Square, as I am staying here for a month. I suppose you have heard that I have lost my darling sister this August and it has left me a very desolate creature. The expenses in consequence have been very great. I should be glad to know if the new edition is selling well. And would you kindly tell me how long the copyright will last.

Yours sincerely,
Hester M. Pater.

164 Frederick Macmillan to Hester Pater, 16 September 1910

MS.: British Library.
Miss Pater, /17 Elm's Avenue, /Eastbourne.

Sept. 16.

Dear Miss Pater,

I was very sorry indeed to see the announcement of your sad loss in August. I did not write to you yourself at the time, as I knew my wife was doing so.

I am glad to say that the profits on the sales of the books this year will be slightly larger than the last, as you will see from the accounts which I send herewith. If it will be any convenience, we shall be glad to send you a cheque for £100 now, although, as you know, the money is strictly speaking not payable till January next. If I hear from you that you would like the cheque, a cheque shall go immediately.

It is impossible to say what the results of future years' sales will be, but I hope that the decrease will not be large for at any rate some time to come. Unfortunately, the copyright in *Studies in the Renaissance*, which is one of the most important of the books, expires in 1915. There is some hope, however, that the new Copyright Bill which the government has prepared, and which is to be brought into parliament next session, may become law. If it does it will be very greatly to your advantage, as by that Bill copyright will last for fifty years from the date of the death of the author.

I am

Yours very sincerely,
Frederick Macmillan.

165 Hester Pater to Frederick Macmillan, 9 January 1911

MS.: British Library.

6 Canning Place, /Kensington Gate, /London. /Jan. 9.

Dear Sir Frederick,

If it would not be inconvenient could you send me the cheque for the book money within the next four days, as I am going away about the middle of the week, and don't know how long I may be away.

With kind regards

Yours sincerely,
Hester M. Pater.

166 Frederick Macmillan to Hester Pater, 10 January 1911

MS.: British Library.
Miss Pater, /6 Canning Place, /Kensington Gate, /London W.

Jan. 10.

Dear Miss Pater,

In reply to your note, I have pleasure in enclosing a cheque for £378.13.6, which is due to you this month.

I am,

Yours very truly,
Frederick Macmillan.

167 Frederick Macmillan to Hester Pater, 4 July 1911

MS.: British Library.
Miss Pater, /6 Canning Place, /Kensington Gate, /London W.

July 4.

Dear Miss Pater,

We are publishing a series of shilling editions of well-known books, with the idea of meeting the demand for cheap copyright literature which seems to be growing, and it has been suggested that *Studies in the Renaissance* would make a very valuable and saleable addition to this series. I am writing therefore to ask whether you will agree to having this done. I do not think that if *The Renaissance* is the only one of your brother's books which is issued at 1/- the publication would be likely to have a serious effect on the sale of the more expensive edition, and, indeed, it might possibly have the result of stimulating the desire to read his books among a public who are at present ignorant of them. At the same time we should not like to make this experiment without your full knowledge and concurrence. If you agree, we can publish the shilling edition either on the present basis of half-profits or, if you prefer, on a royalty of ten per cent of the published price. If the proposal meets with your approval, the new edition will be published, with several other volumes of our Shilling Library, during the coming autumn.

I am,

Yours very truly,
Frederick Macmillan.

168 Frederick Macmillan to Hester Pater, 10 August 1911

MS.: British Library.
Miss Pater, /6 Canning Place, /Kensington Gate, /London W.

Aug. 10.

Dear Miss Pater,

I wrote to you on July 4th to say that we are thinking of including *Studies in the Renaissance* in a series of cheap copyright books which we are putting on the market to meet the demand for such things, but, as I have had no reply, I am afraid that my letter may have miscarried, although in that case it is rather strange that it has not come back to us through the post. However, I now write again to ask if you have any objection to this proposal, and, if not, whether you would prefer that the book should be published on the present half-profits basis or on a ten per cent royalty. My reason for troubling you is that, if the book is to be issued, I wish to get it announced in our Autumn List.

I am,

Yours very truly,
Frederick Macmillan.

169 Frederick Macmillan to Hester Pater, 5 October 1911

MS.: British Library.
Miss Pater, /c/o Miss Strong, /39 Kensington Square,/London W.

Oct. 5.

Dear Miss Pater,

I am sending you the accounts for the sales of your brother's books for the year ending June 30th last. We sent them first to Canning Place, but they came back to us with a note to say that you had left, and we have got the present address from Canon Ottley. I shall be glad to know if it is permanent, or if not, where you would like your letters sent.

You will be glad to see that the result of the publication of the uniform seven-and-sixpenney edition has been very satisfactory.

The fact of your having moved away from Canning Place probably accounts for my not having had a reply to two letters I wrote during the summer with reference to a proposed shilling edition of *Studies in the Renaissance.* We are issuing a certain number of well-known books at this very low price, and have reason to think that a large sale might be obtained for a shilling edition of *Studies in the Renaissance.* At all events, we should like to try it, but do not wish to do so without letting you know, and therefore the thing has been held over. If you do not disapprove, we shall bring out the shilling very shortly. I do not think it would have any bad effect on the sale of the seven-and-sixpenny book, but if we found that it did we could easily withdraw it from sale.

Believe me,

Yours very truly,
Frederick Macmillan.

170 Hester Pater to Frederick Macmillan, 6 October 1911

MS.: British Library.

Oct. 6.

Dear Sir Frederick,

I was very glad to hear that the sale of the new edition of the books has been so very satisfactory. It has relieved my mind of a great deal of trouble and worry. Since I left Canning Place at midsummer I have had no settled address or would have written to you. I have been wandering about in town, and in country, looking for a small house but they seem very difficult to find. The London houses are doleful little places, and those in the country too remote and lonely for me.

I very much approve of bringing out a shilling edition of *The Renaissance.* I think it would be very successful. Till I telegram you of a settled address will you please send letters to Miss Strong, 39 Kensington Square, and she will send them on.

Believe me,

Yours very truly,
Hester M. Pater.

171 Maurice Macmillan to Hester Pater, 31 January 1912

MS.: British Library.
Miss Pater, /51 Earl's Court Road, /Kensington, /London W.

Jan. 31.

Dear Madam,

An American firm of publishers proposes to introduce into Great Britain a work which they have already issued in the United States entitled *The Stoddard Library* comprised in twelve volumes, and made up of extracts from the works of various writers, among which is Mr. Walter Pater's story of 'Cupid and Psyche' and an excerpt from *The Renaissance.*

We have been applied to and have given permission for the use of these extracts, as we do not think that their appearance in a work of this nature, which is only to be sold in sets at a high price, will have any injurious effects upon the sale of Mr. Pater's books. As, however, the proprietors have made us a payment for the right to use these extracts, we beg to enclose for your acceptance a cheque for £9.10.0, representing your share in it.

Yours faithfully,
for Macmillan and Co. Ltd.,
Maurice Macmillan, Director.

172 Hester Pater to George Macmillan, 4 February [1912]

MS.: British Library.

51 Earl's Court Road, /Kensington, /London. /Feb. 4.

Dear Mr. Macmillan,

Thanks for the cheque for the extracts for *The Stoddard Library*. I think it might be an advertisement for my brother's books and so help the sale rather than the reverse.

Yours truly,
Hester M. Pater.

173 Frederick Macmillan to Hester Pater, 28 February 1912

MS.: British Library.

Miss Pater, /51 Earl's Court Road, /Kensington, /London W.

Feb. 28.

Dear Miss Pater,

We have lately arranged to undertake the joint publication, with Mr. Philip Lee Warner, a series of books printed in a special type called the 'Riccardi' fount, which was designed for him some years ago by Mr. Herbert Horne. These editions are limited in number and are never reprinted; they are in fact rather bibliographic toys than books. We should like if possible to bring out in this type a special edition of *Marius the Epicurean*; it would be in two volumes sold at 12s. 6d. each, and would be limited to 1000 copies. I write to ask if you are willing to license us to print this edition in return for an outright payment of £250? If so, we should like to make such an agreement. I need not say that the existence of this edition could not in any way damage the sale of the ordinary seven-and-sixpenny edition.

With kind regards, I am

Yours very truly,
Frederick Macmillan.

174 Hester Pater to Frederick Macmillan, 29 February 1912

MS.: British Library.
Postcard marked: London W., /5:00 p.m., /29 February 1912.

51 Earl's Court Road, /Kensington, /London W.

I am sending three more fragments for you to see that I could not find yesterday.

H.P.

175 Frederick Macmillan to Hester Pater, 1 March 1912

MS.: British Library.
Miss Pater, /51 Earl's Court Road, /Kensington, /London W.

Mar. 1.

Dear Miss Pater,

I have received the packet containing three more fragments, and hope to write to you within a few days making some suggestion as to utilising them. It certainly seems a pity from every point of view that they should not be put into print.

I am

Yours very truly,
Frederick Macmillan.

176 Frederick Macmillan to Hester Pater, 5 March 1912

MS.: British Library.
Miss Pater, /51 Earl's Court Road, /Kensington Gate,/London W.

Mar. 5.

Dear Miss Pater,

I am much obliged to you for your letter accepting our proposal for the 'Riccardi' edition of *Marius the Epicurean*.

With regard to the fragments which you left with me the other day, it seems to me the best way of turning them into money would be to get them, in the first instance at all events, published in a good periodical. My feeling is that the *English Review* would be the most likely to pay a good price for them, and if I have your permission I will at once communicate with Mr. Austin Harrison, the editor, and see what offer I can get. You will of course understand that in this matter I shall be acting for you, and not in any sense for my firm, that is to say, anything that is paid for their serial publication will go to you without deduction.

I am,

Yours very truly,
Frederick Macmillan.

177 Hester Pater to Frederick Macmillan, 6 March [1912]

MS.: British Library.

51 Earl's Court Road, /Kensington, /London W. /Mar. 6.

Dear Sir Frederick,

Thank you for your kind offer of sending the fragments to the *English Review* for me, but I really did not think as much of the money they may bring as that they are too interesting to be lost, and that the people who care for the books generally would be very glad to see them. Do you really think they are finished, and complete, enough as fragments to be published? If so I should be very glad to have them appear in the *Engish Review*. I cannot bear to print anything he might perhaps have not liked to be printed.

With kind regards.

Yours very truly,
H.M. Pater.

178 Frederick Macmillan to Hester Pater, 7 March 1912

MS.: British Library.

Miss Pater, /51 Earl's Court Road, /Kensington, /London W.

Mar. 7.

Dear Miss Pater,

I think that perhaps before sending the fragments to the editor of the

English Review the matter had better have a little more consideration. I propose to ask the advice of a literary friend on whose judgment I rely a good deal, and will let you know what he thinks about it. It certainly would be a pity to print anything which your brother would not have liked to appear over his name.

I am,

Yours very truly,
Frederick Macmillan.

179 Frederick Macmillan to Hester Pater, 8 March 1912

MS.: British Library.
Miss Pater, /51 Earl's Court Road, /Kensington, /London W.

Mar. 8.

Dear Miss Pater,

I put the fragments which you gave me the other day into the hands of a man whose judgment in such matters we think particularly good. I told him that there was an idea of publishing them, and asked him to let me know how the question struck him. I think I cannot do better than send you a copy of his report. I certainly should not like to advise you to publish the fragments, though of course if you are determined to do so we should like to have them out with our imprint. I feel however that the decision as to whether they should be published at all, or not, should be taken by you and not by us.

I am,

Yours very truly,
Frederick Macmillan.

180 Hester Pater to Frederick Macmillan, 19 March [1912]

MS.: British Library.

51 Earl's Court Road, /Kensington, /London W. /Mar. 19.

Dear Sir Frederick,

Thank you so much for the trouble you have taken about the fragments. I shall most certainly take your advice and that contained in the letter you forwarded to me, and *not* publish them.

Yours very truly,
Hester M. Pater.

181 Frederick Macmillan to Hester Pater, 21 March 1912

MS.: British Library.
Miss Pater, /51 Earl's Court Road, /Kensington, /London W.

Mar. 21.

Dear Miss Pater,

I feel that you are quite right in your decision as to the publication of the fragments. I return them herewith.

Yours very truly,
Frederick Macmillan.

182 Hester Pater to Frederick Macmillan, 27 January [1913]

MS.: British Library.

38 Pembroke Square, /Kensington, /London W. /Jan. 27.

Dear Sir Frederick,

In case you are sending me a cheque, can you send it me tomorrow, as I am going away for a little time on Thursday.

Yours sincerely,
H.M. Pater.

183 Frederick Macmillan to Hester Pater, 26 May 1913

MS.: British Library.
Miss Pater, /38 Pembroke Square, /Kensington, /London W.

May 26.

Dear Miss Pater,

You will remember that some time ago we arranged with you for the publication by the Medici Society of a so-called 'Riccardi' edition of *Marius the Epicurean*, for which you were to receive a lump sum of £250. This book will be ready tomorrow, and two presentation copies will be sent to you. In the meantime I have the pleasure to enclose a cheque for £250.

I remain,

Yours very truly,
Frederick Macmillan.

184 Hester Pater to Frederick Macmillan, 30 May [1913]

MS.: British Library.
38 Pembroke Square, /Kensington, /London W. /May 30.

Dear Sir Frederick,

Thanks for the cheque, and the two copies of *Marius*, which I received on Wednesday.

With kind regards.

Yours very truly,
H.M. Pater.

185 Hester Pater to [George] Macmillan, 26 July [1913]

MS.: British Library.
38 Pembroke Square, /Kensington, /London W. /July 26.

Dear Mr. Macmillan,

I received this note yesterday. I don't know the name of the publisher of the shilling booklets. I suppose the copyright is only the copyright of the photograph. Please tell me if I should give them permission for the use of the photograph.

Yours sincerely,
H.M. Pater.

186 George Macmillan to Hester Pater, 28 July 1913

MS.: British Library.
Miss Pater, /38 Pembroke Square, /Kensington, /London W.

July 28.

Dear Miss Pater,

There is no reason why you should not let Messrs. Elliott and Fry give permission to use the photograph of your brother in the little calendar from his writings which we have allowed Mr. Palmer to print. Indeed it is we who referred him to Elliott and Fry as the copyright of the portrait is theirs. It shows good feeling on their part that they should consult you in the matter.

I am,

Yours sincerely,
George A. Macmillan.

187 Hester Pater to Frederick Macmillan, 6 October [1914]

MS.: British Library.
Postcard /38 Pembroke Square, /Kensington, /London. /Oct. 6.
Dear Sir Frederick,

Thank you for sending me the account of the books. I am very glad to find that they are selling well.

With kind regards,

Yours sincerely,
H.M. Pater.

188 Frederick Macmillan to Hester Pater, 9 February 1914

MS.: British Library.
Miss Pater, /38 Pembroke Square, /Kensington, /London W.

Nov. 9.

Dear Miss Pater,

I return Messrs. Jarrold's letter. I do not see what you are to gain by having 'The Child in the House' published in their 'Miniature Classics,' and would advise you not to give them permission to do so.

I am,

Yours very truly,
Frederick Macmillan.

189 Frederick Macmillan to Hester Pater, 7 July 1917

MS.: British Library.
Miss Pater, /38 Pembroke Square, /Kensington, /London W.

July 7.

Dear Miss Pater,

The compiler of the *Calendar* which was published by Mr. Palmer did apply to us some time ago for permission to make everyday quotations from the works of Walter Pater. It seemed to us that it could not do the books any harm, and we therefore gave him the permsission required.

With kind regards, I am,

Yours very truly,
Frederick Macmillan.

EXPLANATORY NOTES

In the notes below, I have tried to identify, and where appropriate to contextualise, the allusions the writers make throughout the letters printed in this volume. Thus, I have annotated titles of books, names of writers, details about publication and distribution, information about publishing forms, and outlines of key issues, including methods of payment and details of copyright, with a view to showcasing the business of 'bookmaking' during the period 1872 to 1912 especially.

page

67 *the papers of which I spoke*: The first edition of *The Renaissance* (1873) contained eight essays, together with a preface and a conclusion. To this point, Pater has published 'Winckelmann,' *Westminster Review* 87 (January 1867): 80-110; 'Notes on Leonardo da Vinci,' *Fortnightly Review* 12 (November 1869): 494-508; 'A Fragment on Sandro Botticelli,' *Fortnightly Review* 14 (August 1870): 155-60; 'Pico della Mirandula,' *Fortnightly Review* 16 (October 1871): 377-86; and 'The Poetry of Michelangelo,' *Fortnightly Review* 16 (November 1871): 559-70. Pater makes no mention of the essay on William Morris, the last six paragraphs of which became the 'Conclusion.' This means that Pater was working on 'Aucassin and Nicolette,' 'Luca della Robbia' and 'Joachim du Bellay,' which are dated 1872 in the third and later editions of *The Renaissance*. Evans (p. 8n) suggests the essay in manuscript may have been the first version of 'The School of Giorgione,' theoretical portions of which enlarge on the doctrine advanced in the 'Preface.' See also Hill, pp. 384-5, and Shuter (1997), p. 3. The essay appeared in the *Fortnightly Review* 28 (October 1877): 526-38, and later in the third (1888) edition of *The Renaissance*. Brake (1976) suggests that the cancelled essay was 'Arezzo,' a MS. in the collection of Pater papers at the Houghton Library, bMS Eng 1150 (24): 274-6. She argues: In this 'extended reverie on a landscape,' Pater explores the Italian art tradition Michelangelo drew on. Inman (1990) contests this view, arguing that 'Arezzo' lacks the finish of the published essays. Inman (pp. 385-6) claims that the essay was 'Wordsworth,' which was written so as to form a conclusion. Quite possibly (Inman adds),

Pater set out to show the reappearance of the spirit of re-birth in the eighteenth century (with Winckelmann) and the nineteenth century (with Wordsworth). See Letters 6 and 7.

a handsome 8vo volume: Books can be defined as folio, quarto (qto) octavo (8vo), duodecimo (12mo), etc., depending upon the number of times a sheet of paper is folded (Jacobi, pp. 25-6). Thus, a folio would be two leaves to the sheet, a quarto would be four leaves, an octavo would be eight, and so on. Sometimes, distinguishing an octavo (say) from a quarto was difficult, but if the book is printed on laid paper, the water-lines that run through the sheet will determine this, i.e., water-lines on a folio, an octavo, and octo-decimo would be perpendicular. The crown octavo book (with uncut or merely trimmed edges) should measure 7.5 ins x 5.0 ins (Glaister, p. 281).

these terms: During the period under consideration, literary property could be dealt with in the following ways (Unwin, 1926): (a) the writer sold it outright for a fixed price; (b) publisher and writer agreed to a profit-sharing arrangement; (c) they agreed to a royalty system, sometimes called the best form of agreement. Of course, it was necessary to know what the proposed royalty meant to both parties and (d) the publisher agreed to publish on a commission basis. All other forms of agreement were combinations of these.

69 *paste-board covers*: From about 1500, bookbinders in Great Britain used paper, rather than wood, in preparing cover boards. Three kinds of boards were used: (a) sheets of rough, low-quality paper pasted together; (b) waterleaves pasted together, possibly in their original wet state to band together as they dried; and (c) pulped paper, usually book-edge shavings. The later (pulpboard) contained foreign materials, including large and interesting pieces of coloured fabric etc. During the second decade of the eighteenth century, pasteboard gave way to rope-fibre millboard, in large part because it was more durable (Middleton, pp. 62-8; Glaister, pp. 35-6).

70 *Mr. Combe's funeral*: Thomas Combe (1797-1872) left (in 1838) Joseph Parker (Oxford), Bookseller to the University, to become Printer to the University and Superintendent of the Clarendon Press. Almost immediately, he showed his new employers that, by virtue of his enterprise and financial ability, he was the right man for the job. Accordingly, he became (in 1841) a partner in the firm and (in 1851)

the senior partner, holding eight shares. In 1855, Combe bought the paper-mill on the river by Wolvercote, having it completely rebuilt and equipped, so that the Press could meet the increasing demand for Bibles. Under Combe's direction, the Press enjoyed its golden age of prosperity. In addition, Combe founded and funded the construction of the church of St. Barnabas in Jericho, to ensure that his employees did not drift into dissent. As well as teaching at the Sunday School, which he had created for the boys at the Press, he also taught classes on secular subjects at the Night School. This strikingly handsome man (contemporaries remarked that, in old age, he bore a remarkable resemblance to Michelangelo's portrait of Moses) was also a patron of the arts. He commissioned (in 1852) John Everett Millais' 'Return of the Dove to the Art' and he bought (in 1853) William Holman Hunt's picture, 'The Light of the World,' which his widow gave (in 1895) to Keble College. Daniel and Alexander regarded Combe as a highly valued friend. He died suddenly at the Press on 30 October 1872. According to some reports, he had amassed a fortune of £80,000 (equivalent to £2,940,800 in 1997). See Macmillan (1908), p. xxxiv; Graves, p. 200; Embury, pp. 66-8; and Sutcliffe, pp. 6, 7, and 18.

the Press: *The Renaissance* was printed at the Clarendon Press, which was managed by Thomas Combe, E. Bensley Gardner (of the London Bound Book Business), Edward Pickard Hall, and John Stacey, Printers to the University until 1884, when the partnership was dissolved. The Clarendon Press, the former name of the Oxford University Press, dates from 1672. Its first home was the upper part of the Sheldonian Theatre at Oxford. The name came from the funds which were generated by the Earl of Clarendon's *History of the Rebellion and Civil Wars in England* (1704), the perpetual copyright of which was given to the press by his son. It is now the publishing department of the OUP in charge of its learned publications. The present Oxford premises of the Clarendon Press in Walton Street were erected during the period 1825-30. All the subsidiary processes of book production, including Bibles, of which it has the right by Royal patent, are managed by the firm on its own premises, while the paper is supplied by the university mills at Wolvercote. See Sutcliffe, pp. 6, 7, 18, 36-7, and 39.

Mr. Wheeler: Rowland Wheeler (1826-98) joined the Clarendon Press in 1841 with a view to learning the business of a compositor. Wheeler devoted most of his life to the Press, working as compositor, accountant, proof-reader (when required), and manager of the composing room.

In 1862, he took charge of that side of the business which was responsible for printing and publishing educational works, such as Anglo-Saxon, Greek, Hebrew, Icelandic, New English, and Sanskrit dictionaries. During the golden age of the Press, i.e., from 1862-82, he was responsible for no fewer than 80 workers. A man of robust health and extraordinary vigour managed, he also managed the Night School in its early days and for many years taught in the Sunday School at the Press. Wheeler retired from the Press late in 1891. See Anon. (1920), 'The Corridors of Time.'

71 *Mr. Hall*: Early in his career, Edward Pickard Hall (1808-86) helped his father run the *Maidstone Journal and Kentish Advertiser*. In 1853, Hall joined the Clarendon Press as a partner, owning four shares. He was responsible for discipline or, in contemporary terms, labour relations. By all accounts, he threw himself into his extra-curricular activities. For example, four nights a week, during winter months, he organized, and taught classes for, the Night School, which might include up to 80 boys, and on weekends, Sundays, and holidays he organized games and singing classes at his home. He also took great pride in the brass band, together with the fife and drum band, he conducted. As well, Hall published *The Oxford Index to the authorised Version of the Bible* (1877). However, he was summarily dismissed in 1884, at 76 years of age. See Sutcliffe, pp. 36, 37, and 63-4.

Mr. MacLehose: James MacLehose (1810-85), friend and confidant of Daniel and Alexander for 50 years, founded (with Robert Nelson) a publishing business at 83 Buchanan Street, Glasgow, in 1838. From 1841, when Nelson retired, MacLehose carried on the business in his own name, becoming Bookseller (in 1862) and Publisher (1872) to the University of Glasgow. In 1881, his nephews, Robert MacLehose and James J. MacLehose, were admitted as partners, and the firm was called James MacLehose and Sons. Daniel and Alexander (from 1848) habitually consulted this 'single-minded' Scot whenever they made an important business decision.

On 6 March 1886, Alexander's daughter Olive (1858-1926) married MacLehose's third son Norman (1859-1931), who edited the *Ophthalmic Review* and published papers on ophthalmic subjects.

The reference here is to *Olrig Grange,* a poem by W.C. Smith, which was published by MacLehose in 1872. See Graves, pp. 166-9, 372 and 373, and *Books Published by James MacLehose from 1838 to 1881 and by James MacLehose and Sons to 1905* (1905).

72 *We enclose a form of agreement*: According to this agreement, dated 4 January 1873, Messrs. Macmillan and Co. contracted to publish at their own expense *Studies in the History of the Renaissance* on condition that, after deducting expenses, the profits remaining be divided equally. See BL Add. MS. 55030, fol. 8.

73 *Sidney Colvin* served as Slade Professor of Fine Art at Cambridge from 1873-85, Director of the Fitzwilliam Museum 1876-84, and Keeper of Paintings and Drawings at the British Museum from 1884-1912. In addition, he edited the work of Robert Louis Stevenson and wrote the life of John Keats. Pater reviewed Colvin's book, *Children in Italian and English Design* (1872) in the *Academy* 3 (July 1872): 267-8. Colvin reviewed (anonymously) *The Renaissance* in the *Pall Mall Gazette*, 1 March 1873: 11-12. See p. 38. The two were friends during the 1870s, but Colvin (1921) does not mention Pater in his autobiography.

75 *Theologia Germanica*: Martin Luther published a short version of this fourteenth-century treatise in 1516 and a complete version in 1518. Susanna Winkworth (1820-84) published the first English translation, together with a Preface by the Rev. Charles Kingsley (1819-75), Rector of Eversley, in 1854. Macmillan and Co. printed (1873) the edition referred to here. Pater alludes to the engraving on the title-page by C.H. Jeens (see note below). The engraving features the head and shoulders of Christ, who is blind-folded and wearing a crown of thorns.

and cheque: The cheque was probably the annual payment representing Pater's share of half-profits. See Evans, p. 19n.

76 *Mr. Jeens*: Charles Henry Jeens (1827-79) grew up in Uley, Gloucestershire, and studied engraving first with John Brain, an engraver of Islington, and then with William Greatbach. In 1848, he started working on his own, producing (for example) designs for postage-stamps for some English colonies, including the Bahamas, South Australia, Queensland, St. Vincent, and Antigua. He executed a number of works for the *Royal Gallery of Art*, edited by S.C. Hall, and a number of plates for the *Art Journal*. However, he produced (during the 1860s and the 1870s) much of his best work, such as beautiful vignettes and portraits, for Macmillan and Co., especially for their 'Golden Treasury' and 'Scientific Worthies' publications. His large work included the plate (1863) for Frank Dicksee's *A Labour of Love* and the plate (1877) for Edward Armitage's *Joseph and Mary*. His small plates are distinguished by a thoroughness and

a perfection of detail which 'at times mitigates against the general effect of his large ones.' The portrait of Daniel serving as the frontispiece to Thomas Hughes's (1833) memoir of Daniel Macmillan was engraved on steel by Jeens, after a painting by Lowes Dickinson. He died (on 22 October 1879) after a long illness. See obituary notice (1870) and Evans, p. 20n.

77 *Stray Studies from England and Italy* (1876) was bound in the same dark-blue cloth Macmillan and Co. used for all of the books Pater published during his lifetime, the only exception being the second (1885) of *Marius the Epicurean*. See Evans, p. 20n.

Alexander met J.R. Green (1837-83), the historian, early in 1862, and they became very close friends (Graves, pp. 183-4). For a time, Green was curate and vicar of two East-End London parishes and then librarian at Lambeth. He developed tuberculosis in 1869, which made all active work impossible. Macmillan and Co. published Green's best-seller, *Short History of the English People* in 1874. Macmillan and Co. reprinted this volume many times. According to Graves, 35,000 copies of this work were sold by March 1876. Alexander and his wife spent the last five weeks of Green's life with the writer at Mentone (Graves, pp. 325, 366).

I should propose 1,000 instead of 1,250: The publication figures were perfectly normal for an author who did not appeal to a very wide public. For example, only one of the first eight books by Henry James which Macmillan and Co. published appeared in an edition of over 1,250 copies, i.e., *Hawthorne* (1879). This book appeared as part of a series published in an edition of 6,000 copies. Initially, Macmillan and Co. published *The Europeans* (1878) and *Daisy Miller* (1879) in editions of 250 copies only. The former was reprinted twice in impressions of 250 copies and the latter was reprinted once before it was reprinted in larger quantities. Complete publications figures for Pater's works for the period 1873-1910 are printed in the Appendix.

78 *size of the vignette*: The vignette, which was added to the title-page of the second (1877) edition and to the page facing the title-page of later editions, was taken from the Leonardesque drawing no. 2252 in the Louvre, 'Head of a Youth.' Pater seems to have this drawing in mind when in the essay on Leonardo he speaks of 'a little drawing in red chalk which every one will remember who has examined at all carefully the drawings by old masters at the Louvre. It is a face of doubtful sex, set in the shadow of its own hair, the cheek-line in high light against it, with

something voluptuous and full in the eyelids and the lips.' See Clark, pp. 16 and 108; Hill, pp. 90-1, 283, 289, and 372-3; and Evans, p. 20n.

John Morley's article: In his review article, 'Mr. Pater's Essays,' which appeared in the *Fortnightly Review* 19 (April 1873): 469-77, Morley speaks of Pater's essays as 'The most remarkable example of [a] younger movement towards a fresh and inner criticism' (p. 471). See p. 30.

79 *my essays on Demeter and Dionysus*: Pater delivered 'Demeter and Persephone: A Study of Art Mythology' as a lecture at the Birmingham, and Midland Institute on Monday, 29 November 1875. The first part of the lecture subsequently appeared in the *Fortnightly Review* 25 (January 1876): 82-95; the second appeared in the *Fortnightly Review* 25 (February 1876): 260-76. Pater revised this essay with a view to publishing it, together with 'A Study of Dionysus.' See Letter 42. The first part of 'A Study of Dionysus' appeared as 'The Spiritual Form of Fire and Dew' in the *Fortnightly Review* 26 (December 1876): 752-72; the second part, 'The Bacchanals of Euripides,' although dated 1878 in *Greek Studies* (1895), appeared much later, in *Macmillan's Magazine* 60 (May 1889): 63-72. See Evans, p. 21n.

It should be remembered that these 'studies' were composed during the period when opposition to *The Renaissance* was especially intense. We can see in these works evidence of Pater trying to appease his critics. Three commentaries on 'Demeter and Persephone' in particular warrant mention here. First, DeLaura (1969) reads the series of studies in Greek myth and art as a re-thinking of Arnold's view of the classical/medieval antagonism, which he had formulated in the essay on Coleridge and then expanded in the essay on Winckelmann (pp. 245-9). Secondly, Dowling (1988) reads the essay as Pater's attempt to combine 'the seemingly unpromising materials' of the new 'human sciences' of mythology, anthropology, and archaeology with the modified familiar essay, which he had already made uniquely his own, with a view to establishing a new basis for humanism. Thirdly, Inman (1990) argues that he wanted his critics to see that he possessed too much religious spirit to pose as a danger to his students; that he firmly supported the institution of the family; and finally that he was no shallow aesthete (pp. 384-5).

the book should be thoroughly advertised: The second edition of *The Renaissance* was advertised in the *Athenaeum*, 19 May 1877: 631; in the *Pall Mall Gazette* 24 May 1877: 13; and in the *Saturday Review*,

26 May 1877: 654. Each notice reprinted an excerpt from Morley's appreciative article. Upon discovering a mistake in referring to the old (and misleading) title, Pater arranged for a fourth notice to appear in the *Pall Mall Gazette*, 31 May 1877: 13. This one reprinted two comments praising Pater's criticism.

80 *what hours on Tuesday next*, i.e., 20 March 1877 (Evans, p. 22n).

Schnaase's History of Sculpture: This is a reference to *Geschichte der bildenden Künste bei den Alten*, by Dr. Carl Julius Schnaase (1798-1875). 7 vols. Dusseldorf: Verlagshandlung von Julius Buddeus, 1843-76. To the best of my knowledge, this work has never been translated into English.

one of my sisters: Clara Pater (see p. 7) distinguished herself for (among other things) her intellectual accomplishments.

81 *Bartolozzi*: Francesco Bartolozzi, R.A. (1725-1815), son of a Florentine goldsmith, studied drawing in Florence and engraving in Venice. He made a name for himself in England as an engraver of exquisitely finished plates. Shortly after his arrival in 1764, he was appointed engraver to the king, with a salary of £300 a year (equivalent to £17,635.50 in 1997), and in 1768 he became a Royal Academician. According to reports, few artists of his generation reached so distinguished a rank in their profession. Bartolozzi produced a prodigious number of plates, capturing the spirit of the most eminent painters. In 1802, he became Director of the National Academy of Lisbon.

82 *the other volume proposed*: Pater and Macmillan met in London on 20 March 1877 to discuss *The School of Giorgione and other Studies*. For a list of the proposed contents see p. 85.

My daughter: Margaret Anne Macmillan (b. 1857), the eldest daughter of the publisher, married Louis Dyer (1851-1908), the American writer and lecturer. Dyer studied classics at the University of Chicago, the University of Munich, and Harvard University, where he graduated B.A. (1874), and at Balliol College, Oxford, where he graduated B.A. (1878) and M.A. (1893). At Balliol, he got to know Margaret's brother Malcolm (see p. 34) very well. He taught Greek and Latin at Harvard from 1877 to 1887, when he returned to Oxford. Shortly after his return, Dyer joined his old college friend (Malcolm) on an extensive tour of

Greece. Margaret and Louis were married in November 1889, and they purchased Sunbury Lodge, Oxford, in 1890. Louis continued to teach (he lectured at Balliol 1893-96) and write, but gradually he shifted his attention to acting as an unofficial liaison between the University of Oxford and the young American students who began flocking to Oxford under the Rhodes Foundation. According to the obituary in *The Times* for 21 July 1908, Margaret and Louis made Sunbury Lodge a center from which radiated kindness, hospitality, and assistance (p. 12). Dyer published a sympathetic (but superficial) account of Pater's life and work in the *Nation* 59 (23 August 1894): 137-9. Margaret helped Graves (1910) prepare his biography of Alexander Macmillan.

see us on your return to England: In a letter to Edmund Gosse (see p. 53) dated 10 September 1877, Pater stated that he and his sisters had just toured Normandy, Brittany, and the Loire, 'which had lain out of the way of [their] previous excursions, including Azay-le-Rideau, the most perfect of all those Loire Châteaux.' He goes on to say that they returned with their minds 'pleasantly full of memories of stained glass, old tapestries, and new wildflowers' (Evans, pp. 25-6). We might add that his head (or notebook) must have been full (Inman, 1990: 400) of the Norman farm and the Norman coast, which he soon recreated in 'An English Poet' (1878). Many years later, May Ottley (1931) published this 'imaginary portrait' in the *Fortnightly Review.*

22 Bradmore Road, Oxford: During the period 1869-77, the house the Paters rented was unnumbered. *Webster's Oxford Directory* (1872) simply lists the address as 'Bradmore Road.' At the start of 1878, the house was listed as no. 22; this system was abandoned a year later; by 1882 the house was listed as no. 2. Accordingly, the address '22 Bradmore Road' appears only in the letters dated 1878. See Evans, p. 27n.

a cheque: £4.17.8 in 1878 is equivalent to £197.95 in 1997.

Malcolm Macmillan: see p. 34.

83 *Mirage*: Julia Constance Fletcher (1858-1938), the daughter of an American clergyman and his Swiss wife, wrote six novels and five plays under the pseudonym George Fleming. Fletcher completed two novels before she was twenty; Macmillan and Co. published both works. The firm published the second, *Mirage,* in October 1877, in three volumes in blue-grey patterned sand-grain cloth, framed in black on the front and

blind on the back, together with very dark brown end-papers. Fletcher dedicated the work to Walter H. Pater, 'with profound admiration for the rare and exquisite quality of his work.' *Mirage* was reprinted in December, and a second edition was issued in August 1878.

Interestingly enough, Constance Fletcher and Oscar Wilde met in Rome in Spring 1877. She caricatured Wilde as Claude Davenant (the aesthete) in *Mirage*. The two may well have lunched with Pater in the common room at BNC on Thursday, 20 June 1878.

During the 1880s and the 1890s, Fletcher divided her time between Venice and London, where she mixed with such literary figures as Thomas Hardy, Henry James, Rudyard Kipling, Vernon Lee, George Moore, Mary Robinson, and Oscar Wilde. She served in the Italian Red Cross during WW II, and was decorated for her work. See Evans, pp. 28 and 30, and Inman (1990): 399-400.

George Macmillan: see p. 33.

Mrs. Humphry Ward: In her long review, which appeared in *Macmillan's Magazine* 52 (June 1885), pp. 132-9, Mary Ward (see p. 8) spoke of *Marius the Epicurean* as a thinly-veiled autobiography. She said that *Marius* conveyed the reflections of 'a real mind' of the nineteenth-century, trying to give expression to the subtleties and the elusiveness of English feeling at a particularly troubled time. Pater reviewed her novel *Robert Elsmere* (1888) favourably in the *Guardian*, 28 March 1888, pp. 468-9.

The Child and the House: This imaginary portrait, the earliest sample of Pater's fiction, was published as 'The Child in the House' in *Macmillan's Magazine* 37 (August 1878): 313-21, and reprinted in *Miscellaneous Studies* (1895).

84 *Messrs. Clay and Sons*: The Clays of Bungay, Suffolk, printed a wide range of books and periodicals for the leading publishers of the day, including Richard Bentley, Archibald Constable, J.M. Dent, Ward Lock, Macmillan and Co., and George Routledge. Richard Clay (1789-1877) founded the firm in 1827, when he took over a printing business in Devonshire Street, London. He had apprenticed (1803-17) at the University Press at Cambridge, the second oldest press in Britain. Here, under the Printer, Richard Watts, he had learned the most up-to-date printing techniques, among them stereotype printing. As luck would have it, his business prospered and in 1829 he moved to larger premises

in Bread Street. By 1839, he was employing 26 printers and training 14 apprentices. The business soon achieved renown for its expert printing of wood engravings. In 1854, his son Richard (1839-90) joined the firm as a partner. He is said to have had a considerable effect on the technical development of the business. Joseph Taylor became a partner in 1857 and Richard's other son, Charles John (1827-1905), joined the business as a partner in 1861. (The latter was also Printer to the University Press at Cambridge from 1854-94.) Under the leadership of Charles John Clay, the Cambridge University Press became a modern publishing house. For a discussion of his service, see Black (1984): 151-71. Clay retired in 1868, and a new partnership was formed, which traded under the name R. Clay, Sons and Taylor. In 1876 the Clays bought Charles Childs' printing business in Bungay, which had become famous for its modern editions of standard authors and its annotated editions of the Bible. Following Taylor's retirement in 1888, a limited company was formed; this firm traded under the title of Richard Clay and Sons Ltd. Today, it trades under the name Richard Clay plc. The Clays printed a wide range of books for Macmillan and Co., from religious to medical, not to mention fiction like *Tom Brown's Schooldays* (1857) and *The Europeans* (1878). One of the most celebrated productions was the original issue of Palgrave's *Golden Treasury*, which they printed in 1861. The Clays printed three periodicals for Macmillan and Co., *Macmillan's Magazine*, from 1859-1907, *Nature*, from 1869-1920, and *Journal of Hellenic Studies*, from 1880-1956. According to Moran (1984), the printing of *Macmillan's Magazine* (see pp. 30-1) constituted the turning points in the firm's development (p. 89).

at the beginning of November: Pater probably called on Saturday, 2 November 1878. See Letter 44.

86 *the beautiful copy of Milton*: Very likely, this is a reference to *The Poetical Works of John Milton*, ed. David Masson, M.A., LL.D., Professor of Rhetoric and English, the University of Edinburgh, an inexpensive edition (in the Globe Series) Macmillan and Co. printed in May 1877. Macmillan and Co. produced an elegant version, on fine paper and with gilt edges and various calf or morocco bindings, in June of the same year. Macmillan and Co. reprinted this work (with minor alterations) in 1878, 1880, 1885, and 1887.

The Europeans: Henry James made London his home in autumn 1876, taking rooms at 3 Bolton Street, Piccadilly. Writing in his Notebooks (five years later), he noted that London was 'the right place' to make his name as a writer. Almost immediately, he realized that London offered him as an observer of the human comedy 'the biggest aggregation of human life – the most complete compendium of the world.' However, he faced a serious problem: How should I make my début? He had already published a number of works in the United States, but in England he was largely unknown. He decided that publishing a volume of essays would not injure his reputation as a writer of fiction. In this way, he planned to gain the time he needed to make a grand entry into English letters. Accordingly, he wrote (7 August 1877) to Macmillan and Co., proposing to collect into a volume a series of papers on contemporary French writers he had published over the previous four or five years in American publications, these 13 or 14 articles of various length making a volume of about 325 pages. In due course, Morley (as the firm's literary advisor) read the manuscript carefully, and reported that, while they were written with great sense and in a thoroughly rational mode, 'the essays *as criticism* were not at all interesting.' When all is said and done, Morley concluded, the book would sell only moderately well; this is 'honest scribble work, and no more' (quoted in Morgan, pp. 114-5).

However, Frederick accepted the work, recognizing in James a productive writer. On 22 August 1877, he wrote to James saying that, although publishing volumes of reprinted essays 'has not been such as to make us very sanguine about the success of the venture, we are willing to take the risk of printing the book, sharing with you any profit that may result from its publication' (Moore, p. 5). Very likely, he wanted to secure the right to publish *The American*, which tells the story of American good overcoming European treachery.

In the meantime, Macmillan and Co. published *French Poets and Novelists*, which included chapters on Alfred de Musset, Theophile Gautier, Charles Baudelaire, Honoré de Balzac, and George Sand, on 19 February 1878, in an edition of 1,250 copies selling for 8s. 6d. each. Macmillan and Co. prepared no separate American edition; instead, the firm sent a number of bound copies of this edition to New York and sold them at $2.50 each. Macmillan and Co. issued the second edition in the uniform Eversley series in January or February 1884 in an edition of 1,000 copies, selling for 4s. 6d. each, equivalent to £9.92 in 1997 (see Edel and Laurence, p. 34).

James then proposed *The Europeans*, which tells the story of two Europeans who travel to the Boston of 1840, where they learn that, ironically, the people of New England possessed no *joie de vivre*. Frederick wrote (31 July 1878) to James accepting this work on the same terms, i.e., 'we will assume the entire risk of the undertaking, and share with you any profits that may arise' (Moore, p. 15). He was more optimistic about this work, and hoped that it would earn an enormous profit. Macmillan and Co. published the novel on 18 September 1878 in two volumes in an edition of 250 copies (printed by Clay and Taylor) selling for 21s. each. Macmillan and Co. issued two additional impressions in October and in November of the same year, these impressions consisting of 250 copies each, lacking any imprint to distinguish them from the first. *The Europeans* impressed readers, in London and in Boston. In April 1879, the firm published the second edition of the novel (in one volume) in an edition of 1,000 copies selling for 6s. each, equivalent to £12.87 in 1997 (Edel and Laurence, pp. 37-8).

Macmillan and Co. published many of James' books in London between 1878-93, and most of them in New York between 1886-98. Unfortunately, they brought neither novelist nor publisher the fortune James had expected (see Morgan, C., p. 115; Nowell-Smith, pp. 167-74; Edel, pp. 204-43; and Moore, pp. 49-50, 147, and 158-61).

On 17 November 1878, James wrote to say that he was very grateful to 'the exquisite' Pater for his compliment about *The Europeans*. Apparently, Alexander passed on Pater's remarks to Frederick, who then passed them on to James (Moore, p. 21).

The two may have been introduced (in January of 1879) by a mutual friend, Julia Fletcher (see pp. 155-6). During the period 1885-93, Pater and James often met at literary parties, especially those given by the family of the poet and translator Mary Robinson, later known as Madame Duclaux and then as Madame Darmesteter (1857-1944), who entertained the celebrities of the day (Sharp. p. 801; Cooper Willis, pp. 152, 224). Apparently, they chatted whenever they met, but never really became close friends. In temperament, they were far apart: James (at the height of his reputation) was socially voluble and Pater was withdrawn, almost on principle (Donoghue, p. 13).

86 *the Oxford Press*: The Oxford University Press, a department of the University of Oxford, is wholly owned by 'the Chancellor, Masters, and Scholars.' It is wholly self-supporting, the profits being employed as a source for working capital and for financing the publication of learned works. Governed by a University committee, its principal departments are the publishing office at Oxford, responsible for the learned and educational books bearing the imprint 'At the Clarendon Press'; the printing works, also at Oxford; and the publishing department in

London, whose functions have included, in addition to the distribution of Clarendon Press books and Oxford Bibles and prayer books, the production of a less academic character, and conveniently differentiated by the general imprint 'Oxford University Press.' It has been suggested that the first book was printed 1478, although the continuous history of the press dates from 1858, when the University approved a loan of £100 (equivalent to £40,064 in 1997) to a local bookseller, Joseph Barnes, to set up a press. The first book printed by Barnes was John Case's book on Aristotle's *Ethics.* Over the next 33 years, Barnes produced some 300 books, mostly tracts or sermons (see Sutcliffe, pp. xiv-xv). In 1863, Alexander Macmillan was appointed Publisher to the University of Oxford, a post he held until 1880, when the Delegates of the University Press abandoned the system of employing a private publisher to manage their publications. See *A Bibliographic Catalogue,* p. vi.

88 *I am glad to hear of your safe return*: George Grove (see p. 30) had spent the period from middle of September to the middle of November travelling in the United States and Canada (Evans, p. 35n).

89 *I enclose a cheque*: £35 in 1878 is equivalent to £1,385.65 in 1997.

90 *E.S. Dodgson*: Edward Spencer Dodgson (1857-1922) matriculated at New College, Oxford, on 22 January 1876. Apparently, he failed the Final Honour School in 1879. After spending several years in New Zealand and Brazil, he became an expert on the Basque language, publishing a number of books on the subject. Later, he was elected an honourary member of the Real Academia de la Historia of Madrid, and as a member of Jesus College he received an honourary M.A. from Oxford in 1907. Little is known of his relationship with Pater (Evans, p. 36n).

Dante: Possibly *Dante's Divine Comedy: The Inferno,* trans. John [Aitken] Carlyle. A literal prose translation: with the text of the original collated from the best editions, and explanatory notes. 2nd edn. London: Chapman and Hall, 1867; *The New Life of Dante Alighieri,* trans. (with essays and notes) Charles Eliot Norton, Boston: Ticknor and Fields, 1867; *The Divine Comedy,* trans. Henry Wadsworth Longfellow. 3 vols. London: George Routledge and Sons, 1867; *The Canzoniere of Dante Alighieri, including the Poems of the Vita Nuova and Convito,* trans. Charles Lyell. London: James Bohn, 1840; *The Vision: or Hell, Purgatory, and Paradise of Dante Alighieri,* trans. the Rev. [Henry Francis] Cary. With a chronological view of the age of Dante and notes. London: Frederick Warne and Co., 1871; and *A Shadow of Dante*: Being an Essay toward studying himself, his World, and his Pilgrimage, by Maria Francesca Rossetti. 2nd edn. London: Rivingtons, 1872.

91 *the magazine*, i.e., *Macmillan's Magazine*. See pp. 30-1 and Evans, p. 55n.

your new book, i.e., *Marius the Epicurean*.

93 *We are working for publication*: *Marius* appeared on 4 March 1885. See Letter 65.

95 *our extract from the Saturday Review*: This is probably a reference to the review of *Marius the Epicurean* that appeared in the *Saturday Review* 59 (14 March 1885): 351-2.

Professor Nettleship: Henry Nettleship (1839-93), the distinguished Latin scholar and academic reformer, was assistant master at Harrow from 1868-73 and classics lecturer at Christ Church College from 1873-78. He was Corpus Professor of Latin at Oxford from 1878-93. Not the sort of scholar to be entirely absorbed in abstruse investigation, Nettleship took a keen interest in the educational advancement of women. His great inspirations were John Conington (1825-69), the first Professor (from 1854) of Latin at Oxford, and the Rev. Mark Pattison, the Rector (from 1861) of Lincoln College, Oxford. Like Pattison, Nettleship believed that a university should be devoted to teaching as well as research. It was probably as a result of Pattison's encouragement that Nettleship spent (1865) a semester at the University of Berlin, to see what a German university was like. Instead of following Conington's example and concentrating on editing and translating, Nettleship studied ancient authors with a view to 'understanding' them in context. He was diverted from these studies in 1877, when he was invited by the Clarendon Press to prepare a new Latin dictionary. Characteristically, he set out not to revise or to improve some existing dictionary but to produce an entirely new one, based on a fresh reading of the ancient texts. Unable to secure collaborators, Nettleship worked on this project singlehandedly for several years before admitting that it was too great for one person. During his tenure as Corpus Professor of Latin, he published a prodigious number of works, including a revised edition (1883) of Conington's *Virgil*. His *Lectures and Essays on Subjects Concerned with Latin Literature and Scholarship* was published

(1885) by the Clarendon Press. He completed (1879) J.R. Green's book on Virgil and he contributed (1882) a prefatory memoir to the Rev. T.H. Steel's book, *Sermons Preached in the Chapel of Harrow and Elsewhere,* for Macmillan and Co. He lived near the Paters at 17 Bradmore Road.

Our idea about a second edition: The second edition of *Marius* was released on 12 November 1885.

John Inglesant: A Romance: Joseph Henry Shorthouse (1834-1903) submitted the MS. of this historical novel set in the time of Charles I to Smith, Elder, and Co. for consideration, but the reader (James Payn) rejected it (Graves, pp. 356-62). In 1880, Shorthouse published the book (which explores old-world phases of the spiritual mind) for private circulation. As luck would have it, the *Guardian* printed a favourable review of the work. Mary Ward was quite struck by the book, and sent a copy to Alexander Macmillan, together with a note suggesting that he publish it (Sutherland, p. 91). He wrote (18 February 1881) to the author to say that he would be honoured to publish it. Macmillan and Co. printed the first edition of *John Inglesant* in May 1881. The work surpassed all expectations, selling nearly 9,000 copies during the first year.

The edition referred to here, that is, the one on hand-made paper, was printed in July 1882.

The *Eversley Series* began in 1881 with a special, high quality edition of Charles Kingsley's *Alton Locke* (1850). Alexander Macmillan regarded Kingsley as 'one of the noblest men' he had ever known (Graves, p. 329). In the end, the Eversley series included almost 200 volumes.

Pater chose the second alternative, and the new edition appeared on 13 November 1885, selling for 12s. Evans points out that the first had sold for a guinea.

96 *There are many minute corrections to make*: Almost immediately after the publication of *Marius,* Pater began to revise the book. He made more than a hundred alterations, primarily in word order and punctuation. However, they are insignificant in comparison to the six thousand textual changes he made for the third edition (1892). See Chandler, pp. 24-5; Fletcher (1984); Monsman (1984); and Small (1985 and 1991).

Might it be printed by Clark: Messrs. R. and R. Clark printed many books for Macmillan and Co., including the first editions of *Imaginary Portraits* and *Appreciations*, as well as the third edition of *The Renaissance* (see Evans, p. 78n).

This printing firm was founded in 1846 by Robert Clark (1825-94), the son of a Montrose solicitor, at Hanover Street, Edinburgh. It established a reputation for producing work of a very high quality in 1852, when it printed an edition of the Waverley novels for Messrs. Adam and Charles Black. For many years, it printed books for the leading publishing houses of the day, including Constable and Co., Macmillan and Co., and Penguin. Thomas Hardy and G. Bernard Shaw among other writers thought highly of the firm. In fact, after Shaw decided to 'manufacture' his own books, he worked closely with the firm's printers. In 1946, the firm passed into the ownership of the University of Edinburgh, becoming printers to the University Press.

cloth binding of the colour enclosed: Evans (p. 62n) tells us that 'a piece of chartreuse fabric and a small triangle of white paper' were pinned to the letter.

Miss Bretherton: The story of 'Miss Bretherton' was suggested to Mary Ward (see p. 8) by the brilliant success in 1883 of a beautiful actress by the name of Mary Anderson. She wrote the story (which describes the artistic growth of a beautiful young actress whose natural gifts are supplemented by an intellectual understanding of drama) during the summer 1884. She informed Morley that she would like to submit this story in lieu of one of the articles she usually submitted to *Macmillan's Magazine*. Morley read the manuscript, but he advised her that the work would not be suitable for serial publication. He claimed that the story lacked 'well-marked action.' However, at Morley's suggestion, Macmillan and Co. published the book – Mary Ward's first novel – in December 1884. By and large, reviewers agreed with Morley's assessment. See Mary Ward, pp. 192-8, and Smith (1980).

97 *the second edition* of *Marius* appeared on 12 November 1885.

Mr. Knowles: James Thomas Knowles (1831-1908), architect, designed many important buildings during the thirty years he practised his profession. His chief commissions included the three churches in Clapham, namely, St. Stephen, St. Saviour, and St. Philip, the Thatched House Club in St. James Street, Tennyson's house at Aldworth, and Sir Erasmus Wilson's enlargement of the Sea Bathing Hospital at Margate. Knowles edited the *Contemporary Review* from 1870-77, the year he founded (and edited) the *Nineteenth Century* in order 'to provide a platform from which men of all parties and persuasions might address the public in their own names.' Pater published 'Some Great Churches of France. I. Notre-Dame d'Amiens' in the *Nineteenth Century* 35 (March 1894): pp. 481-8. For an extended account of Knowles, see Metcalf (1980).

98 *for your new book*, i.e., *Imaginary Portraits*, which appeared on 24 May 1887.

the revised copy of your Renaissance: The third edition of *The Renaissance*, with the 'Conclusion' restored, appeared in January 1888.

99 *a photograph of you*: Frederick refers to the portrait of Pater which was taken in the summer 1889 – possibly for his fiftieth birthday – by Elliott and Fry, two of the most eminent portrait photographers of the age. This study was used as the frontispiece in *Greek Studies* (1895). See Evans, p. 102n.

Joseph John Elliott (1835-1903) ran away to sea at 15, sailing to Australia, where he spent the period 1850-59 looking for gold. In 1863, he and Clarence Edmund Fry formed a partnership, taking premises at 55 Baker Street, London. Elliott brought a shrewd business sense to the enterprise; Fry brought a sound knowledge of photography, technical as well as artistic, to the enterprise. Business prospered, and soon they were forced to expand their premises to include the adjoining house at 56 Baker Street. A team of technicians at their branch at High Barnet, north London, took care of the printing and the finishing. In 1886 a branch was opened in South Kensington. Fry took over the management of this establishment. The partnership was mutually dissolved in 1893.

During the 1880s, the Baker Street Studio had a comfortable look about it, which reassured the uneasy or excited visitor. On his visit, Pater would have found no reception rooms to speak of; from the vestibule, he would walk up a flight of stairs, where he found himself in the first of three galleries. The pictures which graced the walls of the first gallery likewise produced a tranquil effect. One of these was 'The Last Muster,' the painting that brought Hubert von Herkomer his gold medal at the Paris Exhibition. It was only when the visitor left the first gallery and proceeded to the second and the third did he encounter photographs. Among these large photographs were some fine carbon prints upon opal or porcelain. Fry explained that the firm tried 'to show what photography can do with painting in the production of large artistic portraits.' Their light was easterly. This meant that they were able to take advantage of side light as well as top light. Every means of shutting out the light was at hand, together with what were called palm-leaf screens. There were 26 backgrounds in one studio, including a fine view of Windsor Castle, which were lowered like stage sets. The most remarkable sight was the elongated canopy which stretched over the camera. This canopy was no less than 12 feet long, so that the photographer looked at the sitter through a sort of tunnel. According to Pritchard, a camera had never been shaded so successfully. Four rooms served as storing space for negatives and paper. No special care of the negatives was required; Fry thought that, if negatives were properly varnished, they ran no risk whatsoever. The fee for a sitting was one guinea (somewhat higher than average), and the sitter was kept for about 10 minutes. Fry made every effort to put his sitters at ease before going to the studio. No less than seven dressing rooms were fitted up to this end. The guinea entitled the sitter to 18 cartes or 6 cabinets. See Pritchard, pp. 42-5.

some more copy: Pater's suggestions were incorporated into the third edition of *The Renaissance*: four of the nine chapters do not 'end at the end of the page' and 'The School of Giorgione' was inserted as instructed.

99 *I send you a book*: The book mentioned here is *Neaera*, a tale of ancient Rome, which was written by J.W. Graham and published by Macmillan and Co. in 1886. John William Graham (1859-1932) taught mathematics at and was principal of Dalton Hall, Manchester, from 1886-1924, when he turned to travelling and lecturing. He visited the United States five times in the service of the Society of Friends; he lectured on religion to students in India during the winter of 1927-28. Towards the end of his life he frequently spoke and wrote on war. See Graves, pp. 373-4.

I propose to leave England: In August, the Paters travelled to Italy: they visited Milan, Bergamo, and Brescia (see Evans, p. 101n).

102 *I send you final the memoranda of agreement*: According to this agreement, dated 13 September 1889, Messrs. Macmillan and Co. contracted to publish at their own risk *The Renaissance, Marius the Epicurean,* and *Appreciations* on condition that the copyright belong to the publishers and that, after deducting expenses, profits be divided equally. See BL Add. MS. 55030, fol. 52.

103 *Appreciations* was released on 15 November 1889.

104 *you have not yet sent them a corrected copy*: For some reason, Pater lingered over correcting the proofs of *Appreciations*. The second edition appeared in May of 1890.

Francis Lucas: As far as I can tell, Francis Lucas (1830-97) published only one volume of poetry, *Sketches of Rural Life and other Poems*, which Macmillan and Co. issued in London and in New York in 1889. The firm reprinted the book in 1897.

105 *a profit of something over*: £50 in 1890 is equivalent to £2,412.50 in 1997.

106 *The manager of our American branch*: this is George Edward Brett (see p. 32).

an application from somebody who wants to translate: See Letter 95.

M. Lepelletier: This may well be a reference to Edmond Lepelletier (1846-1913), historical novelist, as well as biographer of Emile Zola (1908) and of Paul Verlaine (1913), a close friend.

will pay you £15: £15 in 1890 is equivalent to £723.75 in 1997.

108 The third edition of *Marius* was issued in June of 1892.

109 *the price might be*: 15s. in 1892 is equivalent to £36.19 in 1997.

Mr. C.L. Shadwell: For Shadwell, one of Pater's pupils and lifelong friends, see p. 2.

the Purgatorio: Macmillan and Co. published Shadwell's translation of Cantos 1-27 of the *Purgatorio* in November 1892. Shadwell's 'Experiment in literal verse translation' is based on the quatrain devised by Andrew Marvell for 'An Horatian Ode upon Cromwell's return from Ireland' (1650). This handsome volume includes a prefatory essay by Pater. A reviewer writing for the *Saturday Review* for 28 January 1893 noted that the book was 'beautifully produced' (p. 106).

What recommends this translation (according to Pater) is 'its union of minute and sensitive fidelity almost to the very syllable of the original, with that general sense of composure and breadth of effect' which marks the great Italian classic (p. xxv).

110 *Professor Tyrrell of Dublin*: While at Trinity College, Dublin, Robert Yelverton Tyrrell (1844-1914) distinguished himself as a brilliant classical scholar. Tyrrell graduated (1864) with a double first in classics and logic. In 1871, he became professor of Latin and in 1880 regius professor of Greek. Tyrrell's genius lay in his ability to translate: by instinct, as it were, he knew the right style to adopt and the right one to take, whether translating from the classics into English or the reverse. His lectures were most stimulating, and the influence he exerted on students in literary matters was all-pervading. He was not merely a man of books: he took a keen interest in many kinds of sport. As a conversationalist, he had few peers. In 1901, Tyrrell was chosen one of the first fifty members of the British Academy. Pater's essay, 'The Bacchanals of Euripides,' was printed in *The Bacchae of Euripides: With a Revision of the Text and a Commentary*, ed. R.Y. Tyrrell (1892), pp. lv-lxxxii. Macmillan and Co. published this work in London and New York.

112 *your new volume on Plato*: see pp. 49-52.

open to the pirates: This is a reference to Thomas B. Mosher (1852-1923), the American book-collector who founded (1891) his own press (Mosher Books, Portland ME) in order to print books of high quality in attractive formats selling for popular prices. Over the course of 30 years, he published more than 500 books, and, often, he prepared the Prefaces himself. Collectors have compared these inexpensive but beautiful books to Kelmscott books (Chapman, pp. 229-31). Mosher included many 'unauthorized' reprints of Pater's works among the 'little-known masterpieces of literature,' thereby introducing them to a wider reading public. Aside from reprinting many essays and imaginary portraits separately or in his monthly magazine, *The Bibelot*, which edited for the period 1894 to 1914, he printed (cf. Vilain and Bishop, 1992) 425 copies of *The Child in the House* in 1895; 400 copies of *Essays from 'The Guardian'* in 1897; 450 copies of *Marius the Epicurean* in 1900; 450 and 700 copies of *The Renaissance* in 1902 and 1912 respectively; and 925 copies of *Gaston de Latour* in 1906.

Under the new copyright law: see note on p. 175.

113 *a formal memorandum of agreement*: According to this agreement, dated 13 December 1892, Messrs. Macmillan and Co. contracted to publish at their own risk *Plato and Platonism* on condition that the copyright belong

to the publishers and that, after deducting expenses, profits be divided equally. This agreement also covered the American edition for which Pater was to be paid a royalty of 10 per cent of the retail price per copy. See BL Add. MS. 55030, fol. 57.

114 *Three Short Stories*: see p. 49.

an elaborate thesis: Arnold Guyot Cameron (1864-1947), the gifted editor, studied modern languages at Princeton, graduating A.M. in 1888 and Ph.D. in 1891, and taught at Yale from 1892-97 and at Princeton from 1897-1905, when he gave up teaching in order to pursue a career in public speaking and in writing. During the period 1912-16, he wrote on economic and international matters for the *Wall Street Journal*. His versatility won him a leading place in the world of journalism. He espoused the cause of Latin America and became contributing editor to *Latin America*. He also edited a number of textbooks, including *Contes de Daudet* (1893) and *Selections from Pierre Loti* (1897). Cameron never published the book mentioned in George Macmillan's letter.

Our usual fee for such advice: £2.2 in 1893 is equivalent to £109.58 in 1997.

115 *It was a sudden and unexpected shock*: Pater died rather suddenly, leaving no will. He wrote about death often, but he never prepared for his own. According to Inman (1983), the Certificate of Administration, prepared (19 September 1894) in lieu of a will, names Clara Ann Pater as the Administratix. This means that she inherited all his personal effects, which were valued at £2,493.11.5 (equivalent to £128,340.44 in 1997). The certificate makes no mention of Pater's manuscripts or the books in his library. Hester Maria Pater and Charlotte Byron Green (see p. 52) witnessed the document. See Levey, p. 222.

116 *the amount due*: £110 in 1894 is equivalent to £5,661.70 in 1997; £175 in 1894 is equivalent to £9,007.25 in 1997.

117 *the volume of collected papers*, i.e., *Greek Studies*, which appeared in January of the new year.

a formal memorandum of agreement: According to this agreement, dated 13 September 1894, the publishers agree to publish at their own risk *Greek Studies* and two other volumes of uncollected papers by Pater on condition that the copyright belong to the publishers and that, after deducting expenses, profits be divided equally. This agreement also covered the American edition, for which the Pater sisters were to be paid a royalty of 10 per cent of the retail price per copy. See BL Add. MS. 55030, fol. 65.

Messrs. Warne and Co.: Frederick Warne (1825-1901), publisher, joined (at the age of fourteen) his brother, William Henry Warne (d. 1859), and his brother-in-law, George Routledge (1812-88), in the retail bookselling business the latter had founded (in 1836) in Ryder's Court, Leicester Square. Seven years later, Routledge started a publishing business. In 1851, Warne became a partner in the firm, which was called Routledge, Warne, and Routledge; according to reports, Warne was largely responsible for the success of the firm; he left the firm in 1865 to begin his independent publishing career at 15 Bedford Street, Strand. Warne was joined by E.J. Dodd and A.W. Duret. Eventually, Messrs. Warne and Co. opened (1881) a branch in New York. Warne tells us that he emulated Routledge's ambition to popularise good literature. Accordingly, he inaugurated (1868) the popular 'Chandos Classics.' Ultimately, an edition of Shakespeare numbered 340,000 copies. The 154 volumes in the series sold 5 million copies. Warne focused on the publication of coloured picture books for children. He published works by Edward Lear, artist, traveller, and writer; Kate Greenaway, artist and book illustrator; and Walter Crane, artist. According to reports, Warne set the standard for this kind of publishing during the period 1870-80. In 1902, Warne and Co. introduced Beatrix Potter's (1866-1941) *The Tale of Peter Rabbit*, which she illustrated herself. In the following decades, the 23 Peter Rabbit books sold millions of copies. For more details, see King and Stuart, pp. 47-55.

118 *the only photograph of my brother we have*: This is a reference to the Elliott and Fry study. See p. 164.

the new volume, i.e., *Greek Studies*.

121 *Mr. Allen*: I am unable to identify this London bookseller.

122 *The International Library of Famous Literature* was published in 20 volumes by Merrill and Baker (New York). The *International Library* was described, i.e., on the title page, as 'selections from the world's great writers with biographical and explanatory notes and with an introduction by Donald Mitchell and Andrew Lang.' The compilers are

listed as Nathan Haskell Dole, Forrest Morgan, and Caroline Ticknor. However, a note in the Catalogue in The New York Public Library indicates that Dole 'repudiates the use of his name in connection with this publication.' The set contains about 500 full page illustrations. A selection from *Marius the Epicurean*, entitled 'Marcus Aurelius at Home,' appeared in iii, 1293-1304.

The *Edition de luxe* in 775 sets was issued on 4 September 1901, together with 1,000 copies of *The Essays from 'The Guardian,'* which was printed from the private edition of 1896.

123 *Mr. Gosse*: Gosse (see p. 53) prepared (1896) an edition of 100 copies of *Essays from 'The Guardian'* for 'the inner circle of [Pater's] friends,' and helped obtain for Hester and Clara Pater a Civil List pension from the Crown, i.e., when the sale of Pater's books began to decline markedly. When Hester, alone and 79 years old, experienced hard times financially, Gosse secured an addition of £50 (equivalent to £1,456.50 in 1997) to her pension (Evans, p. xxxvi).

125 *what we actually get*: £25 in 1900 is equivalent to £1,245.25 in 1997.

127 *Mr. Hollyer*: I am unable to identify this printer.

128 *the list you sent us*: Arthur Symons (1865-1945), poet, translator, and critic, produced one of the very first lists of the signed and unsigned reviews that make up Pater's literary journalism. Cf. the *Athenaeum*, 12 June 1897: 769-70. Symons, a spokesman for the Decadent Movement and interpreter of the French Symbolists, was a member of the Rhymers' Club, contributor to the *Yellow Book*, editor of the *Savoy*, and author of several volumes of verse. As a young man, he idolised Pater, and was delighted to discover the latter's favourable review of his first book, *An Introduction to the Study of Browning* (1886). They met in London on 7 August 1888, after corresponding for two years. In Symons, Pater found a genuine disciple, and he used his influence with Macmillan and Co. to publish *Days and Nights* (1889), which is dedicated 'To Walter Pater in all gratitude.' They were close friends until about 1892.

130 *you have been approached by someone*: Early in 1903, Thomas Wright (1859-1936) of Olney, schoolmaster, literary enthusiast, and biographer of William Cowper (1892), Daniel Defoe (1894), and Edward FitzGerald (1904), approached Macmillan and Co. with a request to reprint Pater's

letters in his proposed biography of the writer. Early in 1904, Wright (1936) visited the Pater sisters out of courtesy, to let them see his MS. before publishing the book. Although they rejected his offer, Wright collected biographical information and letters from Pater's cousins, friends, and acquaintances.

In the meantime, they gave their approval to A.C. Benson (1862-1925), Fellow (1904-15) and Master (1915-25) of Magdalene College, Cambridge, who had been commissioned by Macmillan and Co. to write a critical biography for the highly successful 'English Men of Letters' series. They not only gave Benson permission to quote from Pater's letters, they also helped him track down additional correspondence (see Seiler, 1987: 221-4). In *Walter Pater*, Benson (1906) presents an engaging portrait of Pater as the Oxford scholar who lived a singularly ascetic and placid life, but the book fails to delve into such matters as Pater's 'romantic friendships.'

In *The Life of Walter Pater*, Wright (1907) tries to reveal the 'true' Pater, but undiscriminating use of the materials made available to him undermined this goal. In trying to depict Pater was 'one of the most brilliant and most original writers of the Victorian era,' he produced a portrait of a scholar too indolent to get to the bottom of intellectual problems.

131 *Mr. Daniel's request*: A perusal of Madan's memorial volume, *The Daniel Press* (1921), reveals that Daniel never printed 'Aesthetic Poetry.' See pp. 19-20.

Mrs. Robert Ottley: Inman (1983) tells us that, soon after Clara died (9 August 1910), Hester wrote a will leaving all her effects to Robert L. Ottley, the Canon of Christ Church, Oxford, and his wife May Ottley. May had been a pupil at Somerville College when Clara Pater was Tutor and Vice-Principal, and the two became good friends. Hester died on 5 August 1922, and her effects, including manuscripts, books, furniture, and other items from the Pater household, became the property of the Ottleys. These items were valued at £4,957.17.4 (equivalent to £115,964.11 in 1997). May Ottley (1931) pays tribute to the Paters in her preface to an edition of 'Imaginary Portraits. 2. An English Poet. By Walter Pater.' Robert Ottley died on 1 February 1933, leaving his property (and the Pater effects) to his wife. May, together with three of her unmarried daughters, moved to Hove, Sussex, to live with her eldest daughter, Constance Mary Ottley, who was a surgeon. May died on 3 June 1939, leaving her property to Constance. Constance died on

18 May 1981, leaving her property to Agnes May Ottley, the second eldest daughter of Robert and May Ottley. Inman (1983) writes that Constance mentions three other sisters in her will, Lucy Janet Ottley, Ursula Margaret Ottley, and Dorothea Mary Jones, plus two children, Catherine Lucy Jones and Rosamund Ann Jones. Agnes died in 1990, leaving her property to her four nieces, who now hold the Pater copyright. Thus, as Inman makes clear, Pater's property was dispersed in stages. In October 1942, Constance sold Pater's manuscripts to aid the Red Cross, and in May 1972, shortly after Ursula's death, she sold all the books from Pater's personal library that had not been given away by his sisters and others, so that she and her remaining unmarried sisters could move into a small house. I am indebted to Wright (1975), p. 144, and Inman (1983), p. 3, and Inman (1995), pp. 3-8, for this information.

writings by F.D. Maurice: The religious controversies of Frederick Denison Maurice (1805-72), the first theologian to perceive the importance of the great social movements of the day, played a significant part in the development of Macmillan and Co.

Maurice studied at Trinity College and Trinity Hall, Cambridge, but as a Dissenter he left (in 1827) without taking a degree. However, he was baptised (1831) in the Church of England and eventually (1834) ordained priest. He became chaplain at Guy's Hospital and at Lincoln's Inn in 1837 and 1841 respectively. In 1840, he was appointed Professor of English Literature and History and in 1846 he was appointed Professor of Theology at King's College, London. Very rapidly, Maurice – a shy and reserved man – established himself an intellectual as well as a spiritual leader among his ablest contemporaries. During the upheaval of the late 1840s, he argued, as did the chartists and the radicals, that great changes were needed; he claimed, however, that society could be reconstructed only if secularist doctrines were replaced by Christian doctrines. He believed that Christianity was the only foundation of Socialism and that true Socialism was the necessary result of sound Christianity. Maurice's 'Christian Socialism' as it was called provoked considerable opposition. Those engaged in the campaign to discredit him would cite passages from, say, *Theological Essays* (1853), where Maurice stated that the popular belief in the endlessness of future punishment was simply superstition. As a result of the opposition to his heterodoxy Maurice resigned from King's College. To put their theories into practice the leaders of Christian Socialism – F.D. Maurice, Charles Kingsley and Thomas Hughes – founded a Working Men's College, co-operative stores and community workshops, with a view to improving the social and educational opportunities of the underprivileged classes. (These influences merged with those of John Ruskin and William Morris to pave the way for the British Labour Party.) From 1866-72, Maurice was Knightsbridge Professor of Casuistry, Moral Theology and Moral Philosophy at Cambridge.

Daniel and Alexander, among Maurice's most enthusiastic admirers and exponents, found in Maurice the 'Prophet' who could expound the nebulous religiosity of Thomas Carlyle to an unbelieving generation in a systematic and an intelligible way. They believed too that an intellectual renaissance of the sort represented by Maurice was needed in the Church if it was to retain its hold on people. They threw themselves into Maurice's Christian Socialist Movement, and they made every effort to publish his works, beginning with *Theological Essays*. Indeed, Maurice was one of their most prolific authors. At one time his books occupied a page and a half in their catalogue. Through Maurice they acquired Charles Kingsley, who gave them their first spectacular success. See Morgan, pp. 34-7.

132 *Ethel Randall*: Ethel Claire Randall attended the University of Chicago from 1900-10. According to the Office of the Registrar, she was awarded the B. Phil. in 1904 and the M. Phil. in 1906. There is no record of her Ph.D. thesis, possibly the very first piece of scholarship devoted to the life and work of Pater.

Dr. Furnivall: Frederick James Furnivall (1825-1910) earned two honourary degrees, a Ph.D. from the University of Berlin in 1884 and a D.Litt. from the University of Oxford in 1901.

Furnivall studied at Trinity Hall, Cambridge, and Lincoln's Inn, London. After graduation, he worked as a conveyancer. However, he quickly lost interest in the law, as a result of his increasing involvement in the Christian Socialist movement, which championed social and political reform. Motivated by the doctrines of association and co-operation, he dedicated his life to improving the social and the educational opportunities of the working classes. Initially, this meant assisting in the organisation of the Working Men's College in Red Lion Square, London. He spent five nights a week at the college, actively involved in its social, athletic and educational life.

As Furnivall's zeal for teaching intensified, so did his enthusiasm for literary studies. Typically, he tried to adapt his pursuit of the principles of association and co-operation, which he had advocated in other areas of his life. As an active member of the Philological Society (1847-1910), he promoted a variety of reforms, in spelling and in phonetics for example. Two of the major projects to which he devoted his time and effort (c. 1860) was the proposed supplement to Dr Johnson's dictionary, as well as a concise dictionary which would be an abstract of the larger one. (The Press at the University of Oxford took over this enterprise, which became known as the OED, in 1876.) Meanwhile, Furnivall concentrated on early and middle literature, convinced that it was his duty to reprint from manuscripts works which were either unprinted or imperfectly printed. Thus, to promote early and middle English literature for its own sake he formed a number of societies, including the Early English Test Society in 1864, the Chaucer Society in 1868 and the New Shakespere Society in 1873, to facilitate the printing of texts. Furnivall devoted 40 years to the Early English Text Society, as director and editor. One of the texts he edited, *Le Morte Arthur*, edited from the Harleian MS. 2252 in the British Museum, was published in 1864 by Macmillan and Co. By 1910, the society had issued 140 volumes in the original series and 107 in the extra series.

It has been thought that Pater read (13 April 1875) a paper on *Love's Labour's Lost* before the New Shakespeare Society. This would have been an early version of an essay which appeared in *Macmillan's Magazine* 53 (December 1885): 89-91, and later reprinted in *Appreciations* (1889): 167-75, where it is dated 1878. Furnivall may have been impressed, for in May he asked Pater to edit a play, possibly *Romeo and Juliet*. No such edition was ever published by Pater. See Evans, p. 15n.

some sixteen reviews: See p. 132.

133 *I enclose a cheque*: £419.19.8 in 1908 is equivalent to £19,069.93 in 1997.

My wife is in Rome: Frederick Macmillan spent the period from 1871-76 in New York, where he met and married (15 April 1874) Georgina Elizabeth Warrin of Newtown, Long Island.

134 *a new and uniform edition*: 1250 sets of the Library Edition were issued late in 1910.

the existing stereotype plates: a stereotype plate is made by taking an impression from an existing type or perhaps from another plate, in mould or plaster of Paris, papier maché, or flong. Stereotype metal (or an alloy of tin, antimony, and lead) is then poured into the resulting matrix, that is, the impression bearing the mould, the surface of the resulting stereo being made more durable by the process called nickelling. As a process, stereotyping – which saves the original types and the delays by their working loose – was invented in 1727. See Glaister, pp. 387-91.

135 *I have lost my darling sister*: Clara died on 9 August 1910. Her estate, valued at £50.1.8 (equivalent to £2,275.04 in 1997), went to Hester. See Inman (1983).

136 *we shall be glad to send you a cheque*: £100 in 1910 is equivalent to £4,541 in 1997.

the new Copyright Bill: In Britain, the first Copyright Act was passed in 1709. It duly recognised property in books, and gave authors copyright for 14 years, with an additional 14 years if they were still living. At the time, publishers believed that the books would then become their property. However, the Courts construed the Act to mean that, when the term of Copyright expired, the books became anybody's. The Copyright Act of 1842 extended the authors' copyright to 7 years after death or 42 years from the date of publication, whichever was longer. As popular writers soon realised, this Act had no effect in the United States, where unscrupulous publishers circulated thousands of their books without any profit for themselves. Some authors, such as Charles Dickens, crossed the Atlantic with a view to arranging contracts for so-called 'exclusive rights,' but many publishers in New York, Philadelphia, and Boston continued to 'pirate' whatever English books they thought would sell. Agitation for an international copyright act resulted in the Berne Convention of 1886. This act, which was ratified by a number of governments, including the government of Great Britain, granted reciprocal protection for authors' rights. However, the United States ignored this agreement as well. In 1891, an act of Congress provided for mutual copyright arrangements with various countries, including Great Britain. The Copyright Act of 1911 increased the period of copyright to the life of authors and 50 years after their death. According to this Act, after 25 years after death, anyone could produce a work for sale after he gave notice to the holder of the copyright and made a payment of 20 per cent of the published price. This Act also required the delivery of copies of all publications to certain libraries, including the British Museum and the Bodleian.

137 *I have pleasure in enclosing a cheque*: £378.13.6 in 1911 is equivalent to £16,695.64 in 1997.

the shilling edition: A shilling edition of *The Renaissance* appeared in 1912.

139 *Stoddard's Library: A Thousand Hours of Entertainment with the World's Great Writers* in 12 vols., edited by John Lawson Stoddard (1850-1931), traveller, writer, and lecturer, was first published by G.L. Shuman and Co., Chicago and Boston, in 1910. The set was continuously reprinted until 1922. The extract from *Marius the Epicurean*, referred to as 'Cupid and Psyche' in the index, appeared in i, 100-18, and the extract from *The Renaissance* appeared in ix, 328-47.

140 *Mr. Philip Lee Warner*: Philip Henry Lee Warner (1877-1925), an eccentric publisher, studied modern history at University College, Oxford. In 1905, he joined Chatto and Windus as a partner. The fine standards of book production he set during the period he was with the firm have been maintained to this day. Chatto and Windus incorporated the Medici Society in 1908, and Warner became Managing Director and Publisher for the Society until 1921, when he resigned. See Warner (1955) and (Mumby and) Norrie (1974).

the Riccardi fount: Hebert Horne (p. 49) designed three types of importance: the Montallegro, the Florence and the Riccardi. The Riccardi, based on founts cuts by Antonio Miscomini and cut in 1909, was used in the 'Riccardi Press' edition published by the Medici Society. The Riccardi type has been described as elegant yet practical. See Updike, ii, 215, and Fletcher (1970), pp. 117-57.

in return for an outright payment: £250 in 1912 is equivalent to £10,722.50 in 1997.

141 *three more fragments*: These fragments may have been the papers Shadwell refers to in the 'Preface' to *Greek Studies* (1895): 'The papers on Greek sculpture are all that remain of a series which, if Mr. Pater had lived, would, probably, have grown into a still more important work. Such a work would have included one or more essays on Phidias and the Parthenon, of which only a fragment, though an important fragment, can be found amongst his papers; and it was to have been prefaced by an Introduction to Greek Studies, only a page or two of which was ever written' (p. 3). Pater was working on the first fragment, 'The School of Phidias,' during the last months of his life. He may have intended it as a sequel to 'The Age of Athletic Prizemen,' which was published

in the *Contemporary Review* for February 1894 and reprinted in *Greek Studies* (1895), pp. 283-315. Little is known of the manuscript today. The other fragments, including 'Introduction to Greek Studies' and 'The Parthenon,' are among the Pater materials now at the Houghton Library, Harvard University. When photocopied, the materials in 'Walter Pater: Literary and Scholarly Papers' (bMS Eng 1150, 1-35) run to about 750 pages. For more details of these MSS., see Wright (1975): 144-7; Shuter (1990): 1-11; and Bassett (1990): 2-8.

142 *the English Review*: At first, 1908-09, the *English Review* focused on (imaginative) literature, and glanced at current events briefly, offering a non-partisan perspective. Legend has it that, when he heard that Thomas Hardy could not publish his poem, 'A Sunday Morning Tragedy,' because editors in London thought the poem immoral, Ford Madox (Hueffer) Ford (1873-1939), poet, novelist, and critic, quickly translated his resolve to start his own literary periodical into action. Ford (1932) paid Hardy £20 (equivalent to £904.20 in 1997) for the poem, and printed it in the first issue (December 1908) of the *English Review*. He edited 13 issues, but in that time created the most important literary periodical of the period.

Ford (1932) wanted to bring together the most talented writers of the day, established and up-and-coming, who would comprise the nucleus of a movement dedicated to fostering a critical attitude toward literature, thereby reviving English letters (pp. 362-3). Throughout his editorship, Ford employed a simple editorial strategy: (a) mixing sections of imaginative literature and sections literary criticism, together with a small section (at the end) on current events, usually beginning with a section of modern poetry, and (b) mixing the work of established writers with that of up-and-coming writers, in order to hold the reader's interest. Above all, Ford included writing of the highest standard only. Thus, he printed (sometimes for the very first time) work by Thomas Hardy, Henry James, W.H. Hudson, and Vernon Lee, together with that of Joseph Conrad, H.G. Wells, John Galsworthy, Violet Hunt, and Arnold Bennett. Ford demonstrated a knack for discovering new talent. He was the first to introduce the work of D.H. Lawrence, Wyndham Lewis, and Ezra Pound. Now and then, he printed works posthumously, namely, poems by D.G. Rossetti and Francis Thompson. In his own way, Ford played the role of the sympathetic uncle, always willing to assist a young writer.

Artistically, the *English Review* was an extraordinary success, but financially it was a dismal failure. Ford mismanaged such matters as circulation and advertising; alienated established critics by rejecting their work; and quarrelled with contributors, including Conrad, Wells, and Bennett. By August 1909, the periodical had run out of money. Sir Alfred Mond, the wealthy politician, bought the review, but he installed Austin Harrison (see below) as editor.

Under Harrison, editor from 1910-23, the *English Review* focused on current events, including foreign policy, which he treated from a Liberal perspective. Whereas Ford promoted a 'critical' attitude toward 'the arts and matters generally,' Harrison promoted an 'adult' attitude. For example, he printed (in 1911) Frank Harris' controversial article on Japanese morality. Generally, he printed new works by many of the review's famous early contributors, including Richard Aldington, Aldous Huxley, Katherine Mansfield, and Bertrand Russell.

Under Ernest Remnant (1872-1941), editor from 1923-31, the *English Review* focused on current events, which he treated from a Conservative perspective. Remnant promised readers that the review would stand for England and Empire. In the hands of this businessman, the literary contributions declined sharply in quality.

The last number of the *English Review* appeared in July 1937, when it amalgamated with the *National Review* in order to become a more effective exponent of Conservative and National principles. See Goldring, pp. 139-52, and MacShane, pp. 74-91.

Harrison: Austin Harrison (1873-1928), journalist, was the son of Frederic Harrison (1831-1923), the champion of English Positivism. Obituary notices point out that Harrison was a man of unfulfilled promise. He went to Harrow and then attended the universities of Lausanne and Marburg, where studied international affairs. During the period 1900-05, he worked in Berlin as foreign correspondent and (acting) drama critic for the *Daily Mail*. During the period 1905-08, he edited the London *Observer*. Apparently, he lacked the temperament needed to push the newspaper in a direction that would ensure a great circulation. However, he was at his most inspired when writing about current events, as in *The Pan-Germanic Doctrine* (1904) and *Germany and England* (1907). During the period 1910-23, he edited the *English Review* (see above), which served as a vehicle for his Liberal and Reformist views. Like his predecessor, he had a talent for recognising gifted young writers. Harrison tried to write fiction, e.g., *Lifting Mist* (1924), which shows that he lacked the story-teller's gift, but he produced his most enduring work in writing his affectionate biography of his father, *Frederick Harrison: Thoughts and Memories* (1926).

145 *Messrs. Elliott and Fry*: See note on pp. 164-5.

Mr. Palmer: This is a reference to *The Pater Calendar*, which J.M. Kennedy edited and which Frank Palmer of 12-14 Red Lion Court, London, published in October 1913. Kennedy selected a quotation from the works of Pater for each day of the year.

146 *Messrs. Jarrold and Sons Ltd.*: This printing and publishing firm dates from 1823, when John Jarrold (1773-1823) opened a business at 3-5 London Street, Norwich, where for the first while he and his four sons concentrated on such activities as printing, publishing and selling stationery. In 1847 the firm opened an office in London, where large numbers of educational books were produced. One of their best-known books of this period was Anna Sewell's *Black Beauty* (1877). Millions of copies of this novel have been printed. William Thomas Fisher Jarrold (1866-1937) and his brother Thomas Herbert Curteis Jarrold (1868-1936) acted as directors for the period 1888-1937 and 1890-1936 respectively. William and Herbert were described as men of quiet disposition, for whom business was their chief interest in life. They formed a public limited company in 1902.

'The Miniature Classics' were edited by E.G. Goodchild and published in 1914 by Jarrold and Sons Ltd. This series included *The Deserted Village* by Oliver Goldsmith, *A Rime of the Ancient Mariner* by S.T. Coleridge, *The Sensitive Plant* by Percy Bysshe Shelley, *Pippa Passes* and *A Blot in the Scutcheon* by Robert Browning, and *Maud* by Alfred Lord Tennyson. These volumes were thread sewn in 16 page sections. They were not cased but glued into a brown wrap and cut flush to 4.75 ins by 3.00 ins. There is no evidence that 'A Child in the House' appeared in this series.

APPENDIX

Publication Figures of Pater's Works, 1873-1910

The information printed here derives from the Macmillan Archive (BL Add. MSS. 54786 to 56035), specifically the Macmillan Letter Books (55393 to 55542) and the volumes called New Books and New Editions (55909 to 55919). The first column gives the edition, British as well as American; the second gives the date when the printing was ordered; and the last column gives the number of copies printed.

The Renaissance		
First	[February] 1873	[1250]
Second	[March] 1877	1250
American	[January] 1887	[1000]
Third	January 1888	[1500]
American	[1 July] 1890	1000
Fourth	26 June 1893	2000
American	16 October 1894	1000
American	11 March 1897	1000
Reprint	9 June 1899	500
Edition de Luxe	7 June 1900	775
Reprint	16 August 1900	250
American	20 June 1901	600
Fifth	27 July 1901	500
American	11 February 1902	500
Reprint (8vo)	22 July 1902	500
American	10 June 1903	500
Reprint	5 May 1904	1000
American	20 June 1904	500
American	5 June 1905	500
American	15 May 1906	500
Reprint	2 August 1906	500
American	11 February 1907	500
Reprint	19 July 1907	1000

American	5 March 1908	500
American	19 July 1909	500
Library Edition	12 March 1910	1250
Marius the Epicurean		
First	[January] 1885	[1000]
American	[November] 1885	[1000]
Second	12 November 1885	2000
American	8 December 1890	1000
Third	4 June 1892	2000
American	12 January 1893	1000
American	24 May 1895	500
Reprint	31 January 1896	500
American	11 March 1897	1000
Fourth	[19 November] 1897	500
American	27 June 1898	500
Reprint	8 March 1899	250
American	9 June 1899	500
Reprint	23 February 1900	250
Edition de Luxe	7 June 1900	775
Reprint	3 January 1901	350
Reprint	5 February 1901	250
American	20 June 1901	500
Fifth	[6 November] 1901	500
American	21 August 1902	500
Reprint	[August] 1902	[500]
Reprint	9 January 1903	500
American	24 June 1903	500
Reprint	20 July 1904	1000
American	1 March 1905	500
Reprint	[11 October] 1906	1000
American	24 April 1908	500
Reprint	6 April 1909	1000
Library Edition	12 March 1910	1250
Imaginary Portraits		
First	[April] 1887	[1000]
Second	November 1890	[1250]
Reprint	19 October 1894	1000
Third	1 May 1896	500
American	10 January 1899	500

Reprint	8 March 1899	250
Edition de Luxe	7 June 1900	775
Fourth	[1 January] 1901	[500]
American	31 October 1902	500
Reprint	9 June 1903	500
American	5 June 1905	500
Reprint	11 September 1905	500
Reprint	8 January 1907	500
American	9 October 1907	500
Reprint	[13 November] 1908	500
Library Edition	26 May 1910	1250

Appreciation

First	November 1889	[1000]
Second	[23 December] 1889	[1500]
American	[1 July] 1890	1000
Reprint	26 November 1894	1000
Third	3 January 1895	500
Reprint	14 January 1897	250
Reprint	1 July 1897	500
Reprint	[20 December] 1898	500
American	25 October 1898	500
Reprint	21 March 1900	500
Edition de Luxe	7 June 1900	775
Reprint	16 August 1900	250
American	20 June 1901	500
Fourth	7 October 1901	500
American	5 May 1902	500
American	25 September 1903	500
Reprint	[9 December] 1903	1000
American	29 December 1904	500
American	10 February 1906	500
American	26 February 1907	500
Reprint	12 June 1907	1000
American	16 April 1908	500
American	31 November 1909	500
Library Edition	30 June 1910	1250

Plato and Platonism

First	[15 December] 1892	2000
Second	17 May 1895	250

Reprint	26 August 1896	250
Reprint	20 December 1897	500
American	10 January 1899	500
Edition de Luxe	7 June 1901	775
Third	[3 May] 1901	250
American	3 May 1902	500
American	5 July 1902	500
Reprint (8vo)	22 July 1902	500
American	25 September 1903	500
American	5 June 1905	500
Reprint	12 September 1905	500
Reprint	9 May 1907	500
Reprint	10 June 1909	500
Library Edition	30 June 1910	1250
Greek Studies		
First	[19 October] 1894	2000
American	20 May 1899	250
Edition de Luxe	7 June 1900	775
Second	[November] 1900	1000
Reprint	[13 December] 1903	1000
Reprint	13 February 1908	500
Library Edition	17 August 1910	1250
Miscellaneous Studies		
First	20 June 1895	1500
Reprint	29 June 1898	250
Reprint	[29 November] 1898	250
Edition de Luxe	7 June 1900	775
American	14 July 1900	500
Reprint	14 September 1900	500
American	21 October 1902	500
Second	9 June 1904	500
American	6 February 1905	500
Reprint	[5 November] 1906	500
American	23 April 1907	500
Reprint	10 June 1909	500
Library Edition	17 August 1910	1250
Gaston de Latour		
First	20 July 1896	1500

Reprint	14 January 1897	500
Edition de Luxe	7 June 1900	775
Second	16 September 1902	500
Reprint	12 June 1907	500
Library Edition	26 May 1910	1250

Essays from 'The Guardian'

Edition de Luxe	[5 June] 1901	1000
Reprint	[13 August] 1901	500
Extra Crown 8vo	9 June 1903	500
Extra Crown 8vo	2 August 1906	500
Library Edition	26 May 1910	1250

WORKS CITED

Adams, James Eli (1995) *Dandies and Desert Saints: Styles of Victorian Masculinity*, Ithaca and London: Cornell University Press.

Altick, Richard D. (1957) *The English Common Reader: A Social History of the Mass Reading Public, 1800-1900*, Chicago: University of Chicago Press.

Anon. (1894) 'A Note on Walter Pater. By one who knew him.' *Bookman*, 6 (September): 173-5.

Anon. (1920) 'The Corridors of Time: A Retrospect.' *Clarendonian*, 1 (January): 105-7.

Ball, Douglas (1985) *Victorian Publishers' Bindings*, London: The Library Association.

Barber, Giles (1990) 'Rossetti, Rickets, and some English Publishers' Bindings of the Nineties.' *Library*, 25 (March): 314-30.

Bassett, Sharon (1990) 'Dating the Harvard Manuscripts: Part III.' *Pater Newsletter*, no. 25 (Fall): 2-8.

Benson, A.C. (1906) *Walter Pater*, London: Macmillan and Co.

Berry, W. Turner, and Poole, H. Edmund (1966) *Annals of Printing*, Toronto: University of Toronto Press.

A Bibliographic Catalogue of Macmillan and Co.'s Publications from 1843 to 1889 (1892) London: Macmillan and Co.

Black, M.H. (1984) *Cambridge University Press: 1584-1984*, Cambridge: Cambridge University Press.

Blake-Hill, Philip V. (1972) 'The Macmillan Archive.' *British Museum Quarterly*, 36 (Autumn): 74-80.

Brake, Laurel (1976) 'A Commentary on 'Arezzo': An Unpublished Manuscript by Walter Pater.' *Review of English Studies*, n.s. 27 (August): 266-76.

——— 'Judas and the Widow.' (1981) *Prose Studies*, 4 (May): 39-54.

——— (1991) 'The Discourses of Journalism: "Arnold and Pater" again – and Wilde.' In Brake, Laurel and Small, Ian (eds) (1991b) *Pater in the 1990s*, Greensboro, NC: ELT Press, pp. 43-61.

——— (1994) *Walter Pater*, Plymouth: Northcote House Publishers Ltd.

Brake, Laurel and Small, Ian (1991a) 'Pater in the 1990s.' In Brake, Laurel and Small, Ian (eds) (1991b), *Pater in the 1990s*, Greensboro, NC: ELT Press, pp. xv-xxi.

Brake, Laurel, and Small, Ian (eds) (1991b) *Pater in the 1990s*, Greensboro, NC: ELT Press.

Brittain, Vera (1960) *The Women at Oxford: A Fragment of History*, New York: The Macmillan Company.

Buchan, John (1909) 'Nine Brasenose Worthies.' *Brasenose College Quatercentenary Monographs*, 2 vols, Oxford: Clarendon Press, XIV 2(A), pp. 23-30.

Bullen, J.B. (1994) *The Myth of the Renaissance in Nineteenth-century Writing*, Oxford: Clarendon Press.

Bywater, Ingram (1877) *Heracliti Ephesii Relique*, Oxford: Clarendon Press.

Capes, William W. (1873) 'Sermon on the new "humanitarian culture."' *Oxford Undergraduates' Journal*, 27 November 1873: 98-9.

——— (1880) *Stoicism*, London: Pott, Young, and Co.

Chandler, Edmund (1958) *Pater on Style*, Copenhagen: Rosenkilde and Bagger.

Chapman, Alfred K. (1959) 'Thomas Bird Mosher.' *Colby Library Quarterly*, 4 (February): 229-44.

Clark, Kenneth (ed.) (1964) *The Renaissance*, London: Collins.

Cohen, Morton N. and Gandolfo, Anita (eds) (1987) *Lewis Carroll and the House of Macmillan*, Cambridge: Cambridge University Press.

Colvin, Sidney (1921) *Memoirs and Notes of Persons and Places: 1852-1912*, London: E. Arnold.

Comparato, Frank E. (1971) *Books for the Millions: A History of the Men whose Methods and Machines packaged the printed World*, Harrisburg, PA: The Stackpole Company.

Cooper Willis, Irene (ed.) (1937) *Vernon Lee's Letters: With a Preface by her Executor*, London: Privately printed.

Crinkley, Richmond (1970) *Walter Pater: Humanist*, Lexington, KY: The University Press of Kentucky.

DeLaura, David J. (1969) *Hebrew and Hellene in Victorian England: Newman, Arnold, and Pater*, Austin and London: University of Texas Press.

——— (1991) 'Reading Inman Rereading Pater Reading: A Review-Essay.' *Pater Newsletter*, no. 26 (Spring): 2-9.

Dellamora, Richard (1990) *Masculine Desire: The Sexual Politics of Victorian Aestheticism*, Chapel Hill, NC: University of North Carolina Press.

——— (1994) *Apocalyptic Overtures: Sexual Politics and the Sense of Ending*, New Brunswick, NJ: Rutgers University Press.

d'Hangest, Germain (1961) *Walter Pater: l'Homme et l'Oeuvre*, 2 vols, Paris: Didier.

Donoghue, Denis (1995) *Walter Pater: Lover of Strange Souls,* New York: Alfred A. Knopf.

Dowling, Linda (1986) *Language and Decadence in the Victorian Fin de Siecle,* Princeton, NJ: Princeton University Press.

——— (1988) 'Walter Pater and Archaeology: The Reconciliation with Earth.' *Victorian Studies,* 31 (Winter): 209-31.

——— (1994) *Hellenism and Homosexuality in Victorian Oxford,* Ithaca and London: Cornell University Press.

'Dr C.L. Shadwell.' (1919) Obituary. *The Times,* 14 February 1919: 10.

Edel, Leon (1985) *Henry James: A Life,* New York: Harper and Row.

Edel, Leon, and Laurence, Dan H. (1961) *A Bibliography of Henry James,* 2nd edn, London: Rupert Hart-Davis.

Embury, J.W. (1919) 'Fifty Years Ago.' *Clarendonian,* 1 (July): 66-8.

Engel, A.J. (1983) *From Clergyman to Don: The Rise of the Academic Profession in Nineteenth-Century Oxford,* Oxford: Clarendon Press.

Escott, T.H.S. (1895) 'Some Oxford Memories of the Prae-Aesthetic Age.' *National Review,* 24 (October): 232-44.

Evans, Lawrence (ed.) (1970) *Letters of Walter Pater,* Oxford: At the Clarendon Press.

Faber, Geoffrey (1957) *Jowett: A Portrait with Background,* London: Faber and Faber Ltd.

Farrar, Frederic W. (1874) 'The Voice of History.' In his book *The Silence and the Voices of God, with other Sermons,* London: Macmillan and Co., pp. 51-68.

Fletcher, Ian (1959) *Walter Pater*. Reprinted London: Longmans, 1971.

——— (1970) 'Herbert Horne: The Earlier Phase.' *English Miscellany,* 21: 117-57.

——— (1984) 'In the Way of an Introduction: *Marius* Past and Present.' *English Literature in Transition,* 27.1: 5-10.

Ford, Ford Madox (1932) *Return to Yesterday,* New York: Liveright.

Franklin, Colin (1969) *The Private Presses,* London: Studio Vista.

Glaister, Geoffrey Ashall (1960) *Glossary of the Book,* London: George Allen and Unwin Ltd.

Goldring, Douglas (1948) *The Last Pre-Raphaelite: A Record of the Life and Writings of Ford Madox Ford,* London: Macdonald and Co. (Publishers) Ltd.

Gosse, Edmund (1894) 'Walter Pater: A Portrait.' *Contemporary Review,* 67 (September): 795-810.

Graves, Charles L. (1910) *Life and Letters of Alexander Macmillan*, London: Macmillan and Co.

Green, J.R. (1874) *A Short History of the English People*, London: Macmillan and Co.

Grieve, Alastair (1973) 'Rossetti's applied Art Designs (2): Book-Bindings.' *Burlington Magazine*, 115 (February): 79-84.

Gross, John (1969) *The Rise and the Fall of the Man of Letters*, London: Penguin Books.

Grosskurth, Phyllis (1964) *John Addington Symonds: A Biography*, London: Longmans, Green, and Co. Ltd.

Gurr, A.J. (1965) 'Macmillan's Magazine.' *Review of English Literature*, 6 (January): 39-55.

Hill, Donald L. (ed.) (1893) *The Renaissance: Studies in Art and Poetry*, London: Macmillan and Co. Reprinted Berkeley and Los Angeles: The University of California Press, 1980.

Hughes, Thomas (1883) *Memoir of Daniel Macmillan*, London: Macmillan and Co.

Inman, Billie Andrew (1981) *Walter Pater's Reading: A Bibliography of his Library Borrowings and Literary References, 1858-1873*, New York and London: Garland Publishing, Inc.

——— (1983) 'Tracing the Pater Legacy.' *Pater Newsletter*, 11 (Spring): 31.

——— (1990) *Walter Pater and his Reading, 1874-1877, with a Bibliography of his Library Borrowings, 1878-1894*, New York and London: Garland Publishing, Inc.

——— (1991) 'Estrangement and Connection: Walter Pater, Benjamin Jowett, and William M. Hardinge.' In Brake, Laurel and Small, Ian (eds) (1991b) *Pater in the 1990s*, Greensboro, NC: ELT Press, pp. 1-20.

——— (1995) 'Tracing the Pater Legacy, Part II: Posthumous Sales, Manuscripts, and Copyrights.' *Pater Newsletter*, no. 32 (Winter): 3-8.

Jackson, William Walrond (1919) *Ingram Bywater: The Memoir of an Oxford Scholar, 1840-1914*, Oxford: At the Clarendon Press.

Jacobi, Charles T. (1891) *On the Making and Issuing of Books*, London: Elkin Mathews.

James, Elizabeth (1992) 'The Macmillan Archive at the British Library.' In Conference Proceedings: The Colloquium on The Book in Britain (1830-1914), which was held at Trinity College, Cambridge, 4-5 July 1992. *Publishing History* 32: 57-68.

Jowett, Benjamin (ed.) (1871) *The Dialogues of Plato*, trans. into English with analyses and introductions, 4 vols, Oxford: Clarendon Press.

King, A. and Stuart, A.F. (1965) *The House of Warne*, London: Frederick Warne.

Knoepflmacher, U.C. (1965) *Religious Humanism and the Victorian Novel: George Eliot, Walter Pater, and Samuel Butler*, Princeton: University of Princeton Press.

Lee, Vernon (1887) *Juvenilia*, 2 vols, London: T. Fisher Unwin.

Levey, Michael (1978) *The Case of Walter Pater*, London: Thames and Hudson.

Loesberg, Jonathan (1991) *Aestheticism and Deconstruction: Pater, Derrida, and de Man*, Princeton, NJ: Princeton University Press.

MacColl, D.S. (1931) 'A Batch of Memories. XII. Walter Pater.' *Week-End Review*, 4 (December): 759-60.

Mackail, J.W. (1899) *The Life of William Morris*, 2 vols, London: Longmans, Green and Co.

Macmillan, Frederick (1924) *The Net Book Agreement 1899*. Privately printed, Glasgow: Robert MacLehose and Co. Ltd.

Macmillan, George A. (1908) *Letters of Alexander Macmillan*, London: Macmillan and Co.

MacShane, Frank (1965) *The Life and Work of Ford Madox Ford*, London: Routledge and Kegan Paul.

Madan, Falconer (1921) *The Daniel Press: Memorials of C.H.O. Daniel, with a Bibliography of the Press, 1845-1919*, Oxford: the Daniel Press.

Mallet, Charles Edward (1924-27) *A History of the University of Oxford*, 3 vols, London: Methuen and Co.

Mallock, William Hurrell (1877) *The New Republic: Culture, Faith, and Philosophy in an English Country House*, intro. John Lucas, London: Chatto and Windus. Reprinted Leicester: Leicester University Press, 1975.

——— (1920) *Memoirs of Life and Literature*, New York and London: Harper.

Manson, Edward (1906) 'Recollections of Walter Pater.' *Oxford Magazine*, 25 (7 November): 60-1.

Marshall, Alan (1983) *Changing the Word: The Printing Industry in Transition*, London: Comedia Publishing Group.

McGann, Jerome J. (1991) *The Textual Condition*, Princeton, NJ: Princeton University Press.

McLean, Ruari (1972) *Victorian Book Design and Colour Printing*, London: Faber and Faber.

Metcalf, Priscilla (1980) *James Knowles: Victorian Editor and Architect*, Oxford: Clarendon Press.

Middleton, Bernard (1963) *A History of English Craft Bookbinding Technique*, New York and London: Hafner Publishing Company.

Miller, Andrew H. and Adams, James Eli (1996) *Sexualities in Victorian Britain*, Bloomington and Indianapolis: Indianapolis University Press.

Mitchell, B.R. (1988) *British Historical Statistics*, Cambridge: Cambridge University Press.

Monsman, Gerald (1967) *Pater's Portraits: Mythic Patterns in the Fiction of Walter Pater*, Baltimore: The Johns Hopkins Press.

——— (1971) 'Pater's Aesthetic Hero.' *University of Toronto Quarterly*, 40 (Winter): 136-51.

——— (1991) 'Editing *Gaston de Latour*.' In Brake, Laurel and Small, Ian (1991b), *Pater in the 1990s*, Greensboro, NC: ELT Press, pp. 21-31.

——— (ed.) (1995) *Gaston de Latour, by Walter Pater: The Revised Text*, Greensboro, NC: ELT Press.

Moore, Rayburn S. (1993) *The Correspondence of Henry James and the House of Macmillan, 1877-1914*, Baton Rouge: Louisiana State University Press.

Moran, James (1984) *Clays of Bungay*. Revised edition, Bungay: Richard Clay plc.

Morgan, Charles (1943) *The House of Macmillan*, London: Macmillan and Co.

Morgan, Thaïs E. (1996) 'Reimagining Masculinity in Victorian Criticism: Swinburne and Pater.' In Miller, Andrew H. and Adams, James Eli (1996) *Sexualities in Victorian Britain*, Bloomington and Indianapolis: Indianapolis University Press, pp.140-56.

Morris, William (1957) *The Ideal Book* (1893). London: L.C.C. Central School of Arts and Crafts.

'Mr. Charles Henry Jeens' Obituary, *Athenaeum*, 1 November 1879: pp. 568-9.

'Mr. Louis Dyer' Obituary, *The Times*, 21 July 1908: p. 12.

Mumby, Frank Arthur and Ian Norrie (1974) *Publishing and Bookselling*, London: Cape.

Nadel, Ira (1984) 'The 'Fictional' and the 'Real' in *Marius*.' *English Literature in Transition*, 27.2: 140-8.

Nelson, James G. (1971) *The Early Nineties: A View from the Bodley Head*, Cambridge, MA: Harvard University Press.

Nowell-Smith, Simon (1967) *Letters to Macmillan*, London: Macmillan.

Olmert, Michael (1992) *The Smithsonian Book of Books*, Washington, DC: Smithsonian Books.

Ottley, May (ed.) (1931) 'Imaginary Portraits. 2. An English Poet' by Walter Pater. *Fortnightly Review*, 129 (April): 433-48.
Paget, Violet (1883) 'The Responsibilities of Unbelief.' *Contemporary Review*, 43 (May): 685-710.
Pater, Walter H. (1910) *The Renaissance: Studies in Art and Poetry*, (1873). London: Macmillan and Co., Ltd.
——— (1910) *Marius the Epicurean: His Sensations and Ideas*, 2 vols, London: Macmillan and Co., Ltd.
——— (1910) *Imaginary Portraits*, London: Macmillan and Co., Ltd.
——— (1910) *Appreciations: With an Essay on Style*, London: Macmillan and Co., Ltd.
——— (1910) *Plato and Platonism: A Series of Lectures*, London: Macmillan and Co., Ltd.
——— (1910) *Greek Studies: A Series of Essays*, London: Macmillan and Co., Ltd.
——— (1910) *Miscellaneous Studies: A Series of Essays*, London: Macmillan and Co., Ltd.
——— (1910) *Gaston de Latour: An Unfinished Romance*, ed. Charles L. Shadwell, London: Macmillan and Co., Ltd., 1910.
——— (1910) *Essays from 'The Guardian'*, London: Macmillan and Co., Ltd.

Pattison, Mark (1875) *Isaac Casaubon, 1559-1614*, London: Longmans, Green.
——— (1876) 'Philosophy at Oxford.' *Mind*, 1: 82-97.
——— (1885) *Memoirs*, London: Macmillan and Co.
Pennell, Elizabeth R. and Joseph (1908) *The Life of James McNeill Whistler*, 2 vols, London: William Heinemann.
Potts, Alex (1994) *Flesh and the Ideal: Winckelmann and the Origins of Art History*, New Haven and London: Yale University Press.
Pritchard, H. Baden. (1882) *The Photographic Studios of Europe*, New York: Anthony and Co.

Richards, Bernard (1986) 'Walter Pater at Oxford.' In McGrath, Gregory (ed.) *Brasenose College: The Pater Society*, 2nd edn., B.N.C.: The Pater Society, pp. 1-14.
Ricks, Christopher (1977) 'Arnold, Pater, and Misquotation.' *The Times Literary Supplement*, 3948 (25 November): 1383-5.
Robinson, A. Mary F. (1925) 'Souvenirs sur Walter Pater.' *La Revue de Paris*, 1 (15 January): 339-58

Seiler, R.M. (ed.) (1980) *Walter Pater: The Critical Heritage*, London: Routledge and Kegan Paul.

——— (1987) *Walter Pater: A Life Remembered*, Calgary: The University of Calgary Press.

Shairp, John Campbell (1882) 'English Poets and Oxford Critics.' *Quarterly Review*, 153: 431-63.

Sharp, William (1894) 'Some personal Reminiscences of Walter Pater.' *Atlantic Monthly*, 74 (December): 801-14.

Shuter, William F. (1988) 'Pater as Don.' *Prose Studies*, 11 (May 1988): 41-60.

——— (1989) 'Pater's Reshuffled Text.' *Nineteenth Century Literature*, 31: 500-25.

——— (1990) 'Dating the Harvard Manuscripts.' *Pater Newsletter*, no. 24 (Spring): 1-11.

——— (1994) 'The "Outing" of Walter Pater.' *Nineteenth Century Literature*, Electronic edn. 48 (March): 1-30.

——— (1997) *Rereading Walter Pater*, Cambridge: Cambridge University Press.

Small, Ian (1991a) *Conditions for Criticism: Authority, Knowledge, and Literature in the late Nineteenth Century*, Oxford: Clarendon Press.

——— (1991b) 'Editing and Annotating Pater.' In Brake, Laurel and Small, Ian (eds) (1991b) *Pater in the 1990s*, Greensboro, NC: ELT Press, pp. 33-42.

Small, Ian (ed.) (1985) *Marius the Epicurean: His Sensations and Ideas*, London: Macmillan and Co., 1892. Reprinted Oxford: Oxford University Press, 1985.

Smith, Esther Marian Greenwell (1980) *Mrs. Humphry Ward*, Boston: Twayne Publishers.

Sparling, H. Halliday (1924) *The Kelmscott Press and William Morris, master-craftsman*, London: Macmillan.

Stonehill, C.A. and Stonehill, H.W. (eds) (1925) *Bibliographies of Modern Authors*, 2nd series, London: John Castle, pp. 129-40.

Super, R.H. (1966) 'Vivacity and the Philistines.' *Studies in English Literature*, 6: 629-37.

Sussman, Herbert (1995) *Victorian Masculinities: Manhood and Masculine Poetics in early Victorian Literature and Art*, Cambridge: Cambridge University Press.

Sutcliffe, Peter (1978) *The Oxford University Press: An Informal History*, Oxford: At the Clarendon Press.

Sutherland, John (1991) *Mrs. Humphry Ward*, Oxford and London: Oxford University Press.

Symonds, John Addington (1872) *An Introduction to the Study of Dante*, London: Smith, Elder, and Co.

——— (1873) *Studies of the Greek Poets*, London: Smith, Elder, and Co.

——— (1875-86) *Renaissance in Italy*, 7 vols, London: Smith, Elder, and Co.

Symons, Arthur (1906) 'Walter Pater.' *Monthly Review*, 24 (September): 14-24.

Taylor, Basil (1974) *Artists of the Victorian Age*, London: British Broadcasting Corporation.

Taylor, John Russell (1966) *The Art Nouveau Book in Britain*, London: Methuen and Co., Ltd.

Tebbel, John (1972) *A History of Book Publishing in the United States*, 4 vols, New York: R.R. Bowker.

Thompson, Paul (1967) *The Life of William Morris*, London: Heinemann.

Titchener, E.B. (1894) 'Walter Horatio Pater.' *Book Reviews*, 2 (October): 201-5.

Turner, Frank M. (1981) *The Greek Heritage in Victorian Britain*, New Haven and London: Yale University Press.

Tyrwhitt, R. St. John (1877) 'The Greek Spirit in modern Literature.' *Contemporary Review*, 29 (March): 552-66.

Unwin, Stanley (1926) *The Truth about Publishing*, London: George Allen and Unwin Ltd.

Updike, D.B. (1961) *Printing Types: Their History, Form, and Use*, 2 vols, Cambridge, MA: Harvard University Press.

VanArsdel, Rosemary T. (1991) 'Macmillan and Company.' In Anderson, Patricia J. and Rose, Jonathan (eds) *British Literary Publishing Houses, 1820-1880*, Detroit and London: Gale Research Inc., pp. 178-95.

Vilain, Jean-François and Bishop, Philip R. (1992) *Thomas Bird Mosher and the Art of the Book*, Philadelphia, PA: F.A. Davis Co.

Vogeler, Martha Salmon (1964) 'The Religious Meaning of Marius the Epicurean.' *Nineteenth Century Fiction*, 19 (December): 287-99.

Waddington, Samuel (1909) *Chapters of my Life: An Autobiography*, London: Chapman and Hall, Ltd.

Ward, Anthony (1966) *Walter Pater: The Idea in Nature*, London: MacGibbon and Kee Ltd.

Ward, Mrs Humphry (Mary) (1918) *A Writer's Recollections*, London: W. Collins Sons and Co. Ltd.

Ward, T. Humphry (1909) 'Reminiscences. Brasenose, 1864-72.' *Brasenose College Quatercentenary Monographs*, 2 vols, Oxford: Clarendon Press, part XIV, 2(c), pp. 71-5.

Warner, Oliver (1955) *A Century of Writers, 1855-1955*, London: Chatto and Windus.

Waugh, Arthur (1893) 'London Letter.' *Critic*, 22 (25 March): 187.

Weintraub, Stanley (1974) *Whistler: A Biography*, New York: Weybright and Talley.

Williams, Carolyn (1989) *Transformed World: Walter Pater's Aesthetic Historicism*, Ithaca: Cornell University Press.

Woolf, Virginia (1928) 'Slater's Pins have no Points.' N.Y. *Forum* (January): 58-63.

Wordsworth, John (1874) *Fragments and Specimens of Early Latin Language and Literature*, Oxford: Parker.

——— (1878) *University Sermons on Gospel Subjects*, Oxford and London: James Parker and Co.

Wright, Samuel (1975) *A Bibliography of the Writings of Walter H. Pater*, New York and London: Garland Publishing, Inc.

Wright, Thomas (1907) *The Life of Walter Pater*, 2 vols, London: Everett.

——— (1936) *Thomas Wright of Olney: An Autobiography*, London: Herbert Jenkins.

INDEX